NORMAN MAILER

took part in the October 1967 anti-Vietnam march to the Pentagon and was arrested. After his release, he came home to write about the anger, the hangovers, the obscenities, the gurus, the hippies, the bewildered young MP's, the dead-eyed marshals, poets, chaplains, draft-card burners, the walls of the Pentagon, and

NORMAN MAILER.

He has chronicled another kind of war, in a book that is even greater than his first novel, The Naked and the Dead.

World Renowned Authors from SIGNET

(0451)

- ☐ **THE MIRACLE** by Irving Wallace. (135962—$4.50)*
- ☐ **THE CHAPMAN REPORT** by Irving Wallace. (138287—$4.50)*
- ☐ **THE PRIZE** by Irving Wallace. (137590—$4.95)*
- ☐ **THE FABULOUS SHOWMAN** by Irving Wallace. (113853—$2.95)
- ☐ **THE THREE SIRENS** by Irving Wallace. (138295—$4.50)*
- ☐ **THE SECOND LADY** by Irving Wallace. (138279—$4.50)*
- ☐ **THE SINS OF PHILIP FLEMING** by Irving Wallace. (137604—$3.50)*
- ☐ **THE TWENTY-SEVENTH WIFE** by Irving Wallace. (137612—$4.50)*
- ☐ **DANIEL MARTIN** by John Fowles. (122100—$4.50)†
- ☐ **THE EBONY TOWER** by John Fowles. (134648—$3.95)*
- ☐ **THE FRENCH LIEUTENANT'S WOMAN** by John Fowles. (135989—$3.95)*
- ☐ **BREAKFAST AT TIFFANY'S** by Truman Capote. (147308—$2.95)*
- ☐ **THE GRASS HARP and TREE OF NIGHT** by Truman Capote. (140923—$3.50)
- ☐ **MUSIC FOR CHAMELEONS** by Truman Capote. (254639—$6.95)
- ☐ **IN COLD BLOOD** by Truman Capote. (149955—$4.50)
- ☐ **OTHER VOICES, OTHER ROOMS** by Truman Capote. (144635—$3.95)*
- ☐ **THE ARMIES OF THE NIGHT** by Norman Mailer. (140702—$4.95)*

*Prices slightly higher in Canada
†Not available in Canada

Buy them at your local bookstore or use this convenient coupon for ordering.

NEW AMERICAN LIBRARY,
P.O. Box 999, Bergenfield, New Jersey 07621

Please send me the books I have checked above. I am enclosing $_____
(please add $1.00 to this order to cover postage and handling). Send check
or money order—no cash or C.O.D.'s. Prices and numbers are subject to change
without notice.

Name _____

Address_____

City_____ State_____ Zip Code_____

Allow 4-6 weeks for delivery.
This offer is subject to withdrawal without notice.

Norman Mailer

THE ARMIES
OF THE NIGHT

History as a Novel
The Novel as History

A SIGNET BOOK
NEW AMERICAN LIBRARY

Portions of this book were originally published in
Harper's Magazine.

"A Shaky Start," on pages 13 and 14, reprinted by permission
from *Time,* The Weekly Newsmagazine;
Copyright © Time Inc., 1967.
Material on pages 58, 59, and 144 from *Near the Ocean*
by Robert Lowell.
Reprinted with permission of Farrar, Straus & Giroux, Inc.
Copyright © 1967 by Robert Lowell.
Article quoted on pages 313-315 reprinted by permission.
Copyright © 1967 by *The Washington Star.*

This is a reprint of a hardcover edition published by
New American Library.
The hardcover edition was published simultaneously in Canada
by General Publishing Company, Ltd.

To Beverly

An acknowledgment to Sandy Charlebois
for work beyond the call of duty

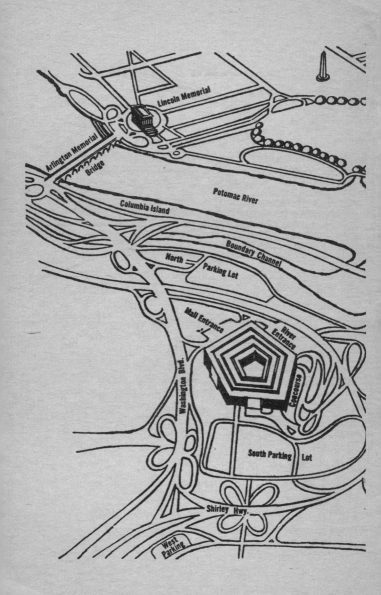

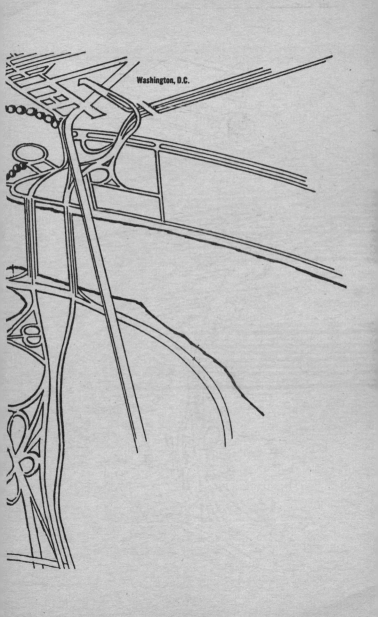

Washington, D.C.

Book One

HISTORY AS A NOVEL:
THE STEPS OF
THE PENTAGON

PART I:

Thursday Evening

1: PEN PALS

From the outset, let us bring you news of your protagonist. The following is from *Time* magazine, October 27, 1967.

A SHAKY START

Washington's scruffy Ambassador Theater, normally a pad for psychedelic frolics, was the scene of an unscheduled scatological solo last week in support of the peace demonstrations. Its antistar was author Norman Mailer, who proved even less prepared to explain Why Are We In Vietnam? than his current novel bearing that title.

Slurping liquor from a coffee mug, Mailer faced an audience of 600, most of them students, who had kicked in $1,900 for a bail fund against Saturday's capers. "I don't want to grandstand unduly," he said, grandly but barely standing.

It was one of his few coherent sentences. Mumbling and spewing obscenities as he staggered about the stage—which he had commandeered by threatening to beat up the previous M.C.—Mailer described in detail his search for a usable privy on the premises. Excretion, in fact, was his preoccupation of the night. "I'm here because I'm like LBJ," was one of Mailer's milder observations. "He's as full of crap as I am." When hecklers mustered the temerity to shout "Publicity hound!" at him, Mailer managed to pronounce

13

flawlessly his all-purpose noun, verb and expletive: "**** you."

Dwight Macdonald, the bearded literary critic, was aghast at the barroom bathos, but failed to argue Mailer off the platform. Macdonald eventually squeezed in the valorous observation that Ho Chi Minh was really no better than Dean Rusk. After more obscenities, Mailer introduced Poet Robert Lowell, who got annoyed at requests to speak louder, "I'll bellow, but it won't do any good," he said, and proceeded to read from *Lord Weary's Castle*.

By the time the action shifted to the Pentagon, Mailer was perky enough to get himself arrested by two Marshals. "I transgressed a police line," he explained with some pride on the way to the lockup, where the toilet facilities are scarce indeed and the coffee mugs low-octane.

Now we may leave *Time* in order to find out what happened.

2: IN THE DEN

On a day somewhat early in September, the year of the first March on the Pentagon, 1967, the phone rang one morning and Norman Mailer, operating on his own principle of war games and random play, picked it up. That was not characteristic of Mailer. Like most people whose nerves are sufficiently sensitive to keep them well-covered with flesh, he detested the telephone. Taken in excess, it drove some psychic equivalent of static into the privacies of the brain; so he kept himself amply defended. He had an answer service, a secretary, and occasional members of his family to pick up the receiver for him—he discouraged

14

his own participation on the phone—sometimes he would not even speak to old friends. Touched by faint intimations of remorse, he would call them back later. He had the idea—it was undeniably oversimple—that if you spent too much time on the phone in the evening, you destroyed some kind of creativity for the dawn. (It was taken for granted that nothing respectable would come out of the day if the morning began on the phone, and indeed for periods when he was writing he looked on transactions via telephone as Arabs look upon pig.)

Still, Mailer had a complex mind of sorts. Like a later generation which was to burn holes in their brain on Speed, he had given his own head the texture of a fine Swiss cheese. Years ago he had made all sorts of erosions in his intellectual firmament by consuming modestly promiscuous amounts of whiskey, marijuana, seconal, and benzedrine. It had given him the illusion he was a genius, as indeed an entire generation of children would so come to see themselves a decade later out on celestial journeys of LSD.

Now, however, that he had again an actively working brain only partially hampered by old bouts of drugs (which revealed their ravages in occasional gaps like the absolutely necessary word for an occasion failing utterly to arrive on time, or a critical crossroad of memory being forever obliterated so that for the safety of his life he could not remember whether some old beloved had helped him or betrayed him on a specific occasion—no small hole *that,* for a novelist!) yes, Mailer was bitter about drugs. If he still took a toke of marijuana from time to time for Auld Lang Syne, or in recognition of the probability that good sex had to be awfully good before it was better than on pot, yes, still!—Mailer was not in approval of any drug, he was virtually conservative about it, having demanded of his eighteen-year-old daughter, a Freshman now at Barnard, that she not take marijuana, and never LSD, until she had completed her education, a mean promise to extract in these apocalyptic times.

Such were the sort of contradictions one could discover. As a corollary of his detestation of the telephone was his necessity to pick it up once in a while. Mailer had the most developed sense of image; if not, he would have been a figure of deficiency, for people had been regarding him by his public image since he was twenty-five years old. He had in fact learned to live in the sarcophagus of his image—at night, in his sleep, he might dart out, and paint improvements on the sarcophagus. During the day, while he was helpless, newspapermen and other assorted bravos of the media and the literary world would carve ugly pictures on the living tomb of his legend. Of necessity, part of Mailer's remaining funds of sensitivity went right into the war of supporting his image and working for it. Sometimes he thought his relation to this image was not unlike some poor fellow who strains his very testicles to bring in emoluments for his wife yet is never favored with carnal knowledge of her. In any event, Mailer worked for the image, and therefore he detested the portrait of himself which would be promulgated if no one could *ever* reach him. So, on impulse, thereby sharpening his instinct as a gambler, he took spot plunges: once in a while he would pick up his own phone.

On this morning in September, 1967, he lost his bet.

No, let us leave it to history whether he lost his bet or eventually won it. But for our record, it had best be stated that his immediate reaction was one of woe—he did not wish to speak to the man on the other end. That man was an author named Mitchell Goodman. Mitch Goodman, as everyone called him, was a worthy fellow, and Mailer had only good things to say of him, indeed Mailer had even given a blurb to Goodman's war novel, a brooding poetic work about World War II which had taken something like eight years to write and had been a book deserving of a blurb. (Although Mailer, with Swiss cheese for memory, could not at the instant recollect the title.) That was not necessarily here nor there. The reason Mailer did not wish to speak to Goodman was that he knew that (1) Goodman had a better character than he did and (2) was going to ask something which would not be easy to refuse but would be expensive to perform. Besides, Goodman was the sort of clear conscience which insists upon being solemn, as if the powers of the universe, concerned that worldly balance not disappear altogether, had decided that if men of good conscience were cheerful, all men might like to grow into good conscience and then the ball game would most certainly be over.

In fact Mailer had known Goodman for twenty years. They had been, if he recollected properly, almost in the same year at Harvard (Mailer was Harvard '43—his 25th Reunion was coming up), they were both from Brooklyn, both married young. They had met in Paris in 1947, Goodman then a tall powerful handsome dark-haired young man with a profound air of defeated gloom. (He looked the way J. D. Salinger would have looked if J. D. Salinger had been tall enough and beefed-up enough to play football, and had fumbled *Catcher in the Rye*.) He was married to a charming and most attractive dark-haired English girl with a characteristic space between her two front teeth. Everyone called her Dinny. Everyone in Paris liked her. She was pure as a bird, delicate yet firm in conscience. Since one did not see them again for years except at parties now and then, it took years to realize that the Denise Levertov of whom everyone spoke as an exceptional and splendid poet was the same Dinny. Bless her, she was still cheerful. Bless Mitch—he was still gloomy. They had been married for twenty years. Of how many could that be said? Not of Mr. Mailer.

In fact, the last time Mailer had heard of Mitch Goodman was when the latter had led a small group of protesters out of the large hotel banquet hall where Hubert Humphrey was about to address the assorted literati and book reviewers of the American writing world at the National Book Award festivities in March, 1967. Mailer had not attended. He had been boycotting the affair for several years—not that it mattered to anyone, but Mailer thought it was the least he could do, since none of his books had ever been considered for an award, let alone given one. But he remembered being glad he had not attended, for if he had, would he have been ready to walk out with Mitch Goodman or not? The war in Vietnam was probably to be protested on every occasion, and any attempt to twist Hubert Humphrey's nose was, in all favorable winds, a venture to applaud, but the exodus from the National Book Award's assembly, as one might have

17

desc

predicted, was small, pilgrim small, by reports not unfar-
cical: Jules Feiffer walked out with the demonstrators,
then sneaked back to go to a party for Humphrey.
Feiffer's comet had not been in ascendance since.

If one was going to take part in a literary demonstration,
it had better work, since novelists like movie stars like to
keep their politics in their pocket rather than wear them
as ashes on the brow: if it is hard for people in the literary world to applaud any act braver or more self-sacrific-
ing than their own, it is impossible for them to forgive any
gallant move which is by consensus unsuccessful. The
measure of the failure on this occasion had been that Ber-
nard Malamud, who won the 1966 award in fiction for
his novel *The Fixer*, did not boycott the Vice-President,
but on the contrary had given his prepared speech in its
proper place. Since Malamud was also opposed to the
war in Vietnam, Goodman's action presumably had failed
to light an outstanding fire in the sympathizers.

Here, therefore, was Mailer now on the phone with an
old friend and lugubrious conscience whose instinct for
the winning move was not—on the face—spectacular.
Mailer hated to put in time with losers. Like many another man of varied affairs considered worthy by some,
worthless by others, there had been all too many years
when he had the reputation of being a loser; it had cost
him much. While he could hardly, at this stage of his career, look back on a succession of well-timed and generally established triumphs, his consolation in those hours
when he was most uncharitable to himself is that taken at
his very worst he was at least still worthy of being a character in a novel by Balzac, win one day, lose the next, and
do it with boom! and baroque in the style. If he had lost
many painful engagements, he had also won a few, and the
damnable habit of consorting with losers was that they
passed their subtle problems on.

Quickly, the conversation, therefore, took a harsh turn.
Before it had been going two minutes, Mailer was scolding Goodman; that was predictable enough, given the request. Goodman had just finished telling Mailer that there
was going to be a March on Washington in about a
month, and Mailer had hardly finished saying he doubted

18

if he would attend since he had no desire to stand in a large meadow and listen to other men make speeches (still furious was Mailer at SANE for an occasion two years ago when they had wanted $50 in contribution from him for a protest in Washington, but did not think enough—or were too dismayed—of the text of a speech he had given in Berkeley about the war in Vietnam to invite him to speak) so, no he did not think he would go to Washington, when Goodman interrupted by saying, "This is going to be different, Norman. Did you read the circular from the Mobilization Committee?"

"I get many circulars, and they're all badly written," Mailer said in a cranky voice.

"Well, this one is a departure," said Mitch Goodman. "Some of us are going to try to invade the corridors of the Pentagon during office hours and close down some of their operation."

Mailer received such news with no particular pleasure. It sounded vaguely and uneasily like a free-for-all with students, state troopers, and Hell's Angels flying in and out of the reports—exactly the sort of operation they seemed to have every other weekend out on the Coast. He felt one little bubble of fear tilt somewhere about the solar plexus.

"Yes, this sounds more interesting," he growled.

"Well, I think it will be," said Goodman. "Anyway, Norman, what I'm calling you about is something else: our group called Resist. On Friday, the day before the Pentagon, we're going to have a demonstration at the Department of Justice to honor students who are turning in their draft cards."

This is about where Mailer began to scold Goodman. He went on for a breath or two on the redundancy of these projects. When was everyone going to cut out the nonsense and get to work, do their own real work? One's own literary work was the only answer to the war in Vietnam. As he was talking, Mailer began to realize that he had not done any real writing in months—he had been making movies—but then it didn't matter, he had done as much in the way of protest about this war as anyone, his speech at Berkeley in 1965 had attacked Johnson at a
19

time when lots of the mob now so much against the war were still singing "Hello, Lyndon." Mailer, filled with such righteous recollections, was therefore scolding Goodman at near to full pedal, when the organ came to a sudden stop. The thought that he was beginning to sound like a righteous old toot came just as suddenly into his head. Mailer had never had a particular age—he carried different ages within him like different models of his experience: parts of him were eighty-one years old, fifty-seven, forty-eight, thirty-six, nineteen, et cetera, et cetera—he now went back abruptly from fifty-seven to thirty-six. "All right, Mitch," he said, "I don't know what I'm arguing for, I'm sure you'll need all your strength to melt some of the real hard heads."

Mitch Goodman chuckled at the other end. It was the first hint between them of memories of somewhat more idealistic days in Paris.

"Mitch, I'll be there," said Mailer, "but I can't pretend I'm happy about it."

A week later some girl called to ask if he would write a form letter to go out under his signature supporting these students. Mailer answered in effect that he was hanging in on this affair by his fingernails and would not try to break them by sending a letter.

A week after that another girl called to ask if he would speak on Thursday night in Washington at a theater with Robert Lowell and Dwight Macdonald and Paul Goodman, not Mitch Goodman this time, *Paul* Goodman. Mailer asked who might be running the meeting. Ed de Grazia was doing that—Mailer knew the name—the thought of seeing de Grazia offered a small but definite pleasure. Warily, he accepted. There would now be three days out of his week, Thursday to speak, Friday at the Department of Justice, and Saturday—it came upon him that something actually was going to be attempted at the Pentagon, and he—if he knew himself—would end up, no matter how, part of such a party. It was going to prove a wasteful weekend he decided with some gloom —he could have spent it more profitably cutting his new movie. He had made a film about cops and crooks (actually about detectives and suspects) which came to more than six possible hours of film and would have to be cut down to three hours or two and a half. Some of the rushes were surprising in their promise; he looked forward to cutting the film; he had directed it and acted in it. In fact he had played a chief of detectives, Lieutenant Francis Xavier Pope, and had been not unbelievable in places. Well, farewell to Francis X. Pope, cheers to you, dear Pentagon: Mailer wished as the Washington weekend approached that the Washington weekend were done.

3: TERMINALS

Thursday afternoon, Dwight Macdonald was on the same plane from New York to Washington, but Mailer and he did not see each other. This could, of course, be made symbolic of the happenings which were to follow at the Ambassador by night, but the probability is that an airplane, serving as some sort of dentist's chair without a drill, does not encourage one's powers of recognition. (In any case they were to meet later at a party, Macdonald, Robert Lowell, Paul Goodman and Mailer.) Ed de Grazia, who was to be M.C. at the Ambassador until dispossessed, was kind enough to meet the novelist at the airport and take him to the Hay-Adams. (People, of course, had been willing to put the guest up. Washingtonians with a spare bedroom and loyal to the cause were not nonexistent after all, but a man who has six children of his own does not necessarily wish to spend his idle moments talking to another man's children on the weekend.) En route, de Grazia explained a little of the temper in the town. It was not in focus, he murmured.

De Grazia was a slim elegant Sicilian with a subtle diffidence in his manner, terribly hesitant, almost a stammer, but he was a Sicilian and somehow inspired the confi-

21

dence that he knew where the next bit of information might reside. Besides, he bore a pleasant resemblance to the way Frank Sinatra looked ten years ago.

Leading lawyer for the Mobilization's Legal Defense Committee, and an old friend from times so recent as the trial in Boston of *Naked Lunch,* where Mailer and he had met, de Grazia as counsel for the book, Allen Ginsberg and Mailer as witnesses to its literary merits, de Grazia expected to be busy on Saturday. No one had any idea of how many arrests would be made, nor of how much violence there would be, neither on the side of the police, nor the demonstrators.

It was a bright late afternoon in Washington, much like a day of Indian summer in September on Cape Cod, the air was good; after New York, surprisingly good. But the car was a convertible, the top was down, and in the shade of taller buildings, waiting for a light, an October cold was in the breeze. Bright and sunny and a hint of cold to bring a whiff of the sinister from the wind. So came idle thoughts: how incredible if in two days one was going to be dead!

The difficulty, de Grazia was explaining, was that there was no center to the March. Unlike the move on Washington in 1963 for civil rights, there was now no central supervisory or coordinating committee to which all organizations would defer, or with whom they would even promise to maintain communication. Something like fifty thousand people were going to arrive and nearly all of them would be unaffiliated or disaffiliated. Nor was the government revealing quite what they were going to do. At the thought of their august power, a vacuum was certainly present in the center of Mailer and de Grazia's mood. Listening to de Grazia talk of the negotiations about the route of march from the Lincoln Memorial to the Pentagon, Mailer learned that first there would be a meeting at Lincoln Memorial similar to the assembly in 1963 when Martin Luther King had said, "I have a dream," and many had whispered that someday he would be President.

Now, for this morning meeting four years later at Lincoln Memorial no one anticipated too much trouble, but afterward tens of thousands of virtually leaderless people were going to walk over Memorial Bridge to Virginia and from there advance to the Pentagon over a road which had still not been selected, no agreement on the route of march having yet been negotiated between the government and the war protesters. There were three roads, de Grazia explained, and the government wished the marchers to use the narrowest of the three. That was one source of trouble. Another—he hesitated. Was what? Well, in discussing police arrangements, which is to say, dispositions of city police, U.S. Marshals, and National Guard, the government representative had indicated there would be other units as well. When queried, the official had given one of those delicate technological replies: he was, he said, not volunteering to indicate what the specific unit might be. "That sounds like paratroopers," said de Grazia. As it turned out, he was right. "Hey, hey," said Mailer, "aren't they just a little bit worried." But *they* were not alone. The sound of paratroopers still had its magic ring. "I want to go out to see it on Saturday," said de Grazia, "but I guess I'll have to stay at the Defense Center." "Oh, that's where you belong," said the Participant, "somebody's got to be there to get us out."

It was now after six, after the rush hour, but in Washington it still seemed like late afternoon and endlessly peaceful. As the afternoon goes on, Washington seems more and more a tender Southern city. The light psychic rust of its iron will, the sense of suffocation (conceivably one chokes to death in Washington more slowly than anywhere else—for some, it takes thirty years) the faded scent of its inhibition, its severity and its concealed corruption (like entering a drawing room plumped with rich middle-aged ladies) all this seemed absent in the golden hovering on such leisurely twilight. Mailer sighed; like most New Yorkers, he usually felt small in Washington. The capital invariably seemed able to take the measure of men like him.

But as Mailer had come to recognize over the years, the modest everyday fellow of his daily round was servant to a wild man in himself: the gent did not appear so very often, sometimes so rarely as once a month, sometimes

23

not even twice a year, and he sometimes came when Mailer was frightened and furious at the fear, sometimes he came just to get a breath of air. He was indispensable, however, and Mailer was even fond of him for the wild man was witty in his own wild way and absolutely fearless—once at the edge of paralysis he had been ready to engage Sonny Liston. He would have been admirable, except that he was an absolute egomaniac, a Beast—no recognition existed of the existence of anything beyond the range of his reach. And when he appeared, it was often with great speed; he gave little warning. Certainly he gave no warning as the Historian checked in at the Hay-Adams, changed his clothes and prepared to give a few thoughtful remarks a little later that night at the Ambassador Theater on the essential insanity of our venture in Vietnam, such remarks designed presumably to encourage happy participation for Saturday's move to invest the Pentagon.

4: THE LIBERAL PARTY

There was a party first, however, given by an attractive liberal couple. Mailer's heart, never buoyant at best, and in fact once with justice called "sodden" by a critic, now collected into a leaden little ball and sank, not to his feet but his stomach. He was aware for the first time this day of a healthy desire to have a drink for the party gave every promise of being dreadful. Mailer was a snob of the worst sort. New York had not spoiled him, because it had not chosen to, but New York had certainly wrecked his tolerance for any party but a very good one. Like most snobs he professed to believe in the aristocracy of achieved quality—"Just give me a hovel with a few young artists, bright-eyed and bold"—in fact, a party lacked

24

flavor for him unless someone very rich or social was present. An evening without a wicked lady in the room was like an opera company without a large voice. Of course there were no wicked ladies when he entered this room. Some reasonably attractive wives to be certain, and a couple of young girls, too young for him, they were still in the late stages of some sort of extraordinary progressive school, and were innocent, decent-spirited, merry, red-cheeked, idealistic, and utterly lobotomized away from the sense of sin. Mailer would not have known what to do with such young ladies—he had spent the first forty-four years of his life in an intimate dialogue, a veritable dialectic with the swoops, spooks, starts, the masks and snarls, the calm lucid abilities of sin, sin was his favorite fellow, his tonic, his jailer, his horse, his sword, say he was not inclined to flirt for an hour with one bright seventeen-year-old or another when they conceived of lust as no more than the gymnasium of love. Mailer had a diatribe against LSD, hippies, and the generation of love, but he was keeping it to himself. (The young girls, incidentally, had been brought by de Grazia. Not for nothing did de Grazia bear a resemblance to Sinatra.)

But we are back with the wives, and the room has not yet been described. It was the sort of room one can see at many a faculty party in places like Berkeley, the University of Chicago, Columbia—the ground of common being is that the faculty man is a liberal. Conservative professors tend to have a private income, so their homes show the flowering of their taste, the articulation of their hobbies, collections adhere to their cabinets and odd statements of whim stand up in the nooks; but liberal instructors, liberal assistant professors, and liberal associate professors are usually poor and programmatic, so secretly they despise the arts of home adornment. Their houses look one like the other, for the wives gave up herculean careers as doctors, analysts, sociologists, anthropologists, labor relations experts—great servants of the Social Program were lost when the women got married and relinquished all for hubber and kids. So the furnishings are functional, the prevailing hues of wall and carpet and cloth are institutional brown and library gray, the paintings and sculpture are stylized abstract, hopeless imitation I. Rice Pereira, Leonard Baskin, Ben Shahn, but bet your twenty-five dollars to win an assured ten dollars that the artist on the wall is a friend of the host, has the right political ideas, and will talk about literature so well, you might think you were being addressed by Maxim Gorky.

Such were the sour and near to unprintable views of the semi-distinguished and semi-notorious author as he entered the room. His deepest detestation was often reserved for the nicest of liberal academics, as if their lives were his own life but a step escaped. Like the scent of the void which comes off the pages of a Xerox copy, so was he always depressed in such homes by their hint of over-security. If the republic was now managing to convert the citizenry to a plastic mass, ready to be attached to any manipulative gung ho, the author was ready to cast much of the blame for such success into the undernourished lap, the overpsychologized loins, of the liberal academic intelligentsia. They were of course politically opposed to the present programs and movements of the republic in Asian foreign policy, but this political difference seemed no more than a quarrel among engineers. Liberal academics had no root of a real war with technology land itself, no, in all likelihood, they were the natural managers of that future air-conditioned vault where the last of human life would still exist. Their only quarrel with the Great Society was that they thought it temporarily deranged, since the Great Society seemed to be serving as instrument to the Goldwater wing of the Republican party, a course of action so very irrational to these liberal technologues that they were faced with bitter necessity to desert all their hard-earned positions of leverage on real power in the Democratic party, a considerable loss to suffer merely because of an irrational development in the design of the Great Society's supermachine. Well, the liberal technologues were not without character or principle. If their living rooms had little to keep them apart from the look of waiting rooms of doctors with a modern practice, it was exactly because the private loves of the ideologues were attached to no gold standard of the psyche. Those

26

true powers of interior decoration—greed, guilt, compassion and trust—were hardly the cornerstones of their family furnishings. No, just as money was a concept, no more, to the liberal academic, and needed no ballast of gold to be considered real, for nothing is more real to the intellectual than a concept! so position or power in society was, to the liberal technologue, also a concept, desirable, but always to be relinquished for a better concept. They were servants of that social machine of the future in which all irrational human conflict would be resolved, all conflict of interest negotiated, and nature's resonance condensed into frequencies which could comfortably phase nature in or out as you please. So they were servants of the moon. Their living rooms looked like offices precisely because they were ready to move to the moon and build Utope cities there—Utope being, one may well suppose, the only appropriate name for pilot models of Utopia in Non-Terrestrial Ecologically Sub-Dependent Non-Charged Staging Areas, that's to say dead planets where the food must be flown in, but the chances for good civil rights and all-out social engineering are one hundred percent zap!

As is invariably the case with sociological ruminations the individual guests at this party disproved the general thesis, at least in part. The hostess was small, for example, almost tiny, but vivid, bright-eyed, suggestive of a fiery temper and a childlike glee. It was to pain Mailer later to refuse her cooking (she had prepared a buffet to be eaten before the move to the theater) but he was drinking with some devotion by then, and mixing seemed fair neither to the food nor the bourbon. It was of course directly unfair to the hostess: Mailer priding himself on his good manners precisely because the legend of his bad manners was so prevalent, hated to cause pain to a hostess, but he had learned from years of speaking in public that an entertainer's first duty was to deliver himself to the stage with the maximum of energy, high focus, and wit—a good heavy dinner on half a pint of bourbon was likely to produce torpor, undue search for the functional phrase, and dry-mouthed maunderings after a little spit. So he apologized to the lady, dared the look of rejection in her eye which was almost balanced on a tear—she was indeed surprisingly adorable and childlike to be found in such a liberal academic coven—tried to cover the general sense of loss by marshaling what he assumed his most radiant look, next assuring her that he would take a rain check on the meal.

"Promise?"

"Next time I'm in Washington," he lied like a psychopath. The arbiter of nicety in him had observed with horror over many a similar occasion that he was absolutely without character for any social situation in which a pause could become the mood's abyss, and so he always filled the moment with the most extravagant amalgams of possibility. Particularly he did this at the home of liberal academics. They were brusque to the world of manners, they had built their hope of heaven on the binary system and the computer, 1 and 0, Yes and No—they had little to do therefore with the spectrum of grace in acceptance and refusal; if you did not do what they wished, you had simply denied them. Now Mailer was often brusque himself, famous for that, but the architecture of his personality bore resemblance to some provincial cathedral which warring orders of the church might have designed separately over several centuries, the particular cathedral falling into the hands of one architect, then his enemy. (Mailer had not been married four times for nothing.) If he was on many an occasion brusque, he was also to himself at least so supersensitive to nuances of manner he sometimes suspected when in no modest mood that Proust had lost a cell mate the day they were born in different bags. (Bag is of course used here to specify milieu and not the exceptional character of the mothers, Mme. Proust and Mrs. I. B. Mailer.) At any rate, boldness, attacks of shyness, rude assertion, and circumlocutions tortured as arthritic fingers working at lace, all took their turn with him, and these shuttlings of mood became most pronounced in their resemblance to the banging and shunting of freight cars when he was with liberal academics. Since he—you are in on the secret—disapproved of them far more than he could afford to reveal (their enmity could be venomous) he therefore exerted himself to

28

push up a synthetic exaggerated sweetness of manner, and his conversations with liberal ideologues on the consequence consisted almost entirely of overcorrections of the previous error.

"I know a friend of yours," says the ideologue. A nervous voice from the novelist for answer. "Yes? Who?" Now the name is given: it is X.

Mailer: I don't know X.

The ideologue proceeds to specify a conversation which M held with X. M recollects. "Oh, yes!" he says; "of course! X!" Burbles of conversation about the merits of X, and his great ebullience. Actually X is close to flat seltzer.

There had been just this sort of dialogue with a stranger at the beginning of the party. So Mailer gave up quickly any thought of circulation. Rather, he huddled first with Dwight Macdonald, but Macdonald was the operative definition of the gregarious and could talk with equal facility and equal lack of personal observation to an Eskimo, a collector from the New York Department of Sanitation, or a UN diplomat—therefore was chatting happily with the world fifteen minutes after his entrance. Hence Mailer and Robert Lowell got into what was by all appearances a deep conversation at the dinner table sometime before food was laid out, Mailer thus doubly wounding the hostess with his later refusal.

We find, therefore, Lowell and Mailer ostensibly locked in converse. In fact, out of the thousand separate enclaves of their very separate personalities, they sensed quickly that they now shared one enclave to the hilt: their secret detestation of liberal academic parties to accompany worthy causes. Yes, their snobbery was on this mountainous face close to identical—each had a delight in exactly the other kind of party, a posh evil social affair, they even supported a similar vein of vanity (Lowell with considerably more justice) that if they were doomed to be revolutionaries, rebels, dissenters, anarchists, protesters, and general champions of one Left cause or another, they were also, in private, *grands conservateurs,* and if the truth be told, poor damn émigré princes. They were willing if necessary (probably) to die

29

for the cause—one could hope the cause might finally at the end have an unexpected hint of wit, a touch of the Lord's last grace—but wit or no, grace or grace failing, it was bitter rue to have to root up one's occupations of the day, the week, and the weekend and trot down to Washington for idiot mass manifestations which could only drench one in the most ineradicable kind of mucked-up publicity and have for compensation nothing at this party which might be representative for some of the Devil's better creations. So Robert Lowell and Norman Mailer feigned deep conversation. They turned their heads to one another at the empty table, ignoring the potentially acolytic drinkers at either elbow, they projected their elbows out in fact like flying buttresses or old Republicans, they exuded waves of Interrruption Repellent from the posture of their backs, and concentrated on their conversation, for indeed they were the only two men of remotely similar status in the room. (Explanations about the position of Paul Goodman will follow later.)

Lowell, whose personal attractiveness was immense (since his features were at once virile and patrician and his characteristic manner turned up facets of the grim, the gallant, the tender and the solicitous as if he were the nicest Boston banker one had ever hoped to meet) was not concerned too much about the evening at the theater. "I'm just going to read some poems," he said. "I suppose you're going to speak, Norman."

"Well, I will."

"Yes, you're awfully good at that."

"Not really." Harumphs, modifications, protestations and denials of the virtue of the ability to speak.

"I'm no good at all at public speaking," said Lowell in the kindest voice. He had indisputably won the first round. Mailer the younger, presumptive, and self-elected prince was left to his great surprise—for he had been exercised this way many times before—with the unmistakable feeling that there was some faint strain of the second-rate in this ability to speak on your feet.

Then they moved on to talk of what concerned them more. It was the subject first introduced to Mailer by Mitch Goodman. Tomorrow, a group of draft resisters, led by William Sloane Coffin, Jr., Chaplain at Yale, were going to march from their meeting place at a church basement, to the Department of Justice, and there a considerable number of draft cards would be deposited in a bag by individual students representing themselves, or their groups at different colleges, at which point Coffin and a selected few would walk into the Department of Justice, turn the cards over to the Attorney General, and await his reply.

"I don't think there'll be much trouble at this, do you?" asked Lowell.

"No, I think it'll be dull, and there'll be a lot of speeches."

"Oh, no," said Lowell with genuine pain, "Coffin's not that kind of fool."

"It's hard to keep people from making speeches."

"Well, you know what they want us to do?" Lowell explained. He had been asked to accompany a draft resister up to the bag in which the draft cards were being dropped. "It seems," said Lowell, with a glint of the oldest Yankee light winging off like a mad laser from his eye, "that they want us to be *big buddy*."

It was agreed this was unsuitable. No, Lowell suggested, it would be better if they each just made a few remarks. "I mean," said Lowell, beginning to stammer a little, "we could just get up and say we respect their action and support it, just to establish, I suppose, that we're there and behind them and so forth."

Mailer nodded. He felt no ease for any of these suggestions. He did not even know if he truly supported the turning in of draft cards. It seemed to him at times that the students who disliked the war most should perhaps be the first to volunteer for the Army in order that their ideas have currency in the Army as well. Without them, the armed forces could more easily become Glamour State for the more mindless regions of the proletariat if indeed the proletariat was not halfway to Storm Troop Junction already. The military could make an elite corps best when the troops were homogenized. On the other hand, no soldier could go into combat with the secret idea that he would not fire a gun. If nothing else, it was

31

unfair to friends in his outfit; besides it suggested the suicidal. No, the iron of the logic doubtless demanded that if you disapproved of the war too much to shoot Vietcong, then your draft card was for burning. But Mailer arrived at this conclusion somewhat used up as we have learned from the number of decisions he had to make at various moral crossroads en route and so felt no enthusiasm whatsoever for the preliminary demonstration at the Department of Justice tomorrow in which he would take part. To the contrary, he wondered if he would burn or surrender his own draft card if he were young enough to own one, and he did not really know the answer. How then could he advise others to take the action, or even associate his name? Still, he was going to be there.

He started to talk of these doubts with Lowell, but he could hear the sound of his own voice, and it offended him. It seemed weak, plaintive, as if his case were—no less incriminating word—phony, he did not quite know why. So he shut up.

A silence.

"You know, Norman," said Lowell in his fondest voice, "Elizabeth and I really think you're the finest journalist in America."

Mailer knew Lowell thought this—Lowell had even sent him a postcard once to state the enthusiasm. But the novelist had been shrewd enough to judge that Lowell sent many postcards to many people—it did not matter that Lowell was by overwhelming consensus judged to be the best, most talented, and most distinguished poet in America—it was still necessary to keep the defense lines in good working order. A good word on a card could keep many a dangerous recalcitrant in the ranks.

Therefore, this practice annoyed Mailer. The first card he'd ever received from Lowell was on a book of poems, *Deaths for the Ladies and other disasters* it had been called, and many people had thought the book a joke which whatever its endless demerits, it was not. Not to the novice poet at least. When Lowell had written that he liked the book, Mailer next waited for some word in print to canonize his thin tome; of course it never came. If Lowell were to begin to award living American poets in critical print, two hundred starving worthies could with fairness hold out their bowl before the escaped Novelist would deserve his turn. Still Mailer was irked. He felt he had been part of a literary game. When the second card came a few years later telling him he was the best journalist in America, he did not answer. Elizabeth Hardwick, Lowell's wife, had just published a review of *An American Dream* in *Partisan Review* which had done its best to disembowel the novel. Lowell's card might have arrived with the best of motives, but its timing suggested to Mailer an exercise in neutralsmanship—neutralize the maximum of possible future risks. Mailer was not critically equipped for the task, but there was always the distant danger that some bright and not unauthoritative voice, irked at Lowell's enduring hegemony, might come along with a long lance and presume to tell America that posterity would judge Allen Ginsberg the greater poet.

This was all doubtless desperately unfair to Lowell who, on the basis of two kind cards, was now judged by Mailer to possess an undue unchristian talent for literary logrolling. But then Mailer was prickly. Let us hope it was not because he had been beaten a little too often by book reviewers, since the fruit of specific brutality is general suspicion.

Still Lowell now made the mistake of repeating his remark. "Yes, Norman, I really think you are the best journalist in America."

The pen may be mightier than the sword, yet at their best, each belong to extravagant men. "Well, Cal," said Mailer, using Lowell's nickname for the first time, "there are days when I think of myself as being the best writer in America."

The effect was equal to walloping a roundhouse right into the heart of an English boxer who has been hitherto right up on his toes. Consternation, not Britannia, now ruled the waves. Perhaps Lowell had a moment when he wondered who was guilty of declaring war on the minuet. "Oh, Norman, oh, certainly," he said, "I didn't mean to imply, heavens no, it's just I have such *respect* for good journalism."

"Well, I don't know that I do," said Mailer. "It's much

harder to write"—the next said with great and false graciousness—"a good poem."

"Yes, of course."

Chuckles. Headmastermanship.

Chuckles. Fellow headmastermanship.

They were both now somewhat spoiled for each other. Mailer got up abruptly to get a drink. He was shrewd enough to know that Lowell, like many another aristocrat before him, respected abrupt departures. The pain of unexpected rejection is the last sweet vice left to an aristocrat (unless they should happen to be not aristocrats, but secret monarchs—then watch for your head!).

Next, Mailer ran into Paul Goodman at the bar—a short sentence which contains two errors and a misrepresentation. The assumption is that Goodman was drinking alcohol but he was not; by report, Goodman never took a drink. The bar, so-called, was a table with a white tablecloth, set up near the archway between the dining room where Lowell and Mailer had been talking and the living room where most of the party was being enacted—to the tune of ten couples perhaps—so the bar did not qualify as a bar, just a poor table with a cloth to support Mailer's irritated eye. Finally he did not run into Goodman. Goodman and Mailer had no particular love for one another—they tended to slide about each other at a party. In fact, they hardly knew each other.

Their lack of cordiality had begun on the occasion of a piece written by Goodman for *Dissent* which had discussed Washington in the early days of the Kennedy Administration. Goodman had found much to displease him then, and kept referring to the "wargasms" of this Kennedy Administration which wargasms he attached with no excessive intellectual jugglery to the existential and Reichian notions of the orgasm which Mailer had promulgated in his piece *The White Negro*. (Goodman was a sexologue—that is, an ideologue about sex—Mailer was then also a sexologue; no war so rich without quarter as the war between two sexologues.) Goodman, at any rate, had scored off Mailer almost at will, something to the general effect that the false prophet of the orgasm was naturally attached to the false hero of Washington who went in for wargasms. Writing for a scholarly Socialist quarterly like *Dissent,* it was hard to miss. The magnetic field of *Dissent*—hostile to Kennedy at the time—bent every wild shot to the target. So Mailer wrote a letter in reply. It was short, sought to be urbane, and was delivered exactly to the jugular, for it began by asserting that he could not judge the merits of Goodman's intellectual points since the other had made a cardinal point of emphasizing Mailer's own incapacity to reason and Goodman was doubtless correct, but Mailer did nonetheless feel competent to comment on the literary experience of encountering Goodman's style and that was not unrelated to the journeys one undertook in the company of a laundry bag . . . Great ferment in scholarly Socialist quarters! A small delegation of the Editors assured Mailer they would print his letter if he insisted, but the hope was that he would not. Mailer had always thought it senseless to undertake an attack unless you made certain it was printed, for otherwise you were left with a determined enemy who was an unmarked man, and therefore able to repay you at leisure and by the lift of an eyebrow. Mailer acceded however. He was fond of the Editors of *Dissent,* although his private mixture of Marxism, conservatism, nihilism, and large parts of existentialism could no longer produce any polemical gravies for the digestive apparatus of scholarly Scialist minds; nonetheless Mailer had never been asked to leave the Board, and would not have resigned on his own since that would have suggested a public attack on the ideas of people with whom he had no intellectual accord but of whom he was personally fond.

Nonetheless, from that day, Mailer and Goodman slid around one another at parties and waved languid hands in greeting. It was just as well. Each seemed to have the instinct a discussion would use up intellectual ordnance best reserved for articles. Besides, they had each doubtless read very little of the other.

Mailer, of course, was not without respect for Goodman. He thought Goodman had had an enormous influence in the colleges and much of it had been, from his own point of view, very much to the good. Paul Goodman had been the first to talk of the absurd and empty

35

nature of work and education in America, and a generation of college students had formed around the core of his militancy. But, oh, the style! It set Mailer's teeth on edge to read it; he was inclined to think that the body of students who followed Goodman must have something deanimalized to put up with the style or at least such was Mailer's bigoted view. His fundamental animus to Goodman was still, unhappily, on sex. Goodman's ideas tended to declare in rough that heterosexuality, homosexuality, and onanism were equal valid forms of activity, best denuded of guilt. Mailer, with his neo-Victorianism, thought that if there was anything worse than homosexuality and masturbation, it was putting the two together. The super-hygiene of all this mental prophylaxis offended him profoundly. Super-hygiene impregnated the air with medicated Vaseline—there was nothing dirty in the damn stuff; and sex to Mailer's idea of it was better off dirty, damned, even slavish! than clean, and without guilt. For guilt was the existential edge of sex. Without guilt, sex was meaningless. One advanced into sex against one's sense of guilt, and each time guilt was successfully defied, one had learned a little more about the contractual relation of one's own existence to the unheard thunders of the deep —each time guilt herded one back with its authority, some primitive awe—hence some creative clue to the rages of the deep—was left to brood about. Onanism and homosexuality were not, to Mailer, light vices—to him it sometimes seemed that much of life and most of society were designed precisely to drive men deep into onanism and homosexuality; one defied such a fate by sweeping up the psychic profit which derived from the existential assertion of yourself—which was a way of saying that nobody was born a man; you earned manhood provided you were good enough, bold enough.

This most conservative and warlike credo could hardly have meaning to a scientific humanist like Goodman for whom all obstacles to the good life derived precisely from guilt: guilt which was invariably so irrational—for it derived from the warped burden of the past. Goodman therefore said hello mildly to Mailer, who answered in as mild a voice, and that was all they had to say. Lowell,

36

following, expressed his condolences to Goodman on the recent death of his son, and Mailer after depressing the hostess by his refusal to eat, went on to talk to Macdonald.

That was most brief. They were old friends, who had a somewhat comic relation, for Macdonald—at least as Mailer saw it—was forever disapproving of the younger author until the moment they came together at one or another party or meeting. Then Macdonald would discover he was glad to see Mailer. In fact, Macdonald could hardly help himself. Of all the younger American writers, Mailer was the one who had probably been influenced most by Macdonald, not so much from the contents of Macdonald's ideas which were always going in and out of phase with Mailer's, but rather by the style of Macdonald's attack. Macdonald was forever referring the act of writing to his sense of personal standards which demanded craft, care, devotion, lack of humbug, and simple *a fortiori* honesty of sentiment. All this was a little too simple for Mailer's temper. Nonetheless, Macdonald had given him an essential clue which was: look to the feel of the phenomenon. If it feels bad, it *is* bad. Mailer could have learned this as easily from Hemingway, as many another novelist had, but he had begun as a young ideologue—his mind had been militant with positions fixed in concrete, and Macdonald's method had worked like Zen for him—at the least it had helped to get his guns loose. Macdonald had given the hint that the clue to discovery was not in the substance of one's idea, but in what was learned from the style of one's attack. (Which was one reason Mailer's style changed for every project.) So, the younger author was unquenchably fond of Macdonald, and it showed. Not a minute would go by before he would be poking Macdonald's massive belly with a finger.

But for now, they were ill at ease. Macdonald was in the process of reviewing Mailer's new novel *Why Are We In Vietnam?* for *The New Yorker*, and there was an empty space in the presence of the mood. Mailer was certain Macdonald did not like the new novel, and was going to do a negative review. He had seemed professionally unfriendly these past few weeks. The Novelist would have liked to assure the Critic that the review could not possibly affect their good feeling for one another, but he did not dare, for such a remark would break a rule, since it would encourage Macdonald to talk about what was in his review, or at worst trick him into an unwilling but revealing reply. Besides, Mailer did not trust himself to speak calmly about the matter. Although Macdonald would not admit it, he was in secret carrying on a passionate love affair with *The New Yorker*—Disraeli on his knees before Victoria. But the Novelist did not share Macdonald's infatuation at all—*The New Yorker* had not printed a line in review of *The Presidential Papers, An American Dream,* or *Cannibals and Christians,* and *that,* Mailer had long ago decided, was an indication of some of the worst things to be said about the magazine. He had once had a correspondence with Lillian Ross who asked him why he did not do a piece for *The New Yorker.* "Because they would not let me use the word 'shit,' " he had written back. Miss Ross suggested that all liberty was his if only he understood where liberty resided. True liberty, Mailer had responded, consisted of his right to say shit in *The New Yorker.* So there was old rage behind the arms-length bantering about Dwight's review of Norman's book, and Mailer finally left the conversation. Macdonald was beginning to like him again, and that was dangerous. Macdonald was so full of the very beans of that old-time Wasp integrity, that he would certainly bend over much too far backward if for a moment while reviewing the book he might have the thought he was sufficiently fond of Norman to conceivably be giving him too-gentle treatment. "No," thought the Novelist, "let him keep thinking he disapproves of me until the review is written."

Among his acquaintances at the party, this now left de Grazia. As has been indicated, they were old friends of the most superficial sort, which is to say that they hardly knew each other, and yet always felt like old friends when they met. Perhaps it was no more than the ability of each man to inspire an odd sense of intimacy. At any rate they never wasted time in needless conversation, since they were each too clever about the other to be penned in position by an evasion.

"How would you like to be the first speaker of the evening?" de Grazia asked.

"There'll be nothing interesting to follow me."

De Grazia's eyes showed pleasure. "Then I thought of starting with Macdonald."

"Dwight is conceivably the world's worst speaker." It was true. Macdonald's authority left him at the entrance to the aura of the podium. In that light he gesticulated awkwardly, squinted at his text, laughed at his own jokes, looked like a giant stork, whinnied, shrilled, and was often inaudible. When he spoke extempore, he was sometimes better, often worse.

"Well," said de Grazia, "I can't start with Lowell."

"No, no, no, you must save him."

"That leaves Goodman."

They nodded wisely. "Yes, let's get rid of Goodman first," said Mailer. But then the thought of that captive audience tuned to their first awareness of the evening by the pious drone of Goodman's voice injured every showman's instinct for the opening. "Who is going to be M.C.?" Mailer asked.

"Unless you want to, I thought I might be."

"I've never been an M.C." said Mailer, "but maybe I should be. I could warm the audience up before Goodman drops them." De Grazia looked uneasily at Mailer's bourbon. "For Christ's sakes, Ed," said Mailer.

"Well, all right," said de Grazia.

Mailer was already composing his introductory remarks, percolating along on thoughts of the subtle annoyance his role as Master of Ceremonies would cause the other speakers.

5 : TOWARD A THEATER OF IDEAS

The guests were beginning to leave the party for the Ambassador, which was two blocks away. Mailer did not know this yet, but the audience there had been waiting almost an hour. They were being entertained by an electronic folk rock guitar group, so presumably the young were more or less happy, and the middle-aged dim. Mailer was feeling the high sense of clarity which accompanies the light show of the aurora borealis when it is projected upon the inner universe of the chest, the lungs, and the heart. He was happy. On leaving, he had appropriated a coffee mug and filled it with bourbon. The fresh air illumined the bourbon, gave it a cerebrative edge; words entered his brain with the agreeable authority of fresh minted coins. Like all good professionals, he was stimulated by the chance to try a new if related line of work. Just as professional football players love sex because it is so close to football, so he was fond of speaking in public because it was thus near to writing. An extravagant analogy? Consider that a good half of writing consists of being sufficiently sensitive to the moment to reach for the next promise which is usually hidden in some word or phrase just a shift to the side of one's conscious intent. (Consciousness, that blunt tool, bucks in the general direction of the truth: instinct plucks the feather. Cheers!) Where public speaking is an exercise from prepared texts to demonstrate how successfully a low order of consciousness can beat upon the back of a collective flesh, public speaking being, therefore, a sullen expression of human possibility metaphorically equal to a bugger on his victim, speaking-in-public (as Mailer liked to describe any speech which was more or less improvised, impromptu, or dangerously written) was an activity like writing; one had to trick or seize or submit to the grace of each moment, which, except for those unexpected and sometimes well-deserved moments when consciousness and grace came together (and one felt on the consequence, heroic) were usually occasions of some mystery. The pleasure of speaking in public was the sensitivity it offered: with every phrase one was better or worse, close or less close to the existential promise of truth, *it feels true*, which hovers on good occasions like a presence between speaker and audience. Sometimes one was better, and worse, at the same moment; so strategic choices on the continuation of the attack would soon have to be decided, a moment to know the blood of the gambler in oneself.

Intimations of this approaching experience, obviously one of Mailer's preferred pleasures in life, at least when he did it well, were now connected to the professional sense of intrigue at the new task: tonight he would be both speaker and master of ceremonies. The two would conflict, but interestingly. Already he was looking in his mind for kind even celebrative remarks about Paul Goodman which would not violate every reservation he had about Goodman's dank glory. But he had it. It would be possible with no violation of truth to begin by saying that the first speaker looked very much like Nelson Algren, because in fact the first speaker was Paul Goodman, and both Nelson Algren and Paul Goodman looked like old cons. Ladies and Gentlemen, without further ado let me introduce one of young America's favorite old cons, Paul Goodman! (It would not be necessary to add that where Nelson Algren looked like the sort of skinny old con who was in on every make in the joint, and would sign away Grandma's farm to stay in the game, Goodman looked like the sort of old con who had first gotten into trouble in the YMCA, and hadn't spoken to anyone since.)

All this while, Mailer had in clutch *Why Are We In Vietnam?* He had neglected to bring his own copy to Washington and so had borrowed the book from his hostess on the promise he would inscribe it. (Later he was

41

actually to lose it—working apparently on the principle that if you cannot make a hostess happy, the next best charity is to be so evil that the hostess may dine out on tales of your misconduct.) But the copy of the book is now noted because Mailer, holding it in one hand and the mug of whisky in the other, was obliged to notice on entering the Ambassador Theater that he has an overwhelming urge to micturate. The impulse to pass urine, being for some reason more difficult to restrain when both hands are occupied, there was no thought in the Master of Ceremonies' mind about the alternatives—he would have to find The Room before he went on stage.

That was not so immediately simple as one would have thought. The twenty guests from the party, looking a fair piece subdued under the fluorescent lights, had therefore the not unhaggard look of people who have arrived an hour late at the theater. No matter that the theater was by every evidence sleazy (for neighborhood movie houses built on the dream of the owner that some day Garbo or Harlow or Lombard would give a look in, aged immediately they were not used for movies anymore) no matter, the guests had the uneasiness of very late arrivals. Apologetic, they were therefore in haste for the speakers to begin.

Mailer did not know this. He was off already in search of The Room, which, it developed was up on the balcony floor. Imbued with the importance of his first gig as Master of Ceremonies, he felt such incandescence of purpose that he could not quite conceive it necessary to notify de Grazia he would be gone for a minute. Incandescence is the *satori* of the Romantic spirit which spirit would insist —this is the essence of the Romantic—on accelerating time. The greater the power of any subjective state, the more total is a Romantic's assumption that everyone understands exactly what he is about to do, therefore waste not a moment by stopping to tell them.

Flush with his incandescence, happy in all the anticipation of liberty which this Götterdämmerung of a urination was soon to provide, Mailer did not know, but he had already and unwitting to himself metamorphosed into the Beast. Wait and see!

He was met on the stairs by a young man from *Time* magazine, a stringer presumably, for the young man lacked that I-am-damned look in the eye and rep tie of those whose work for *Time* has become a life addiction. The young man had a somewhat ill-dressed look, a map showed on his skin of an old adolescent acne, and he gave off the unhappy furtive presence of a fraternity member on probation for the wrong thing, some grievous mis-deposit of vomit, some hanky panky with frat-house tickets.

But the Beast was in a great good mood. He was soon to speak; that was food for all. So the Beast greeted the *Time* man with the geniality of a surrogate Hemingway unbending for the Luce-ites (Loo-sights was the pun) made some genial cryptic remark or two about finding Herr John, said cheerfully in answer to why he was in Washington that he had come to protest the war in Vietnam, and taking a sip of bourbon from the mug he kept to keep all fires idling right, stepped off into the darkness of the top balcony floor, went through a door into a pitch-black men's room, and was alone with his need. No chance to find the light switch for he had no matches, he did not smoke. It was therefore a matter of locating what's what with the probing of his toes. He found something finally which seemed appropriate, and pleased with the precision of these generally unused senses in his feet, took aim between them at a point twelve inches ahead, and heard in the darkness the sound of his water striking the floor. Some damn mistake had been made, an assault from the side doubtless instead of the front, the bowl was relocated now, and Master of Ceremonies breathed deep of the great reveries of this utterly non-Sisyphian release —at last!!—and thoroughly enjoyed the next forty-five seconds, being left on the aftermath not a note depressed by the condition of the premises. No, he was off on the Romantic's great military dream, which is: seize defeat, convert it to triumph. Of course, pissing on the floor was bad; very bad; the attendant would probably gossip to the police (if the *Time* man did not sniff it out first) and The Uniformed in turn would report it to The Press who were sure to write about the scandalous condition in which this meeting had left the toilets. And all of this contretemps

43

merely because the management, bitter with their lost dream of Garbo and Harlow and Lombard, were now so pocked and stingy they doused the lights. (Out of such stuff is a novelist's brain.)

Well, he could convert this deficiency to an asset. From gap to gain is very American. He would confess straight out to all aloud that he was the one who wet the floor in the men's room, he alone! While the audience was recovering from the existential anxiety of encountering an orator who confessed to such a crime, he would be able—their attention now riveted—to bring them up to a contemplation of deeper problems, of, indeed, the deepest problems, the most chilling alternatives, and would from there seek to bring them back to a restorative view of man. Man might be a fool who peed in the wrong pot, man was also a scrupulous servant of the self-damaging admission; man was therefore a philosopher who possessed the magic stone; he could turn loss to philosophical gain, and so illumine the deeps, find the poles, and eventually learn to cultivate his most special fool's garden: *satori,* incandescence, and the hard gem-like flame of bourbon burning in the furnaces of metabolism.

Thus composed, illumined by these first stages of Emersonian transcendence, Mailer left the men's room, descended the stairs, entered the back of the orchestra, all opening remarks held close file in his mind like troops ranked in order before the parade, and then suddenly, most suddenly saw, with a cancerous swoop of albatross wings, that de Grazia was on the stage, was acting as M.C., was—no calling it back—launched into the conclusion of a gentle stammering stumbling—small orator, de Grazia!—introduction of Paul Goodman. All lost! The magnificent opening remarks about the forces gathered here to assemble on Saturday before the Pentagon, this historic occasion, let us hold it in our mind and focus on a puddle of passed water on the floor above and see if we assembled here can as leftists and proud dissenters contain within our minds the grandeur of the two—all lost! —no chance to do more than pick up later—later! after de Grazia and Goodman had finished dead-assing the crowd. Traitor de Grazia! Sicilian de Grazia!

44

As Mailer picked his way between people sitting on the stone floor (orchestra seats had been removed—the movie house was a dance hall now with a stage) he made a considerable stir in the orchestra. Mailer had been entering theaters for years, mounting stages—now that he had put on weight, it would probably have been fair to say that he came to the rostrum like a poor man's version of Orson Welles, some minor note of the same contemplative presence. A titter and rise of expectation followed him. He could not resist its appeal. As he passed de Grazia, he scowled, threw a look from Lower Shakesperia "Et tu Bruté," and proceeded to slap the back of his hand against de Grazia's solar plexus. It was not a heavy blow, but then de Grazia was not a heavy man; he wilted some hint of an inch. And the audience pinched off a howl, squeaked on their squeal. It was not certain to them what had taken place.

Picture the scene two minutes later from the orchestra floor. Paul Goodman, now up at the microphone with no podium or rostrum, is reading the following lines:

> . . . these days my contempt
> for the misrulers of my country
> is icy and my indignation raucous.

It is impossible to tell what he is reading. Off at the wing of the stage where the others are collected—stout Macdonald, noble Lowell, beleaguered de Grazia, and Mailer, Prince of Bourbon, the acoustics are atrocious. One cannot hear a word the speaker is saying. Nor are there enough seats. If de Grazia and Macdonald are sitting in folding chairs, Mailer is squatting on his haunches, or kneeling on one knee like a player about to go back into the ball game. Lowell has the expression on his face of a dues payer who is just about keeping up with the interest on some enormous debt. As he sits on the floor with his long arms clasped mournfully about his long Yankee legs, "I am here," says his expression, "but I do not have to pretend I like what I see." The hollows in his cheeks give a hint of the hanging judge. Lowell is of a good weight, not too heavy, not too light, but the hollows

45

speak of the great Puritan gloom in which the country was founded—man was simply not good enough for God.

At this moment, it is hard not to agree with Lowell. The cavern of the theater seems to resonate behind the glare of the footlights, but this is no resonance of a fine bass voice—it is rather electronics on the march. The public address system hisses, then rings in a random chorus of electronic music, sound of a cerebral mastication from some horror machine of Outer Space (where all that electricity doubtless comes from, child!) then a hum like the squeak in the hinges of the gates of Hell—we are in the penumbra of psychedelic netherworlds, ghost-odysseys from the dead brain cells of adolescent trysts with LSD, some ultrapurple spotlight from the balcony (not ultraviolet—ultrapurple, deepest purple one could conceive) there out in the dark like some neon eye of the night, the media is the message, and the message is purple, speaks of the monarchies of Heaven, madnesses of God, and clam-vaults of people on a stone floor. Mailer's senses are now tuned to absolute pitch or sheer error—he marks a ballot for absolute pitch—he is certain there is a profound pall in the audience. Yes, they sit there, stricken, inert, in terror of what Saturday will bring, and so are unable to rise to a word the speaker is offering them. It will take dynamite to bring life. The shroud of burned-out psychedelic dreams is in this audience, Cancer Gulch with open maw—and Mailer thinks of the vigor and the light (from marijuana?) in the eyes of those American soldiers in Vietnam who have been picked by the newsreel cameras to say their piece, and the happy healthy never unintelligent faces of all those professional football players he studies so assiduously on television come Sunday (he has neglected to put his bets in this week) and wonders how they would poll out on sentiment for the war.

HAWKS 95   DOVES 6
NFL Footballers Approve Vietnam War

Doubtless. All the healthy Marines, state troopers, professional athletes, movie stars, rednecks, sensuous

46

life-loving Mafia, cops, mill workers, city officials, nice healthy-looking easy-grafting politicians full of the light (from marijuana?) in their eye of a life they enjoy—yes, they would be for the war in Vietnam. Arrayed against them as hard-core troops: an elite! the Freud-ridden embers of Marxism, good old American anxiety strata—the urban middle-class with their proliferated monumental adenoidal resentments, their secret slavish love for the oncoming hegemony of the computer and the suburb, yes, they and their children, by the sheer ironies, the sheer ineptitude, the *kinks* of history, were now being compressed into more and more militant stands, their resistance to the war some hopeless melange, somehow firmed, of Pacifism and closet Communism. And their children—on a freak-out from the suburbs to a love-in on the Pentagon wall.

It was the children in whom Mailer had some hope, a gloomy hope. These mad middle-class children with their lobotomies from sin, their nihilistic embezzlement of all middle-class moral funds, their innocence, their lust for apocalypse, their unbelievable indifference to waste: twenty generations of buried hopes perhaps engraved in their chromosomes, and now conceivably burning like faggots in the secret inquisitional fires of LSD. It was a devil's drug—designed by the Devil to consume the love of the best, and leave them liver-wasted, weeds of the big city. If there had been a player piano, Mailer might have put in a quarter to hear "In the Heart of the City Which Has No Heart."

Yes, these were the troops: middle-class cancer-pushers and drug-gutted flower children. And Paul Goodman to lead them. Was he now reading this?

> Once American faces
> were beautiful to me
> but now they look cruel
> and as if they had narrow thoughts.

Not much poetry, but well put prose. And yet there was always Goodman's damnable tolerance for all the varieties of sex. Did he know nothing of evil or entropy? Sex was the superhighway to your own soul's entropy if it was used without a constant sharpening of the taste. And orgies? What did Goodman know of orgies, real ones, not lib-lab college orgies to carry out the higher program of the Great Society, but real ones with murder in the air, and witches on the shoulder. The collected Tory in Mailer came roaring to the surface like a docked hat in a royal coach.

"When Goodman finishes, I'm going to take over as M.C.," he whispered to de Grazia. (The revery we have just attended took no more in fact that a second. Mailer's melancholy assessment of the forces now mounting in America took place between two consecutive lines of Goodman's poem—not because Mailer cerebrated that instantly, but because he had had the revery many a time before—he had to do no more than sense the audience, whisper Cancer Gulch to himself and the revery went by with a mental ch-ch-ch Click! reviewed again.) In truth, Mailer was now in a state. He had been prepared to open the evening with apocalyptic salvos to announce the real gravity of the situation, and the intensely peculiar American aspect of it—which is that the urban and suburban middle class were to be offered on Saturday an opportunity for glory—what other nation could boast of such option for its middle class? Instead—lost! The benignity and good humor of his planned opening remarks now subjugated to the electronic hawking and squabbling *hum* of the P.A., the maniacal necessity to *wait* was on this hiatus transformed into a violent concentration of purpose, all intentions reversed. He glared at de Grazia. "How could you do this?" he whispered to his ear.

De Grazia looked somewhat confused at the intensity. Meetings to de Grazia were obviously just meetings, assemblages of people who coughed up for large admissions or kicked in for the pitch; at best, some meetings were less boring than others. De Grazia was much too wise and guilty-spirited to brood on apocalypse. "I couldn't find you," he whispered back.

"You didn't trust me long enough to wait one minute?"

"We were over an hour late," de Grazia whispered again. "We had to begin."

Mailer was all for having the conversation right then

48

on stage: to hell with reciprocal rights and polite incline of the ear to the speaker. The Beast was ready to grapple with the world. "Did you think I wouldn't show up?" he asked de Grazia.

"Well, I was wondering."

In what sort of mumbo-jumbo of promise and betrayal did de Grazia live? How could de Grazia ever suppose he would not show up? He had spent his life showing up at the most boring and onerous places. He gave a blast of his eyes to de Grazia. But Macdonald gave a look at Mailer, as if to say, "You're creating disturbance."

Now Goodman was done.

Mailer walked to the stage. He did not have any idea any longer of what he would say, his mind was empty, but in a fine calm, taking for these five instants a total rest. While there was no danger of Mailer ever becoming a demagogue since if the first idea he offered could appeal to a mob, the second in compensation would be sure to enrage them, he might, nonetheless have made a fair country orator, for he loved to speak, he loved in fact to holler, and liked to hear a crowd holler back. (Of how many New York intellectuals may that be said?)

"I'm here as your original M.C., temporarily displaced owing to a contretemps"—which was pronounced purposefully as contretempse—"in the men's room," he said into the microphone for opening, but the gentle high-strung beast of a device pushed into a panic by the electric presence of a real Beast, let loose a squeal which shook the welds in the old foundation of the Ambassador. Mailer immediately decided he had had enough of public address systems, electronic fields of phase, impedance, and spooks in the circuitry. A hex on collaborating with Cancer Gulch. He pushed the microphone away, squared off before the audience. "Can you hear me?" he bellowed.

"Yes."

"Can you hear me in the balcony?"

"Yes."

"Then let's do away with electronics," he called out.

Cries of laughter came back. A very small pattern of applause. (Not too many on his side for electrocuting the public address system, or so his orator's ear recorded the vote.)

"Now I missed the beginning of this occasion, or I would have been here to introduce Paul Goodman, for which we're all sorry, right?"

Confused titters. Small reaction.

"What are you, dead-heads?" he bellowed at the audience. "Or are you all"—here he put on his false Irish accent—"in the nature of becoming dead ahsses?" Small laughs. A whistle or two. "No," he said, replying to the whistles, "I invoke these dead asses as part of the gravity of the occasion. The middle class plus one hippie surrealistic symbolic absolutely insane March on the Pentagon, bless us all," beginning of a big applause which offended Mailer for it came on "bless" and that was too cheap a way to win votes, "bless us all—shit!" he shouted, "I'm trying to say the middle class plus shit, I mean plus revolution, is equal to one big collective dead ass." Some yells of approval, but much shocked curious rather stricken silence. He had broken the shank of his oratorical charge. Now he would have to sweep the audience together again. (Perhaps he felt like a surgeon delivering a difficult breech—nothing to do but plunge to the elbows again.)

"To resume our exposition," a good warm titter, then a ripple of laughter, not unsympathetic to his ear; the humor had been unwitting, but what was the life of an orator without some bonus? "To resume this orderly marshalling of concepts"—a conscious attempt at humor which worked less well; he was beginning to recognize for the first time that bellowing without a mike demanded a more forthright style—"I shall now *engage* in confession." More Irish accent. (He blessed Brendan Behan for what he had learned from him.) "A public speaker may offer you two opportunities. Instruction or confession." Laughter now. "Well, you're all college heads, so my instruction would be as pearls before—I dare not say it." Laughs. Boos. A voice from the balcony: "Come on, Norman, say something!"

"Is there a black man in the house?" asked Mailer. He strode up and down the stage pretending to peer at the audience. But in fact they were illumined just well enough

50

to emphasize one sad discovery—if black faces there were they were certainly not in plenty. "Well ah'll just have to be the *impromptu* Black Power for tonight. Woo-eeeeee! Woo-eeeeee! HMmmmmmm." He grunted with some partial success, showing hints of Cassius Clay. "Get your white butts moving."

"The confession. The confession!" screamed some adolescents from up front.

He came to a stop, shifted his voice. Now he spoke in a relaxed tone. "The confession, yeah!" Well, at least the audience was awake. He felt as if he had driven away some sepulchral phantoms of a variety which inhabited the profound middle-class schist. Now to charge the center of vested spookery.

"Say," he called out into the semidarkness with the ultrapurple light coming off the psychedelic lamp on the rail of the balcony, and the spotlights blaring against his eyes, "say," all happiness again, "I think of Saturday, and that March and do you know, fellow carriers of the holy unendurable grail, for the first time in my life I don't know whether I have the piss or the shit scared out of me most." It was an interesting concept, thought Mailer, for there was a difference between the two kinds of fear—pursue the thought, he would, in quieter times—"we are up, face this, all of you, against an existential situation—we do not know how it is going to turn out, and what is even more inspiring of dread is that the government doesn't know either."

Beginning of a real hand, a couple of rebel yells. "We're going to try to stick it up the government's ass," he shouted, "right into the sphincter of the Pentagon." Wild yells and chills of silence from different reaches of the crowd. Yeah, he was cooking now. "Will reporters please get every word accurately," he called out dryly to warm the chill.

But humor may have been too late. *The New Yorker* did not have strictures against the use of sh*t for nothing; nor did Dwight Macdonald love *The New Yorker* for nothing, he also had strictures against sh*t's metaphorical associations. Mailer looked to his right to see Macdonald approaching, a book in his hands, arms at his side, a sor-

51

rowing look of concern in his face. "Norman," said Macdonald quietly, "I can't possibly follow you after all this. Please introduce me, and get it over with."

Mailer was near to stricken. On the one hand interrupted on a flight; on the other, he had fulfilled no duty whatsoever as M.C. He threw a look at Macdonald which said: give me this. I'll owe you one.

But de Grazia was there as well. "Norman, let me be M.C. now," he said.

They were being monstrous unfair, thought Mailer. They didn't understand what he had been doing, how good he had been, what he would do next. Fatal to walk off now—the verdict would claim he was unbalanced. Still, he could not hold the stage by force. That was unthinkably worse.

For the virtuous, however, deliverance (like buttercups) pops up everywhere. Mailer now took the microphone and turned to the audience. He was careful to speak in a relaxed voice. "We are having a disagreement about the value of the proceedings. Some think de Grazia should resume his post as Master of Ceremnies. I would like to keep the position. It is an existential moment. We do not know how it will turn out. So let us vote on it." Happy laughter from the audience at these comic effects. Actually Mailer did not believe it was an existential situation any longer. He reckoned the vote would be well in his favor. "Will those," he asked, "who are in favor of Mr. de Grazia succeeding me as Master of Ceremonies please say aye."

A good sound number said aye.

Now for the ovation. "Will those opposed to this, please say no." The no's to Mailer's lack of pleasure were no greater in volume. "It seems the ayes and no's are about equal," said Mailer. (He was thinking to himself that he had posed the issue all wrong—the ayes should have been reserved for those who would keep him in office.) "Under the circumstances," he announced, "I will keep the chair." Laughter at this easy cheek. He stepped into the middle of such laughter. "You have all just learned an invaluable political lesson." He waved the microphone at the audience. "In the absence of a definitive vote, the man who holds the power, keeps it."

"Hey, de Grazia," someone yelled from the audience, "why do you let him have it?"

Mailer extended the microphone to de Grazia who smiled sweetly into it. "Because if I don't," he said in a gentle voice, "he'll beat the shit out of me." The dread word had been used again.

"Please, Norman," said Macdonald retreating.

So Mailer gave his introduction to Macdonald. It was less than he would have attempted if the flight had not been grounded, but it was certainly respectable. Under the military circumstances, it was a decent cleanup operation. For about a minute he proceeded to introduce Macdonald as a man with whom one might seldom agree, but could never disrespect because he always told the truth as he saw the truth, a man therefore of the most incorruptible integrity. "Pray heaven, I am right," said Mailer to himself, and walked past Macdonald who was on his way to the mike. Both men nodded coolly to each other.

In the wing, visible to the audience, Paul Goodman sat on a chair clearly avoiding any contaminatory encounter with The Existentialist. De Grazia gave his "It's tough all over" smile. Lowell sat in a mournful hunch on the floor, his eyes peering over his glasses to scrutinize the metaphysical substance of his boot, now hide? now machine? now, where the joining and to what? foot to foot, boot to earth—cease all speculations as to what was in Lowell's head. "The one mind a novelist cannot enter is the mind of a novelist superior to himself," said once to Mailer by Jean Malaquais. So, by corollary, the one mind a minor poet may not enter . . .

Lowell looked most unhappy. Mailer, minor poet, had often observed that Lowell had the most disconcerting mixture of strength and weakness in his presence, a blending so dramatic in its visible sign of conflict that one had to assume he would be sensationally attractive to women. He had something untouchable, all insane in its force; one felt immediately there were any number of causes for which the man would be ready to die, and for some he would fight, with an axe in his hand and a

Cromwellian light in his eye. It was even possible that physically he was very strong—one couldn't tell at all—he might be fragile, he might have the sort of farm mechanic's strength which could manhandle the rear axle and differential off a car and into the back of a pickup. But physical strength or no, his nerves were all too apparently delicate. Obviously spoiled by everyone for years, he seemed nonetheless to need the spoiling. These nerves—the nerves of a consummate poet—were not tuned to any battering. The squalls of the mike, now riding up a storm on the erratic piping breath of Macdonald's voice, seemed to tear along Lowell's back like a gale. He detested tumult—obviously. And therefore saw everything which was hopeless in a rife situation: the dank middle-class depths of the audience, the strident squalor of the mike, the absurdity of talent gathered to raise money—for what, dear God? who could finally know what this March might convey, or worse, purvey, and worst of all—to be associated now with Mailer's butcher boy attack. Lowell's eyes looked up from the shoe, and passed one withering glance by the novelist, saying much, saying, "Every single bad thing I have ever heard about you is not exaggerated."

Mailer, looking back, thought bitter words he would not say: "You, Lowell, beloved poet of many, what do you know of the dirt and the dark deliveries of the necessary? What do you know of dignity hard-achieved, and dignity lost through innocence, and dignity lost by sacrifice for a cause one cannot name. What do you know about getting fat against your will, and turning into a clown of an arriviste baron when you would rather be an eagle or a count, or rarest of all, some natural aristocrat from these damned democratic states. No, the only subject we share, you and I, is that species of perception which shows that if we are not very loyal to our unendurable and most exigent inner light, then some day we may burn. How dare you condemn me! You know the diseases which inhabit the audience in this accursed psychedelic house. How dare you scorn the explosive I employ?"

And Lowell with a look of the greatest sorrow as if all this *mess* were finally too shapeless for the hard Protestant smith of his own brain, which would indeed burst if it could not forge his experience into the iron edge of the very best words and the most unsinkable relation of words, now threw up his eyes like an epileptic as if turned out of orbit by a turn of the vision—and fell backward, his head striking the floor with no last instant hesitation to cushion the blow, but like a baby, downright sudden, savagely to himself, as if from the height of a foot he had taken a pumpkin and dropped it splat on the floor. "There, much-regarded, much-protected brain, you have finally taken a blow," Lowell might have said to himself, for he proceeded to lie there, resting quietly, while Macdonald went on reading from "The White Man's Burden," Lowell seeming as content as if he had just tested the back of his cranium against a policeman's club. What a royal head they had all to lose!

6: A TRANSFER OF POWER

The evening went on. It was in fact far from climax. Lowell, resting in the wing on the floor of the stage, Lowell recuperating from the crack he had given his head, was a dreamy figure of peace in the corner of the proscenium, a reclining shepherd contemplating his flute, although a Washington newspaper was to condemn him on Saturday in company with Mailer for "slobbish behavior" at this unseemly lounging.

Now Macdonald finished. What with the delays, the unmanageable public address system, and the choppy waters of the audience at his commencement, for Mailer had obviously done him no good, Macdonald had been somewhat less impressive than ever. A few people had shown audible boredom with him. (Old-line Communists perhaps. Dwight was now one of the oldest anti-Communists in America.)

> Take up the White Man's burden—
> Ye dare not stoop to less—
> Nor call too loud on Freedom
> To cloak your weariness;
> By all ye cry or whisper,
> By all ye leave or do,
> The silent, sullen peoples
> Shall weigh your Gods and you.

read Macdonald from Kipling's poem, and the wit was in the selection, never the presentation.

He was done. He walked back to the wings with an air of no great satisfaction in himself, at most the sense of an obligation accomplished. Lowell's turn had arrived. Mailer stood up to introduce him.

The novelist gave a fulsome welcome to the poet. He did not speak of his poetry (with which he was not conspicuously familiar) nor of his prose which he thought excellent—Mailer told instead of why he had respect for Lowell as a man. A couple of years ago, the poet had refused an invitation from President Johnson to attend a garden party for artists and intellectuals, and it had attracted much attention at the time for it was one of the first dramatic acts of protest against the war in Vietnam, and Lowell was the only invited artist of first rank who had refused. Saul Bellow, for example, had attended the garden party. Lowell's refusal could not have been easy, the novelist suggested, because artists were attracted to formal afternoons of such elevated kind since that kind of experience was often stimulating to new perception and new work. So, an honorific occasion in full panoply was not easy for the mature artist to eschew. Capital! Lowell had therefore bypassed the most direct sort of literary capital. Ergo, Mailer respected him—he could not be certain he would have done the same himself, although, of course, he assured the audience he would not probably have ever had the opportunity to refuse. (Hints of merriment in the crowd at the thought of Mailer on the White House lawn.)

If the presentation had been formal up to here, it had

also been somewhat graceless. On the consequence, our audience's amusement tipped the slumbering Beast. Mailer now cranked up a vaudeville clown for finale to Lowell's introduction. "Ladies and gentlemen, if novelists come from the middle class, poets tend to derive from the bottom and the top. We all know good poets at the bot' —ladies and gentlemen, here is a poet from the top, Mr. Robert Lowell." A large and vigorous hand of applause, genuine enthusiasm for Lowell, some standing ovation.

But Mailer was depressed. He had betrayed himself again. The end of the introduction belonged in a burlesque house—he worked his own worst veins, like a man on the edge of bankruptcy trying to collect hopeless debts. He was fatally vulgar! Lowell passing him on the stage had recovered sufficiently to cast him a nullifying look. At this moment, they were obviously far from friends.

Lowell's shoulders had a slump, his modest stomach was pushed forward a hint, his chin was dropped to his chest as he stood at the microphone, pondering for a moment. One did not achieve the languid grandeurs of that slouch in one generation—the grandsons of the first sons had best go through the best troughs in the best eating clubs at Harvard before anyone in the family could try for such elegant note. It was now apparent to Mailer that Lowell would move by instinct, ability, and certainly by choice, in the direction most opposite from himself.

"Well," said Lowell, softly to the audience, his voice dry and gentle as any New England executioner might ever hope to be, "this has been a zany evening." Laughter came back, perhaps a little too much. It was as if Lowell wished to reprove Mailer, not humiliate him. So he shifted, and talked a bit uneasily for perhaps a minute about very little. Perhaps it was too little. Some of the audience, encouraged by earlier examples, now whistled. "We can't hear you," they shouted, "speak louder."

Lowell was annoyed. "I'll bellow," he said, "but it won't do any good." His firmness, his distaste for the occasion, communicated some subtle but impressive sense of his superiority. Audiences are moved by many cues but the most satisfactory of them is probably the voice of their abdomen. There are speakers who give a sense of security to the abdomen, and they always elicit the warmest kind of applause. Mailer was not this sort of speaker; Lowell was. The hand of applause which followed this remark was fortifying. Lowell now proceeded to read some poetry.

He was not a splendid reader, merely decent to his own lines, and he read from that slouch, that personification of ivy climbing a column, he was even diffident, he looked a trifle helpless under the lights. Still, he made no effort to win the audience, seduce them, dominate them, bully them, amuse them, no, they were there for him, to please *him,* a sounding board for the plucked string of his poetic line, and so he endeared himself to them. They adored him—for his talent, his modesty, his superiority, his melancholy, his petulance, his weakness, his painful, almost stammering shyness, his noble strength—*there* was the string behind other strings.

> O to break loose, like the chinook
> salmon jumping and falling back,
> nosing up to the impossible
> stone and bone-crushing waterfall—
> raw-jawed, weak-fleshed there, stopped by ten
> steps of the roaring ladder, and then
> to clear the top on the last try,
> alive enough to spawn and die.

Mailer discovered he was jealous. Not of the talent. Lowell's talent was very large, but then Mailer was a bulldog about the value of his own talent. No, Mailer was jealous because he had worked for this audience, and Lowell without effort seemed to have stolen them: Mailer did not know if he was contemptuous of Lowell for playing *grand maître,* or admiring of his ability to do it. Mailer knew his own version of *grand maître* did not compare. Of course no one would be there to accept his version either. The pain of bad reviews was not in the sting, but in the subsequent pressure which, like water on a joint, collected over the decade. People who had not read your books in fifteen years were certain they were missing nothing of merit. A buried sorrow, not very attractive, (for bile was in it and the bitterness of unrequited literary injustice) released itself from some ducts of the heart, and Mailer felt hot anger at how Lowell was loved and he was not, a pure and surprising recognition of how much emotion, how much simple and childlike bitter sorrowing emotion had been concealed from himself for years under the manhole cover of his contempt for bad reviews.

> Pity the planet, all joy gone
> from this sweet volcanic cone;
> peace to our children when they fall
> in small war on the heels of small
> war—until the end of time
> to police the earth, a ghost
> orbiting forever lost
> in our monotonous sublime.

They gave Lowell a good standing ovation, much heartiness in it, much obvious pleasure that they were there on a night in Washington when Robert Lowell had read from his work—it was as nice as that—and then Lowell walked back to the wings, and Mailer walked forward. Lowell did not seem particularly triumphant. He looked still modest, still depressed, as if he had been applauded too much for too little and so the reservoir of guilt was still untapped.

Nonetheless, to Mailer it was now *mano a mano*. Once, on a vastly larger scale of applause, perhaps people had reacted to Manolete not unlike the way they reacted to Lowell, so stirred by the deeps of sorrow in the man, that the smallest move produced the largest emotion. If there was any value to the comparison then Mailer was kin to the young Dominguin, taking raucous chances, spitting in the eye of the bull, an excess of variety in his passes. But probably there was no parallel at all. He may have felt like a matador in the flush of full competition, going out to do his work after the other torero has had a triumph, but for fact he was probably less close in essence now to the bullfighter than the bull. We must not forget the Beast. He had been sipping the last of the bourbon out of the mug. He had been delayed, piqued, twisted from his purpose and without anything to eat in close to ten hours. He was on the hunt. For what, he hardly knew. It is possible the hunt existed long before the victim was ever conceived.

"Now, you may wonder who I am," he said to the audience, or bellowed to them, for again he was not using the mike, "and you may wonder why I'm talking in a Southern accent which is phony"—the Southern accent as it sounded to him in his throat, was actually not too bad at this moment—"and the reason is that I want to make a presentation to you." He did not have a notion of what he would say next, but it never occurred to him something would not come. His impatience, his sorrow, his jealousy were gone, he just wanted to live on the edge of that rhetorical sword he would soon try to run through the heart of the audience. "We are gathered here"— shades of Lincoln in hippieland—"to make a move on Saturday to invest the Pentagon and halt and slow down its workings, and this will be at once a symbolic act and a real act"—he was roaring—"for real heads may possibly get hurt, and soldiers will be there to hold us back, and some of us may be arrested"—how, wondered the wise voice at the rear of this roaring voice, could one ever leave Washington now without going to jail?—"some blood conceivably will be shed. If I were the man in the government responsible for controlling this March, I would not know what to do." Sonorously—"I would not wish to arrest too many or hurt anyone for fear the repercussions in the world would be too large for my bureaucrat's heart to bear—it's so full of shit." Roars and chills from the audience again. He was off into obscenity. It gave a heartiness like the blood of beef tea to his associations. There was no villainy in obscenity for him, just— paradoxically, characteristically—his love for America: he had first come to love America when he served in the U.S. Army, not the America of course of the flag, the patriotic unendurable fix of the television programs and the newspapers, no, long before he was ever aware of the institutional oleo of the most suffocating American ideas he had come to love what editorial writers were fond of calling the democratic principle with its faith in the common man. He found that principle and that man in the Army, but what none of the editorial writers ever mentioned was that that noble common man was obscene as an old goat, and his obscenity was what saved him. The sanity of said common democratic man was in his humor, his humor was in his obscenity. And his philosophy as well—a reductive philosophy which looked to restore the hard edge of proportion to the overblown values overhanging each small military existence—viz: being forced to salute an overconscientious officer with your back stiffened into an exaggerated posture. "That Lieutenant is chickenshit," would be the platoon verdict, and a blow had somehow been struck for democracy and the sanity of good temper. Mailer once heard a private end an argument about the merits of a general by saying, "his spit don't smell like ice cream either," only the private was not speaking of spit. Mailer thought enough of the line to put it into *The Naked and the Dead,* along with a good many other such lines the characters in his mind and his memory of the Army had begun to offer him. The common discovery of America was probably that Americans were the first people on earth to live for their humor; nothing was so important to Americans as humor. In Brooklyn, he had taken this for granted, at Harvard he had thought it was a by-product of being at Harvard, but in the Army he discovered that the humor was probably in the veins and the roots of the local history of every state and county in America—the truth of the way it really felt over the years passed on a river of obscenity from small-town storyteller to storyteller there down below the bankers and the books and the educators and the legislators—so Mailer never felt more like an American than when he was naturally obscene—all the gifts of the American language came out in the happy play of obscenity upon concept, which enabled one to go back to concept again. What was magnificent about the word shit is that it enabled you to use the word noble: a skinny Southern cracker with a beatific smile on his face saying in the dawn in a Filipino rice paddy, "Man, I just managed to take me a noble shit." Yeah, that was Mailer's America. If he was going to love something in the country, he would love that. So after years of keeping obscene language off to one corner of his work, as if to prove after *The Naked and the Dead* that he had many an arrow in his literary quiver, he had come back to obscenity again in the last year—he had kicked goodbye in his novel *Why Are We In Vietnam?* to the old literary corset of good taste, letting his sense of language play on obscenity as freely as it wished, so discovering that everything he knew about the American language (with its incommensurable resources) went flying in and out of the line of his prose with the happiest beating of wings—it was the first time his style seemed at once very American to him and very literary in the best way, at least as he saw the best way. But the reception of the book had been disappointing. Not because many of the reviews were bad (he had learned, despite all sudden discoveries of sorrow, to live with that as one lived with smog) no, what was disappointing was the crankiness across the country. Where fusty conservative old critics had once defended the obscenity in *The Naked and the Dead,* they, or their sons, now condemned it in the new book, and that *was* disappointing. The country was not growing up so much as getting a premature case of arthritis.

At any rate, he had come to the point where he liked to use a little obscenity in his public speaking. Once people got over the shock, they were sometimes able to discover that the humor it provided was not less powerful than the damage of the pain. Of course he did not do it often and he tried not to do it unless he was in good voice—Mailer was under no illusion that public speaking was equal to candid conversation; an obscenity uttered in a voice too weak for its freight was obscene, since obscenity probably resides in the quick conversion of excitement to nausea—which is why Lyndon's Johnson's speeches are called obscene by some. The excitement of listening to the American President alters abruptly into the nausea of wandering down the blind alleys of his voice.

This has been a considerable defense of the point, but then the point was at the center of his argument and it could be put thus: the American corporation executive, who was after all the foremost representative of Man in the world today, was perfectly capable of burning unseen women and children in the Vietnamese jungles, yet felt a large displeasure and fairly final disapproval at the generous use of obscenity in literature and in public.

The apology may now be well taken, but what in fact did Mailer say on the stage of the Ambassador before the evening was out? Well, not so very much, just about enough to be the stuff of which footnotes are made, for he did his best to imitate a most high and executive voice.

"I had an experience as I came to the theater to speak to all of you, which is that before appearing on this stage I went upstairs to the men's room as a prelude to beginning this oratory so beneficial to all"—laughs and catcalls —"and it was dark, so—ahem—I missed the bowl—all men will know what I mean. Forgiveness might reign. But tomorrow, they will blame that puddle of water on Communists which is the way we do things here in Amurrica, anyone of you pinko poos want to object, lemme tell ya, the reason nobody was in the men's room, and it so dark, is that if there been a light they'd had to put a CIA man in there and the hippies would grope him silly, see here, you know who I am, why it just came to me, ah'm so phony, I'm as full of shit as Lyndon Johnson. Why, man, I'm nothing but his little old alter ego. That's what you got right here working for you, Lyndon Johnson's little old *dwarf* alter ego. How you like him? How you like him?" (Shades of Cassius Clay again.)

And in the privacy of his brain, quiet in the glare of all that sound and spotlight, Mailer thought quietly, "My God, that is probably exactly what you are at this moment, Lyndon Johnson with all his sores, sorrows, and vanity, squeezed down to five foot eight," and Mailer felt for the instant possessed, as if he had seized some of the President's secret soul, or the President seized some of his —the bourbon was as luminous as moonshine to the spores of insanity in the flesh of his brain, a smoke of menace swished in the air, and something felt real, almost as if he had caught Lyndon Johnson by the toe and now indeed, bugger the rhyme, should never let him go.

"Publicity hound," shouted someone from the upper balcony.

"Fuck you," cried Mailer back with absolute delight, all the force of the Texas presidency in his being. Or was it Lucifer's fire? But let us use asterisks for these obscenities to emphasize how happily he used the words, they went off like fireworks in his orator's heart, and asterisks look like rocket-bursts and the orbs from Roman candles ***. F*ck you he said to the heckler but with such gusto the vowel was doubled. F*-*ck you! was more like it. So, doubtless, had the President disposed of all opposition in private session. Well, Mailer was here to bring the presidency to the public.

"This yere dwarf alter ego has been telling you about his imbroglio with the p*ssarooney up on the top floor, and will all the reporters please note that I did not talk about defecation commonly known as sheeee-it!"—full imitation of LBJ was attempted there—"but to the contrary, speak of you-rye-nation! I p*ssed on the floor. Hoo-ee! Hoo-ee! How's that for Black Power full of white p*ss? You just know all those reporters are going to say it was sh*t tomorrow. F*ck them. F*ck all of them. Reporters, will you stand up and be counted?"

A wail of delight from the students in the audience. What would the reporters do? Would they stand?

One lone figure arose.

"Where are *you* from?" asked Mailer.

"Washington *Free Press*." A roar of delight from the crowd. It was obviously some student or hippie paper.

"Ah want *The Washington Post*," said Mailer in his best Texas tones, "and the *Star*. Ah know there's a *Time* magazine man here for one, and twenty more like him no doubt." But no one stood. So Mailer went into a diatribe. "Yeah, people," he said, "watch the reporting which follows. Yeah, these reporters will kiss Lyndon Johnson's *ss and Dean Rusk's *ss and Man Mountain Mc- Namara's *ss, they will rush to kiss it, but will they stand up in public? No! Because they are the silent assassins of the Republic. They alone have done more to destroy this nation than any force in it." They will certainly destroy me in the morning, he was thinking. But it was for this moment worth it, as if two very different rivers, one external, one subjective, had come together; the frustrated bile, piss, pus, and poison he had felt at the progressive contamination of all American life in the abscess of Vietnam, all of that, all heaped in lighted coals of brimstone on the press' collective ear, represented one river, and the other was the frustrated actor in Mailer—ever since seeing *All the King's Men* years ago he had wanted to come on in public as a Southern demagogue.

The speech went on, and a few fine things possibly were said next to a few equally obscene words, and then Mailer thought in passing of reading a passage from *Why Are We In Vietnam?* but the passage was full of plays of repetition on the most famous four-letter word of them all, and Mailer thought that was conceivably redundant now and so he ended modestly with a final, "See you on Saturday!"

The applause was fair. Not weak, but empty of large demonstration. No standing ovation for certain. He felt cool, and in a quiet, pleasant, slightly depressed mood. Since there was not much conversation between Macdonald, Lowell, and himself, he turned after a moment, left the stage, and walked along the floor where the audience had sat. A few people gathered about him, thanked him, shook his hand. He was quiet and reserved now, with genial slightly muted attempts to be cordial. He had noticed this shift in mood before, even after readings or lectures which had been less eventful. There was a mutual embarrassment between speaker and audience once the speaker had left the stage and walked through the crowd. It was due no doubt to the intimacy—that most special intimacy—which can live between a speaker and the people he has addressed, yes they had been so intimate then, that the encounter now, afterward, was like the eye-to-the-side maneuvers of client and whore once the act is over and dressing is done.

Mailer went on from there to a party of more liberal academics, and drank a good bit more and joked with Macdonald about the superiority of the introduction he

65

had given to Lowell over the introduction Dwight had received.

"Next time don't interrupt me," he teased Macdonald, "and I'll give you a better introduction."

"Goodness, I couldn't hear a word you said," said Macdonald, "you just sounded awful. Do you know, Norman, the acoustics were terrible on the wing. I don't think any of us heard anything anyone else said."

Some time in the early morning, or not so early, Mailer got to bed at the Hay-Adams and fell asleep to dream no doubt of fancy parties in Georgetown when the Federal period in architecture was young. Of course if this were a novel, Mailer would spend the rest of the night with a lady. But it is history, and so the Novelist is for once blissfully removed from any descripion of the hump-your-backs of sex. Rather he can leave such matters to the happy or unhappy imagination of the reader.

PART II

Friday Afternoon

1: THE HISTORIAN

To write an intimate history of an event which places its focus on a central figure who is not central to the event, is to inspire immediate questions about the competence of the historian. Or, indeed, his honorable motive. The figure he has selected may be convenient to him rather than critical to the history. Such cynical remarks obviously suggest themselves in the choice of our particular protagonist. It could be said that for this historian, there is no other choice. While that might not be necessarily inaccurate, nonetheless a presentation of his good motives had best be offered now.

The March on the Pentagon was an ambiguous event whose essential value or absurdity may not be established for ten or twenty years, or indeed ever. So to place the real principals, the founders or designers of the March, men like David Dellinger, or Jerry Rubin, in the center of our portrait could prove misleading. They were serious men, devoted to hard detailed work; their position in these affairs, precisely because it was central, can resolve nothing of the ambiguity. For that, an eyewitness who is a participant but not a vested partisan is required, further he must be not only involved, but ambiguous in his own proportions, a comic hero, which is to say, one cannot happily resolve the emphasis of the category—is he finally comic, a ludicrous figure with mock-heroic associations; or is he not unheroic, and therefore embedded somewhat tragically in the comic? Or is he both at once, and all at once? These questions, which probably are not much more answerable than the very ambiguities of the event, at least help to recapture the precise feel of the ambiguity of the event and its monumental disproportions. Mailer is a figure of monumental disproportions and so serves willy-nilly as the bridge—many will say the *pons asinorum*—into the crazy house, the crazy mansion, of that historic moment when a mass of the citizenry—not much more than a mob—marched on a bastion which symbolized the military might of the Republic, marching not to capture it, but to wound it *symbolically;* the forces defending that bastion reacted as if a symbolic wound could prove as mortal as any other combative rent. In the midst of a technological century, close to its apogee, a medieval, nay, a primitive mode of warfare was reinvigorated, and the nations of the world stood in grave observation. Either the century was entrenching itself more deeply into the absurd, or the absurd was delivering evidence that it was possessed of some of the nutritive mysteries of a marrow which would yet feed the armies of the absurd. So if the event took place in one of the crazy mansions, or indeed *the* crazy house of history, it is fitting that any ambiguous comic hero of such history should be not only off very much to the side of the history, but that he should be an egotist of the most startling misproportions, outrageously and often unhappily self-assertive, yet in command of a detachment classic in severity (for he was a novelist and so in need of studying every last lineament of the fine, the noble, the frantic, and the foolish in others and in himself). Such egotism being two-headed, thrusting itself forward the better to study itself, finds itself therefore at home in a house of mirrors, since it has habits, even the talent, to regard itself. Once History inhabits a crazy house, egotism may be the last tool left to History.

Let us then make our comic hero the narrative vehicle for the March on the Pentagon. Let us follow further. He is awakening Friday morning in his room at the Hay-Adams after his night on the stage of the Ambassador and the party thereafter. One may wonder if the Adams in the name of his hotel bore any relation to Henry; we need not be concerned with Hay who was a memorable and accomplished gentleman from the nineteenth century (then Secretary of State to McKinley and Roosevelt)

68

other than to say that the hotel looked like its name, and was indeed the staunchest advocate of that happy if heavy style in Washington architecture which spoke of a time when men and events were solid, comprehensible, often obedient to a code of values, and resolutely nonelectronic. Mailer awakening with a thunderous electronic headache began his morning revery with a conclusion that the Georgian period in architecture was not resolutely suited to himself.

2: THE CITIZEN

writer

subject

All right, let us look into his mind. It has been burned out by the gouts of bourbon he has taken into himself the night before (in fact, one of the reasons he detests napalm is that he assumes its effect on the countryside is comparable to the ravages of booze on the better foliage of his brain) however, one can make too much of a hangover, these are comic profits which should perhaps be reinvested—his headache is in truth not thunderous so much as definite and ineradicable until late afternoon, when whiskey wastes half-cleared, he will feel legitimized to take another drink. In the meantime, he must stir his stupefied message center into sufficient activity to give him a mind to meet the minds he would encounter this day, for this day, Friday, was—you will remember—the occasion on which he would lend the dubious substance of his name to those young men brave enough, idealistic enough, (and doubtless vegetarian enough!) to give their draft cards back to the government on the steps of the Department of Justice. Mailer detested the thought of getting through the oncoming hours. Under the best of circumstances the nature of these heroics was too dry, too dignified, too obviously severed from bravura to make the

69

Novelist happy (not for nothing had an eminent critic once said that Mailer was as fond of his style as an Italian tenor is fond of his vocal chords) no, he liked good character when it issued into action which was visually tumultuous rather than inspiring awe in the legal mind. To the extent any revolution was legalistic, Mailer detested it, cursed those logics of commitment which carried him into such formal lines of protest.

Of course, the alternatives did not appeal to him on this morning either. His head delicate, he could not help remembering that these affairs were not always so dignified; there had been occasional small riots between pro- and anti-war demonstrators, and the past week had had its associated excitements in Oakland, Chicago, at the University of Wisconsin, Reed College, Brooklyn College, on Boston Common where four thousand demonstrators had massed at a draft-card burning. ("67 men," *Time* was later to report, "ignited their cards with a candlestick once owned by William Ellery Channing.") In some of these places there had been violence with the police, broken heads, the use of Mace by the Oakland police, a particularly nasty chemical spray which blinded people for a few hours. (Indeed its name was appropriate for Batman.) Mailer's eyesight was not good—the thought of Mace in his hard-used eyes inspired a small horror. He did not expect the demonstrations to reach such proportions today, but on Saturday . . . well, he simply did not wish to get Mace in his eyes. As for broken heads—he had been struck once with a policeman's billy and it had opened a cut worth thirteen stitches; Mailer still remembered how disagreeable the subsequent hours in prison had been with his head bleeding, and his brain in the stupefactions of a near to overpowering headache. It was not inspirational to add the memory of that headache to his present one. Still, Mailer could hardly conceive of trouble in Washington on the steps of the Department of Justice —the police would doubtless be superior to their fine colleagues in Brooklyn, Oakland, and Wisconsin.

Revolutionaries-for-a-weekend should never get hangovers. Mailer detected that he was secretly comforted by the thought there would probably be no violence today;

70

even worse, he was comforted by the conclusion that the best police in Washington would be at the Department of Justice to maintain order. His exertions of the night before had been perfect for delivering him of some weeks of concentrated rage, perhaps even violence, at a variety of frustrations, he felt cleansed of the kind of hatred which leaves one leaden or tense, and his voice—which he did not dare to use yet, not even in an attempt to clear his throat—was clearly extinguished down to a whisper by last night's vocal exertions without a mike. Even his chest, chronic captive of a mysterious iron vise upon his lungs (which is why he had given up smoking) was relaxed this morning. Yelling on stage seemed literally to have loosened the screw of the vise. To his surprise, Mailer realized he felt gentle—in fact, this morning, he felt like a damn Quaker, which was no way for a revolutionary to feel, unless he was—mark this conjunction—going to consort with pacifists and draft-card burners.

The trouble with being gentle is that one has no defense against shame. Mailer was beginning to remember what he had said last night—he could not tell himself he was altogether happy about the confidential specifications concerning the men's room; if the memory of that was balmed by the recollection of presenting himself as Lyndon Johnson's dwarf alter ego, well, the general memory of the evening (like a deep bruise which might yet prove languorous and not unpleasant in the intimations of its pain or, to the contrary, directly nauseating) was still a little too delicate to probe. Mailer left the memories alone. He was a suggestion uneasy about the newspapers.

They, however, could have been significantly worse. Reading *The Washington Post* downstairs, over breakfast, Mailer decided he had gotten away with it, and so enjoyed his food and ate with large appetite, an ability he almost always possessed no matter how much he had drunk the night before—the best reason perhaps why he never considered it possible to become an alcoholic.

In the dining room were friends and acquaintances, a political writer, Jack Newfield, who did a column for *The Village Voice,* and Jacob Brackman, a young writer for *The New Yorker.* There were friends and wives and relatives about—a muted festivity was in the air, almost as if the hotel were headquarters for a small convention of gentle professionals, editors let us say, of numismatic magazines—something to offer small aggregations of security to one's years.

The program for the day was presented in a leaflet which Mailer had brought with him to Washington. In a typical anxiety at his essential lack of orientation to the protean forms of these protests he had put a folder of mailings, leaflets, programs, reprints, and associated letters for money in his attaché case—each morning he whipped through the folder selecting what seemed appropriate for the occasion. Even a protest against the 10 percent increase in income tax had gotten into this—Mailer had to put it aside each morning. Since he had taken the oath not to pay the 10 percent increase in the event it was passed (for the increase had been announced as a surtax to meet the costs of the war in Vietnam) he anticipated with no particular joy that the Department of Internal Revenue would examine his returns in the years ahead with no ordinary tolerance. (In fact he fully expected his financial tidbits to be fried.) Stating this supposition with his own variety of gallows humor had been the most direct pleasure in a letter he had written to James Baldwin, Bruce Jay Friedman, Philip Roth, Joseph Heller, Tennessee Williams, Edward Albee, Jack Richardson, Robert Lowell, Truman Capote, Nelson Algren, James Jones, Gore Vidal, Arthur Miller, Lillian Hellman, Lillian Ross, Vance Bourjaily, Mary McCarthy, and Jules Feiffer, asking them to join this protest.

Actually, he had hated the thought of signing the protest, he had piped up every variety of the extraordinarily sound argument that his work was the real answer to Vietnam, and these mass demonstrations, sideshows, and bloody income tax protests just took energy and *money* away from the real thing—getting the work out. But for such an argument to succeed, it was necessary to have work which absorbed all one's effort, and a sense of happy status with oneself. Mailer had had neither for the last year or two. His work had been good—there were some who thought *Why Are We In Vietnam?* was the best book he had ever written, but no project had seemed to cost him enough, and he had been suffering more and more in the past few years from the private conviction that he was getting a little soft, a hint curdled, perhaps an almost invisible rim of corruption was growing around the edges. His career, his legend, his idea of himself— were they stale? So he had no real alternative—he was not sufficiently virtuous to eschew the income tax protest, and had signed, and to his surprise had been repaid immediately by the abrupt departure of a measurable quantity of moral congestion, a noticeable lowering of his spiritual flatulence and a reduction in his New York fever, that ferocious inflammation which New York seemed always to encourage: envy, greed, claustrophobia, excitement, bourbon, broads, action, ego, jousts, cruelty and too-rich food in expensive hateful restaurants. Yes, signing the protest had been good for him. (He hoped he remembered in future years when the penalty might have to be paid.) But now, going through his attaché case, he could grin in the mirror, for if he had only known in September that shortly, so shortly, he was going to be an in-cometaxnik, he could have told Mitch Goodman where to shove his RESISTANCE. (Or was it called RESIST?— even with the pamphlets Mailer could not get the names right, there were so many and they changed so rapidly.) "Yes, Mitch," he could have said, "I think your RESIS-TANCE is first rate! first rate! but I'm putting my energy these days into the income tax drive. You have your going-to-jail bag—now I have mine." Of course, on the other hand, if he had only joined RESIST? RESIS-TANCE? with a little good grace he could have told the tax protest people . . .

This was vast humor perhaps to no one else, but in the middle of his hangover, Mailer was still remotely delighted by the mock dialogue of all this: yessir, boss, we'se gonna get in all the jail bags before day is done.

So over the tag-ends of breakfast, he read once more right over the following literature:

WE ARE PLANNING AN ACT OF DIRECT CREATIVE RE-SISTANCE TO THE WAR AND THE DRAFT IN WASHING-

TON ON FRIDAY, OCTOBER 20. The locale of our action will be the Department of Justice. We will gather at the First United Congregational Church of Christ, 10th and G Streets, N.W., Washington (near Pennsylvania Avenue), at 1 P.M. We will appear at the Justice Department together with 30 or 40 young men brought by us to Washington to represent the 24 Resistance groups from all over the country. There we will present to the Attorney General the draft cards turned in locally by these groups on October 16. (Those of us who want to include their own draft cards will be able to do so.) We will, in a clear, simple ceremony make concrete our affirmation of support for these young men who are the spearhead of direct resistance to the war and all of its machinery.

The draft law commands that we shall not aid, abet or counsel men to refuse the draft. But as a group of the clergy have recently said, when young men refuse to allow their conscience to be violated by an unjust law and a criminal war, then it is necessary for their elders—their teachers, ministers, friends—to make clear their commitment, in conscience, to *aid, abet, and counsel* them against conscription. Most of us have already done this privately. Now publicly we will demonstrate, side by side with these young men, our determination to continue to do so.

Mitchell Goodman, Henry Braun, Denise Levertov, Noam Chomsky, William Sloane Coffin, Dwight Macdonald

NOTE: Among the hundreds already committed to this action are Robert Lowell, Norman Mailer, Ashley Montagu, Arthur Waskow, and professors from most of the major colleges and universities in the East.

3: THE CHURCH

The pamphlet had contained a misstatement. The place for the gathering had been changed to the Church of the Reformation, 212 E. Capitol Street, thus removing the opening scene from the traffic of G Street to the lawn of a house of worship in a residential neighborhood. It was a warm sunny day, and having walked initially from the Hay-Adams to the First United Congregational Church of Christ (had the churches given their mode of nomenclature to the banks of America, or was the reverse true?) and then walked a greater distance to the second church, he had thereby baked his hangover which left his brain like a fresh loaf, the feeling empty but preferable to the uncrusted wound of the headache. A meeting of sorts was in progress on the lawn as he came up, in fact it was almost over, but it continued just long enough to make a small mark on Mailer. The thirty or forty young men there in Washington to represent the twenty-four Resistance groups in the country were sitting in a group on the lawn talking among themselves. Their leader (whose name he subsequently learned was Dickie Harris) turned out to be a Negro with goatee and horn-rimmed glasses, not very tall, slim, wearing dungarees and a shirt open at the neck. He had a smile which spoke of a wry sly humor, and his voice was easy and remarkably relaxed. He was at the end of an orientation on what they were planning later in the evening at a meeting in another church. "This is all good what we're going to do this afternoon," said Harris, "in fact it's sort of nice"—he laughed easily—"but tonight we ought to sit down and see how many ideas there are on how to continue this, so it isn't just a one-shot action, I mean like how many

75

times can you keep turning in the same old draft card?" This brought laughter from many of them, as if their draft cards had been burned months ago, reburned in effigy months later, and numerous signed statements to attest the fact had abounded as a form of hard moral currency ever since.

They were a pleasant group. They had a self-reliant humor which was sufficiently subtle and private to suggest it had been forged in other campaigns in other places. Harris, the Negro, had the dash, the panache (as an English journalist had once described it) of the old cadres in SNCC who used to drive all day from one Deep South town to another, rallying, organizing, slipping messages back and forth across the state, packing a piece or two, then to come in later at night, dusty, tired, yet not without tasty choice in what they wore, a long thin feather in the hat, shade of a Virginia cavalier, or an old pair of boots with turned-up toes. They had flair. Harris had this, too, as well as most of the other student leaders on the grass—their clothes must have cost less on an average than $20 a man, most of them were in shirts and dungarees, but they had managed to work up a style. Some had good belts; others had odd shirts or capes; one or two seemed to have buckskin vests; a college senior with an old jazzeboo plaid jacket was wearing a straw boater.

A cool sat over their assembly, an easiness, a sense of superiority—they seemed clearly indifferent to the numerous onlookers, now forming a modest mob in front of the church of sympathizers, journalists, witnesses, police, detectives, FBI men presumably—the student leaders did not care if they were overheard, photographed, mapped, clocked, or even admired; they were there and a sense of communion was natural to them, taken most naturally for granted as a psychic by-product of their job. Half of them in fact looked as if they had been hitchhiking for three or four days and not sleeping much, which—their expression seemed to say—was a nice trip if you knew how to make it, how to make it, that is, on no sleep.

Just about the time Mailer had decided he was romanticizing these young men in tribute for his English vest and suit, his avoirdupois, his hangover, his endless blendings of virtue and corruption—Harris did something which nailed down the case. A few loaves of bread, a jar of peanut butter, and a couple of quarts of milk were being passed around. No one took very much—numerous subtle manifestations were present of a collective philosophy, which for many of them might even have included a casual abstemiousness about food—at any rate, the meager rations seemed more than enough for the group. The neat remains came back eventually to Harris' feet. Since he had just finished asking if everything was clear about the action at the Department of Justice in the afternoon and the meeting to discuss further action at night, he now stared out at the listening onlookers, picked up the bread and said, "Anyone like some food? It's . . . uh . . ." he pretended to look at it, "it's . . . uh . . . *white* bread." The sliced loaf half-collapsed in its wax wrapper was the comic embodiment now of a dozen little ideas, of corporation-land which took the taste and crust out of bread and wrapped the remains in wax paper, and was, at the far extension of this same process, the same mentality which was out in Asia escalating, defoliating, orientating; yeah; and the white bread was also television, the fun of situation comedy shows with commercials, the humor they had shared as adolescents when pop art was being birthed; the white bread was the infiltrated enemy who had a grip on them everywhere, forced them to collaborate if only by imbibing the bread (and substance) of that enemy with his food processing, enriched flours, vitamin supplements, added nutrients; finally, and this probably was why Harris chuckled when he said it, the bread was *white* bread, not black bread—a way to remind them all that he was one of the very few Negroes here. Who knew what it might have cost him in wonder about his own allegiances not to be out there somewhere now agitating for Black Power. Here he was instead with White bread—White money, White methods, even White illegalities. It was exorbitant, Mailer decided glumly, to watch such virtuosity with a hangover.

Now they all began to leave the lawn and go around the side of the church into the basement, a meeting hall with folding chairs, where people were assembling. Half the people in the room congregated up front, talking to each other in the open space in front of the chairs, which would later serve as the working stage.

He saw Mitch Goodman and went up to say hello, about to make some sheepish reference to their last conversation on the phone, but Goodman simply smiled pleasantly, obviously with many a matter on his mind at this moment. After a word or two, Mailer walked off and took a seat. He was possibly more offended than relieved that he had not been asked to speak later. One would have expected that with his general innocence of the subject, his reluctance to join the cause, the hoarse weak whisper of his used-up voice, and the wrung-out echo of his booze-blasted brain that nothing should have pleased him better. As well ask an old actor if he does not wish a role! Mailer's hangover was definitely not improved by the suspicion he had been slighted.

Nor was this suspicion improved by the sight of Dwight Macdonald and Robert Lowell standing in the open area at the front of the room not ten feet away from where he was now sitting. Busy in conversation with friends, they gave no recognition that they had seen him at all, thereby establishing the most painful sense of indeterminacy in Mailer; he did not know whether it would be worse to believe they had chosen not to recognize him, or that he was merely sufficiently paranoid to assume such a decision. What aggravated this small matter was the generally cool treatment he was receiving, since no one of the two hundred or more people sitting and standing about had come up to introduce themselves and mention that they liked his work or wished to say hello, an occurrence normally so common and so conventionally annoying to a score of the most established American authors that they feel unmanned when it fails to occur.

But most of social life has built-in automatic cut-ins to avoid relational rupture and shearing—Lowell and Macdonald were inclined to work him rather than to ostracize him. In the next minute, Dwight met his eye, gave a chilly nod, and came over to where Mailer was sitting. Yes, the fact was there, and little securities could be grounded on it: Macdonald would not escape his fondness for Mailer.

"Well, Norman," he said reprovingly, "did you see the newspapers?"

"They weren't so bad, I thought."

But Macdonald was in his grand manner. "Not so bad for you. Why they practically made you a *hero*"—this last said with full rolling combers—"but my God, what they did to me!" Mailer remembered now—in one of the accounts there had been a short but cutting reference to Macdonald, and he laughed.

Macdonald was enjoying himself as well. "Yes, it's all very funny," he cried out in his big ringing voice (where his public voice was thin and small, his argumentative voice was sometimes strong, cracked and ringing—rather agreeable) "for *you*, my God it is, you stand up there and carry on like some absolute *hybrid* between William Burroughs and Brendan *Behan*, and don't even let Lowell and me *speak* and act like you're the white H. Rap *Brown!* and *then* the newspapers beat poor Lowell and *me* to death." He was enjoying this hugely. "Seriously, Norman," he said, "I really had too much to drink at that party afterward."

"I did too," Mailer confessed.

"Yes, but you didn't have to listen to Paul Goodman carry on about *you* and *your* performance over breakfast. What did you *do* to the man? He had absolutely *nothing* good to say about you. *Seriously,* Norman, that's an awful lot to have to listen to over breakfast. Why Paul Goodman is *merciless*. He doesn't *drink!* He's a frightening fellow!" said Macdonald beaming, and now poking a finger on Mailer's chest, "and he told us, in fact, he *reminded* us, how very bad you had been. It was the *last* thing I wanted to hear about. Really! What did you ever mean by saying you were Lyndon Johnson's dwarf alter ego. What does *that* mean?"

Ever since Macdonald had shared the editorship of *Encounter* with Stephen Spender, he had prided himself on adopting the "I am dumb" school of English interrogation. Pushed far enough he was capable of asking, "What do you mean by naturalism?"—a dull manifestation of British wickedness, Mailer had always thought, and put the blame on Spender for giving Macdonald bad habits:

Spender, in the summer of 1960, had been capable of asking questions like, "Tell me, what is the significance of Kennedy being Catholic?"

After the conversation with Macdonald, he had a short word with Lowell.

"Hungover?" Lowell had asked, after a pause.

"Pretty bad."

Lowell gave a commiserative nod. Then next he asked casually, studying Mailer, "See the papers?"

"Yes."

"Not so nice."

"I guess not. They'll be worse," said Mailer.

Lowell made a face. He had an expression in his eyes which only a fellow writer could comprehend—it said, "We are lambs—helpless before them." It was true. One could not communicate the horror to anyone who did not write well. The papers distorted one's actions, and that was painful enough, but they wrenched and garbled and twisted and broke one's words and sentences until a good author always sounded like an incoherent overcharged idiot in newsprint—there was even a corollary: the more one might have to say in a sentence, the worse one would probably sound. Henry James would have come off in a modern interview like a hippie who had taken a correspondence course in forensics. It really did not matter what was said—dependably one was always elliptic, incomprehensible, asinine. So a great wall of total miscomprehension was built over the years between a writer, and the audience reached by a newspaper—which meant eventually most of America. So a particular sadness slipped sooner or later into every good writer—they were kept further removed from uneducated readers by the general horrors of journalistic mistranscription than by the difficulty of their work. Ergo, they suffered. Because every time they did something which got into the papers, the motive for their action was distorted and their words were tortured; since they made their living by trying to put words together well, this was as painful to them as the sight of an ugly photograph of herself on the front page must be to a beauty.

Over the years one came to live with a recognition that

the average reporter could not get a sentence straight if it were phrased more subtly than his own mind could make phrases. Nuances were forever being munched like peanuts. After a while one gave up, one did one's little turn for whatever project was up, a cause, a new book, an action, and suffered the publicity which at best was hopeless, at worst gave promise of burying you alive. Some of this was in Lowell's eye—it was obvious the appearance or mis-appearance of public remarks by him in a newspaper was close to physical torment for the poet. And Lowell must have assumed Mailer understood, for he now nodded jocularly at the awesome damage done every time one's name came up on a daily page.

There was a way, of course, to deal with the papers. If the ears of the reporters were geared to capture accurately the mediocre remarks of mediocre men, then one had to look for simple salient statements, so poetically bare, but so irreducible, that they would stick in the reporter's mind like a thorn. It was the only way to talk to a reporter. If one could not learn how to do it, then the only recourse was flight from any situation where a journalist might be present. But brilliance, with a reporter, was to be shunned. Salience, not brilliance, Mailer told himself—he was parenthetically to have an opportunity to test his new method in the next few days.

An impromptu meeting was now opened by Mitch Goodman, who made a few hesitant decent solemn remarks of greeting, and then passed the hand-microphone (which was attached to a floor wire which was in turn attached to a portable speaker held up by a volunteer) over to a well-knit man about thirty-five who had removed his jacket and was wearing an Oxford shirt with the sleeves neatly rolled up. He had on a pair of light brown tortoise-shell glasses, and they sat with comfortable presence above a short nose and hard, strong, well-dimpled chin. His voice had a tough reedy almost barking quality, dry with humor. People had begun to ask him questions even before the microphone had been successfully passed to him; with the well-balanced grin of a man who is as confident with an audience as an executive of regular habit is with the morning shower, he said in his barking, dry

81

voice, "You'll be able to hear me better just as soon as Mitch Goodman gets his foot off the microphone wire." Goodman, looking down, smiled in natural confusion that the wire was in fact trapped under his shoe, the transfer was successfully made, and the man went on to speak. "The police officer in charge of the detachment assigned to us by the District of Columbia said to me, 'Your group looks like it can regulate itself,' and I assured him"—very dry now—"that as a matter of fact, we *could*." Polite happy laughter from this convening of pacifists, professors, and students of principle. He went on to discuss the route of the March, and the order of events which would take place at the Department of Justice, his manner hard, quick, deft, and assured, his remarks purposeful, even salient—yes, he would be the kind of man who would know how to talk to reporters. He had a voice which sounded close to the savvy self-educated tones of a labor union organizer, but there was the irreducible substance of Ivy League in it as well, the barking quality, not unlike a coxswain—except the speaker was too large for that—the coach of a crew perhaps. Mailer was not unimpressed. "Who is that?" he asked Macdonald, who looked back with some surprise. "Why, Bill Coffin," Macdonald said with a hiss since it was not natural for him to speak in whispers.

William Sloane Coffin, Jr., Chaplain at Yale. Mailer had some recollection that Coffin had been arrested in the South on one civil rights affair or another, perhaps in Selma. The man was not unimpressive at all; Mailer felt a dim increase of cheer: our Yale Chaplain looked like a winner.

The meeting broke up in good humor, Coffin informing them that anyone who was not physically well and wished a ride for the mile and a half to the Department of Justice would find a bus outside. Much badinage followed about who was too old and who was not.

They set out. It was an uneventful walk. They strolled along in a column of two, extended for hundreds of feet —by now there were several hundred of them, and the police flanked them in the street. There were not a great many police, but none seemed necessary at all for the

82

route took them along quiet residential streets, part of the way through a middle-class Negro neighborhood, the occasional pedestrian staring at them in some bewilderment. Occasionally, one of the marchers would hold up his fingers in the V for Victory sign which Churchill had made famous for the Allies in World War II. Now it was coming back—sign of a new resistance movement.

But Mailer could feel no sense of belonging to any of these people. They were much too nice and much too principled for him. There seemed as many professors and middle-aged faculty present as students, maybe more, and there was an air of Ivy League intimacy to the quiet conversations on this walk—it could not really be called a March. Despite the occasional adjurations of the police to move it up, or keep in twos, there was a successful informality about the progression. The sun was out, and that made for quiet good spirits, and a gentle sense of gravity. On the several occasions when Mailer had found himself with pacifists there had been invariably just this mixture of gravity, gentleness of mood, and quiet good humor. That was all very well if you were a Christian and liked to be reminded of the air, no doubt, of childhood Sundays in church, but Mailer had recognized long ago that he was sufficiently devil-ridden to need a little action from time to time, and the promise of these pacifistic moods seemed to be that they would go on forever. They were certainly the last mood to encounter with a hangover. Then the sight of Robert Lowell chatting with old friends farther up the line did not lift his depression. He was remembering that Lowell had been a conscientious objector in World War II, and had served time in jail. Perhaps he was now reminiscing with old pacifist friends. But Mailer thought not—it was more a damn Ivy League convocation that Lowell seemed to be having; he looked for the moment like one Harvard dean talking to another, that same genteel confidential gracious hunch of the shoulder toward each other. No dean at Harvard had ever talked to *him* that way, Mailer now decided bitterly. But this was exactly the price of hangovers, he concluded, they reduced you to the meanest side of yourself where the old wounds had not exactly healed. That was self-evident, but counsel to the wise drinker might suggest that the hours for curing a hangover are best spent in the company of ignoble men rather than these fine academic embodiments of everything principled and austere in the American character. But he was dropped out of these ruminations into a conversation begun with him by a young English instructor with eyeglasses and a beard who wanted to query Mailer about some of the literary mechanisms in his work. This sort of literary operation, never agreeable to the novelist at best (since he had a primitive regard by now for the power of symbols and suspected a discussion of their nature was next to defacing them) certainly was unsuitable under the circumstances: cerebrations, such as these, would open the few restored tissues of his brain to all the overstimulation of new adrenalin for new intellectual matters—Mailer resolved the impossibility by muttering, "Excuse me," and jogged abruptly up the line. Finally, he found a friendly face. It was Gordon Rogoff, an old friend from Actors Studio, now teaching at the Yale Drama School; they talked idly about theatrical matters for a while. Rogoff hardly qualified as an ignoble man, but he was at least witty, pleasant, intelligent, and with a firm edge to his critical opinions. So the last of this March had for Mailer the sort of dialogue one might pursue at lunch or dinner in a Manhattan restaurant.

Which reminded him that his stomach was empty. That was probably to the good—he would be forced to lose a pound today, but his hunger did not help the tranquil process of the cure.

4: JUSTICE

Well, they were now at the steps—one of the set of steps in any case. It all seemed a hint undramatic. When he had first heard of the action from Mitch Goodman, pictures had crossed his mind of charged disagreeable encounters with FBI men in the corridors of the Department of Justice, now instead there was not a government man in sight if one did not count the number of FBI and CIA agents doubtless circulating among the press as photographers, newsreel men, TV cameramen, and newspapermen, there to mug and map every subversive face in sight. The nearest representative of any potential violence face to face was a stand of five American Nazis wearing swastikas for armbands, and kept by the police off to one side of the proceedings. All through the afternoon the Nazis kept chanting slogans. "We want dead Reds," was the clearest.

Here was the disposition of bodies: on a corner of the steps of the Department of Justice were gathered about fifteen men, most of whom were going to speak for a minute or two. Facing them, just below the steps, was a phalanx of mass-media representatives, and they were going through a preliminary boxing out and jockeying in for position between newsreel, still and television cameras. To the sides of them, and behind them, was a group of four or five hundred people who for the most part cheered politely although with distinct well-bred fervor at remarks they particularly liked.

Coffin gave the main address. He began speaking of the procedure to be followed. After a few short speeches, those students representing themselves or organizations of students who might wish to turn in their draft cards, would come forward one by one and deposit their cards in a bag. Then, any individuals in the audience, student, faculty, or onlookers who thought to hand in their draft cards as well could join. At that point, Mitch Goodman, Coffin, Dr. Spock, and seven other demonstrators would "disappear for a while and enter the Department of Justice Building. Once inside," said Coffin, "we will proceed to the Office of the Attorney General and there hand over the cards and notify him of our intention which is that we hereby publicly counsel these young men to continue in their refusal to serve in the Armed Forces as long as the war in Vietnam continues, and we pledge ourselves to aid and abet them in all the ways we can."

There were cheers. "At that point," Coffin went on, "depending on how we are received, we shall either leave, and rejoin you here to report our conversation, or if there are difficulties, we may be delayed." It was impossible to tell if he was hinting they might be arrested. "If we do not reappear quickly, I would ask you all to wait and divert yourselves with speeches"—small titter—"or song." More amusement. "If it takes too long, and we are not able to send word out, I would then suggest you disperse and those interested can come together tonight at the meeting already signified, for a full account."

Then he gave his prepared speech. It was reasonable in length, the points clearly made, his indignation kept nicely in leash but nonetheless vibrant. His sentences had a nonpoetic bony statement of meaning which made them exactly suitable for newspaper quotation.

". . . in our view it is not wild-eyed idealism but clear-eyed revulsion that brings us here. For as one of our number put it: 'If what the United States is doing in Vietnam is right, what is there left to be called wrong?'

"Many of us are veterans, and all of us have the highest sympathy for our boys in Vietnam. They know what a dirty, bloody war it is. But they have been told that the ends justify the means, and that the cleansing water of victory will wash clean their hands of all the blood and dirt. No wonder they hate us who say 'There must be no cleansing water.' But what they must strive to understand, hard as it is, is that there can be no cleansing water if military victory spells moral defeat.

"We have the highest sympathy also for those who back the war because their sons or lovers or husbands are fighting or have died in Vietnam. But they too must understand a very basic thing—that sacrifice in and of itself confers no sanctity. Even if half a million of our boys were to die in Vietnam that would not make the cause one whit more sacred. Yet we realize how hard that knowledge is to appropriate when one's husband is numbered among the sacrificed."

Had he, Mailer was ready to wonder, come from a long line of New England ministers whose pride resided partly in their ability to extract practical methods from working in the world? It was a Protestant discipline of which our Participant knew little, and it had made in his opinion for a great deal of waste in the world, since America's corporations were in Mailer's opinion more guilty than the Communists of polluting the air, fields, and streams, debasing the value of manufactured products, transmuting faith into science, technology, and medicine, while all embarked on scandalous foreign adventures with their eminently practical methods—yes, all that might have come by panning the homely practical silt out of the tumultuous rivers of Christian experience in the world. What was fascinating to Mailer is that the Yale Chaplain had one of those faces you expected to see on the cover of *Time* or *Fortune*, there as the candidate for Young Executive of the Year, he had that same flint of the eye, single-mindedness in purpose, courage to bear responsibility, that same hard humor about the details in the program under consideration, that same suggestion of an absolute lack of humor once the line which enclosed his true Wasp temper had been breached. He was one full example of the masculine principle at work in the cloth.

"As the law now stands, for a man to qualify as a conscientious objector he must believe in God. Could anything be more ethically absurd? Have humanists no conscience? Why,—and as a Christian I say this with contrition—some of the most outstanding humanists I know would think they were slipping from their high ideals were they to take steps towards conversion. As a Christian I am convinced it is a gross misfortune not to believe in God, but it is not automatically an ethical default.

"Then despite numerous appeals by numerous religious bodies, Congress last spring chose to provide alternative service only for the absolute pacifist. This too is absurd, for the rights of a man whose conscience forbids him to participate in a particular war are as deserving of respect as the rights of a man whose conscience forbids him to participate in any war at all."

This drew the largest applause of his speech. Just as in the thirties when the success of every Communist meeting was absolutely dependent upon the victory talk being given by a man with a fine Irish brogue—"Down with the doorty capitalist system say I!"—so the conscientious objection of the non-religious would be advanced consummately in the hands of a minister. Indeed, who else?

"The law of the land is clear. Section 12 of the National Selective Service Act declares that anyone 'who knowingly counsels, aids, or abets another to refuse or evade registration or service in the armed forces . . . shall be liable to imprisonment for not more than five years or a fine of ten thousand dollars or both.'

"We hereby publicly counsel these young men to continue in their refusal to serve in the armed forces as long as the war in Vietnam continues, and we pledge ourselves to aid and abet them in all the ways we can. This means that if they are now arrested for failing to comply with a law that violates their consciences, we too must be arrested, for in the sight of that law we are now as guilty as they."

There were a few more speeches, all short. Mitch Goodman made one, Dr. Spock made one, and then three or four other people whose names Mailer did not recognize and to whose speeches he hardly listened. It was turning cold, the sun had gone back of a cloud, and his hangover had settled in for a bout. It would not leave now until the proceedings were over, and he could go somewhere to get a drink. He had no idea if they would call upon him in a little while to speak, although he judged not. Probably Mitch Goodman had passed word that Mailer was attending, but with no especial good grace.

In the middle of these speakers, Robert Lowell was called up. He had been leaning against a wall in his habitual slumped over position, deep in revery at the side of the steps—and of course had been photographed as a figure of dejection—the call for him to say a few words caught him partly by surprise. He now held the portable hand microphone with a delicate lack of intimacy as if it were some valuable, huge, and rare tropical spider which he was obliged to examine but did not have to enjoy. "I was asked earlier today," he began in his fine stammering voice which gave the impression that the life rushed at him like a series of hurdles and some he succeeded in jumping and some he did not, "I was asked earlier this afternoon by a reporter why I was not turning in my draft card," Lowell said with the beginnings of a pilgrim's passion, "and I did not tell him it was a stupid question, although I was tempted to. I thought he should have known that I am now too old to have a draft card, but that it makes no difference. When some of us pledge ourselves to counsel and aid and abet any young men who wish to turn in their cards, why then you may be certain we are aware of the possible consequences and do not try to hide behind the technicality of whether we literally have a draft card or not. So I'm now saying to the gentlemen of the press that unlike the authorities who are running this country, we are not searching for tricks, we try to think of ourselves as serious men, if the press, that is, can comprehend such an effort, and we will protest this war by every means available to our conscience, and therefore not try to avoid whatever may arise in the way of retribution."

It was said softly, on a current of intense indignation and Lowell had never looked more dignified nor more admirable. Each word seemed to come on a separate journey from the poet's mind to his voice, along a winding route or through an exorbitant gate. Each word cost him much—Lowell's fine grace was in the value words had for him, he seemed to emit a horror at the possibility of squandering them or leaving them abused, and political speeches had never seemed more difficult for him, and on the consequence, more necessary for statement.

So Mailer applauded when Lowell was done. And suddenly liked him enormously for his speech, and decided he liked him truly. Beneath all snobbery, affectations of weariness, literary logrollermanship, neutralsmanship, and whatever other fatal snob-infested baggage of the literary world was by now willy-nilly in the poet's system, worked down intimately close to all his best and most careful traditions and standards, all flaws considered, Lowell was still a fine, good, and honorable man, and Norman Mailer was happy to be linked in a cause with him.

But now much began to happen to Mailer on the aftermath of this speech. For shortly afterward students began to file up the steps to deposit their solitary or collective draft cards in the bag, and this procession soon became a ceremony. Each man came up, gave his name, and the state or area or college he represented, and then proceeded to name the number of draft cards he had been entrusted to turn in. The numbers were larger than one might have expected. There were almost two hundred from New York, there were much more than two hundred from Boston, and a good number from Yale. As these numbers were announced, the crowd being when all is said, good Americans, gave murmurs of pleasure, an academic distance from the cry they had given as children to the acrobats of the circus, but not entirely unrelated, for there was something of the flying trapeze in these maneuvers now; by handing in draft cards, these young men were committing their future either to prison, emigration, frustration, or at best, years where everything must be unknown, and that spoke of a readiness to take moral leaps which the acrobat must know when he flies off into space—one has to have faith in one's ability to react with grace en route, one has ultimately, it may be supposed, to believe in some kind of grace.

On the *a fortiori* evidence, then, they were young men with souls of interesting dimension, and their faces did nothing to disprove this. None of them looked alike; they had a surprising individuality in their appearance. Some were scholarly and slight, dressed conservatively, and looked like clerks; others were in dungarees, and possessed, like Dickie Harris, the Negro on the grass, that private élan reminiscent of the old cavaliers of SNCC; a few were sports and looked to have eight hobbies, custom cars, pot, draft cards, skiing, guitar, surfboard, chicks, and scuba—not many of these, but Mailer had been expecting none. One tall student from the West, California no doubt, even looked like one's image of the President of the Young Republicans at Stanford, he was handsome enough in conventional measure to have been Number 1 Deke in Delta Kappa Eps. After he dropped his card in the bag, he gave a little talk to the effect that many of these students had been scared when first they burned their cards, months ago—they had said goodbye to their girls and family and waited for the clang of the jail gate. But the jail gate never came. "Now we think the government might be afraid to go near us. That gets around. A lot of kids who were afraid to join us last year won't be afraid this year. So every bit helps. If we get arrested, we make our point, and people won't forget it—our point being that with good careers ahead of us, we still hate this war so much that we go to jail—if they show they're reluctant to arrest us, then others are in more of a hurry to join us." He was almost too good to be true. The suspicion came up for a moment that the CIA had doubtless not stopped their recruiting in colleges, and would certainly be happy to infiltrate here, an unpleasant thought, but then (1) Mailer came from New York where unpleasant thoughts were common, and (2) the writer in him was intrigued at the thought of a short novel about a young American leading a double life in college as a secret policeman. What a good novel that could make! About once a week Mailer bypassed wistfully around the excitements of the new book which had just come into his head. He would leave it to his detractors to decide that the ones he did not write were better than the ones he did.

Another student came by, then another. One of them, slight, with a sharp face, wearing a sport shirt and dark glasses had the appearance of a Hollywood hustler, but that was misleading; he wore the dark glasses because his eyes were still weak from the Mace squirted in them by police at Oakland. This student had a Berkeley style which Mailer did not like altogether: it was cocky, knowledgeable and quick to mock the generations over thirty. Predictably, this was about the first item on which the kid began to scold the multitude. "You want to come along with us," he told the Over-Thirties, "that's okay, that's your thing, but we've got our thing, and we're going to do it alone whether you come with us or not." Mailer always wanted to give a kick into the seat of all reflection when he was told he had his thing—one did not look forward to a revolution which would substitute "thing" for better words.

Still, the boy from Berkeley proved to have a fair wit. He had begun to tell about Mace. To correct the hint of self-pity in his voice (which had an adenoidal complacency reminiscent of any number of old-line Party speakers who were never so unbearable as when bona fide martyrs) he made the little point that while the suffering was great, the reporting, for once, had also been great. "You see," he said, "the reporters were on our side." He looked down boldly now on the fifty or more assorted media men in front of him, and said, "They didn't want to be particularly, but the cops were so dumb they couldn't tell the reporters from the demonstrators, so the reporters got the Mace in their eyes too. For once, instead of putting down our big threat to the American flag, the cops were the villains, that is: the cops were the villains as soon as the reporters could see well enough to go back and write their story, which took a couple of hours, I can assure you. That Mace is rough on the eyes."

On they came, twenty-four to thirty of them, one by one, making for the most part short dry single sentences for statement, as for example, "I am ready to turn in my draft card, but can't because I burned it in Kansas City several months ago so am here submitting an affidavit with my name and address so the government can find me."

In a little more than a half hour, the students were done. Now began the faculty. They too came up one by one, but now there was no particular sense offered of an internal organization. Unlike the students, they had not debated these matters in open forum for months, organized, proselyted, or been overcome by argument, no, most of them had served as advisers to the students, had counseled them, and been picked up, many of them, and brought along by the rush of this moral stream much as a small piece of river bank might separate from the shore and go down the line of the flood. It must have been painful for these academics. They were older, certainly less suited for jail, aware more precisely of how and where their careers would be diverted or impeded, they had families many of them, they were liberal academics, technologues, they were being forced to abdicate from the machines they had chosen for their life. Their decision to turn in draft cards must have come for many in the middle of the night; for others it must have come even last night, or as they stood here debating with themselves. Many of them seemed to stand irresolutely near the steps for long periods, then move up at last. Rogoff, standing next to Mailer, hugging his thin chest in the October air, now cold, finally took out his card and, with a grin at Mailer, said, "I guess I'm going to turn this in. But you know the ridiculous part of it is that I'm 4-F." So they came up one by one, not in solidarity, but as individuals, each breaking the shield or the fence or the mold or the home or even the construct of his own security. And as they did this, a deep gloom began to work on Mailer, because a deep modesty was on its way to him, he could feel himself becoming more and more of a modest man as he stood there in the cold with his hangover, and he hated this because modesty was an old family relative, he had been born to a modest family, had been a modest boy, a modest young man, and he hated that, he loved the pride and the arrogance and the confidence and the egocentricity he had acquired over the years, that was his force and his luxury and the iron in his greed, the richest sugar of his pleasure, the strength of his competitive force, he had lived long enough to know that the intimation one was being steeped in a new psychical condition (like this oncoming modest grace) was never to be disregarded, permanent new states could come into one on just so light a breeze. He stood in the cold watching the faculty men come up, yes always one by one, and felt his hangover which had come in part out of his imperfectly swallowed contempt for them the night before, and in part out of his fear, yes now he saw it, fear of the consequences of this weekend in Washington, for he had known from the beginning it could disrupt his life for a season or more and in some way the danger was there it could change him forever. He was forty-four years old, and it had taken him most of those forty-four years to begin to be able to enjoy his pleasures where he found them, rather than worry about those pleasures which eluded him—it was obviously no time to embark on ventures which could eventually give one more than a few years in jail.

Yet, there was no escape. As if some final cherished rare innocence of childhood still preserved intact in him was brought finally to the surface and there expired, so he lost at that instant the last secret delight he retained in life as a game where finally you never got hurt if you played the game well enough. For years he had envisioned himself in some final cataclysm, as an underground leader in the city, or a guerrilla with a gun in the hills, and had scorned the organizational aspects of revolution, the speeches, mimeograph machines, the hard dull forging of new parties and programs, the dull maneuvering to keep power, the intolerable obedience required before the over-all intellectual necessities of each objective period, and had scorned it, yes, had spit at it, and perhaps had been right, certainly had been right, such revolutions were the womb and cradle of technology land, no the only revolutionary truth was a gun in the hills, and that would not be his, he would be too old by then, and too incompetent, yes, too incompetent said the new modesty, and too showboat, too lacking in essential judgment—besides, he was too well-known! He would pay for the pleasures of his notoriety in the impossibility of disguise. No gun in the hills, no taste for organization, no, he was a figurehead, and therefore he was expendable, said the new modesty—not a future leader, but a future victim: *there* would be his real value. He could go to jail for protest, and spend some years if it came to it, possibly his life, for if the war went on, and America put its hot martial tongue across the Chinese border, well, jail was the probable perspective, detention camps, dissociation centers, liquidation alleys, that would be his portion, and it would come about the time he had learned how to live.

The depth of this gloom and this modesty came down on Mailer, and he watched the delegation take the bag into the Department of Justice with 994 cards contained inside, and listened to the speeches while they waited, and was eventually called up himself to make a speech, and made a modest one in a voice so used by the stentorian demonstrations of the night before that he was happy for the mike since otherwise he might have communicated in

94

a whisper. He said a little of what he had thought while watching the others: that he had recognized on this afternoon that the time had come when Americans, many Americans, would have to face the possibility of going to jail for their ideas, and this was a prospect with no cheer because prisons were unattractive places where much of the best in oneself was slowly extinguished, but it could be there was no choice. The war in Vietnam was an obscene war, the worst war the nation had ever been in, and so its logic might compel sacrifice from those who were not so accustomed. And, out of hardly more than a sense of old habit and old anger, he scolded the press for their lies, and their misrepresentation, for their guilt in creating a psychology over the last twenty years in the average American which made wars like Vietnam possible; then he surrendered the mike and stepped down and the applause was pleasant.

After a period, Coffin came out from the Department of Justice with his delegation. He made a short announcement. The draft cards had not been accepted. A game of bureaucratic evasion had been played. In fact, the Attorney General had not even been there, instead his assistant. "The assistant simply refused to take our cards," said Coffin. "Consider this! Here was an officer of the law facing clear evidence of an alleged crime, and refusing to accept that evidence. He was derelict in his duty." There was a contained anger in Coffin, much like lawyer's anger, as if some subtle game had been played in which a combination had been based on a gambit, but the government had refused the gambit, so now the combination was halted.

Further reports were given by Dr. Spock, and one or two other members of the delegation. Then the meeting dispersed. Macdonald, Lowell, and Mailer going off for well-earned drinks at the nearest bar, ended up having dinner together. For all his newly inherited modesty, Mailer had nonetheless a merry meal. Liquor, it seemed, was still given special dispensation by the new regime of discipline, asceticism, moderation and self-sacrifice. Yet before dinner was over, the three men had agreed they would go out together tomorrow on the March to the Pentagon, and that they would probably—all consideration given—seek to get arrested. Mailer's hangover was now about gone. The evening went its agreeable way.

PART III:

Saturday Matinée

1: THE NEXT STEP

Next morning, Macdonald and Lowell met Mailer in the dining room of the Hay-Adams for breakfast. There was a crowd about now. In the lobby, a mood prevailed of well-dressed people come together for a collective celebration—a homecoming game or civic testimonial, or class reunion. Everybody was saying hello to people they had not seen in years, and everybody looked good. The thousand days of John Kennedy had done much to change the style of America; nowhere perhaps more than to the sartorial sense of the liberals and Left Wing intellectuals now gathering for breakfast—some drabness had quit them since the fifties, some sense of power had touched them with subtle concomitants of power—a hint of elegance. The city was awake. On the way to the hotel last night, somewhat after midnight, Mailer thought the streets of downtown Washington held a hint of Times Square in the early morning hours, that same offering of fevers not abated, echo of voices a block away which promised violence—if not for tonight, then for another. The whores were out: not a common sight in Washington. The Capital was usually about as lively at 1 A.M. as the center of Cincinnati late at night, but now there were motorcycles gunning up and down the avenues with their whine of constant climax looping into the new whine of higher climax—one waits for them to explode, they never do, they go gunning for the night. The air was violent, yet full of amusement; out of focus. Mailer had no idea whether this atmosphere was actually now typical of Washington on Friday night (as lately of more than one other quiet

American city) or whether this mood came in with the weekend migrants from New York; or if indeed some of the Under-Thirties in Washington were warming up to repel the invasion. There was a hint of hurricane calm, then wind-bursts, gut-roars from the hogs. If the novelist had never heard of Hell's Angels or motorcycle gangs, he would still have predicted, no, rather *invented* motorcycle orgies, because the orgy and technology seemed to come together in the sound of 1200 cc's on two wheels, that exacerbation of flesh, torsion of lust, rhythm in the pistons, stink of gasoline, yeah, oil as the last excrement of putrefactions buried a million years in Mother Earth, yes indeed, that funky redolence of gasoline was not derived from nothing, no, doubtless it was the stench of the river Styx (a punning metaphor appropriate to John Updike no doubt) but Mailer, weak in Greek, had nonetheless some passing cloudy unresolved image now of man as Charon on that river of gasoline Styx wandering between earth and the holy mills of the machine. Like most cloudy metaphors, this served to get him home—there is nothing like the search for a clear figure of speech to induce gyroscopic intensity sufficient for the compass to work.

Actually, Mailer had not been that drunk. Speak of the river Styx, the whiskey earlier that evening had worked like balming oil for the collective ego of Macdonald, Lowell, and Mailer. In the late afternoooon they had all been naturally weary when speeches were done, but not unsatisfied with themselves. "It was a good day, wasn't it, Norman," Lowell kept asking. In the best of gentle moods, his nerves seemed out of their rack, and his wit had plays of light, his literary allusions always near to private, were now full of glee. In one sprawling bar-restaurant where they went at random to drink, a plump young waitress with a strong perfume, who looked nonetheless a goddess of a bucket for a one-night stand, caught Mailer the novelist's eye—he flirted with the sense of gravity Buddhists reserve for the cow. "Good God, Norman, what do you see in her?" Macdonald had to know. Mailer, conceivably, could have told him, but they talked instead of cheap perfume—why it was offensive to some, aphrodisiac to others.

Lowell remarked, "I like cheap perfume, Norman, don't you?" But he said this last as if he were talking about some grotto in Italy he had blundered into all by himself. It was a difficult remark to make without some faint strain of dry-as-sachet faggotry, but Lowell brought it off. The mixture of integrity (Cromwellian axe of light in the eye!) in company with his characteristic gentleness, enabled him to make just about any remark without slithering. It was as if he had arrived at the recognition, nothing lost, that cheap perfume might be one of the hundred odd scents of mystery in the poet's apothecary—let us not, however, forget the smell of gasoline which Mailer in his turn had pondered. Gasoline and cheap perfume—half the smell in American adventure.

But in fact what must have been contributing to his good mood was the knowledge that Norman Mailer seemed to like him. Robert Lowell gave off at times the unwilling haunted saintliness of a man who was repaying *desc* the moral debts of ten generations of ancestors. So his guilt must have been a tyrant of a chemical in his blood always ready to obliterate the best of his moods. Just as danger is a Turk to a coward and the snub a disembowelment to the social climber, so Lowell was vulnerable to not being liked by anyone remotely a peer. In the poet's loneliness—the homely assumption is that all talent is lonely to the degree it is exalted—Lowell was at the mercy of anyone he considered of value, for only they might judge his guilt, and so relieve the intolerable dread which accompanies this excessive assumption of the old moral debts of the ancestors. Who knows what they might be? We may only be certain that the moral debt of the Puritan is no mean affair: agglutinations of incest, abominations upon God, kissing the *sub cauda* of the midnight cat—Lowell's brain at its most painful must have been equal to an overdose of LSD on Halloween.

There had been, however, a happy conversation somewhat earlier and it had made a difference in Lowell's good mood. As they were coming down the steps from the Department of Justice in the now late cold October afternoon, Lowell had said, "I was most impressed with your speech, Norman."

"Well, glad you liked it, Cal," Mailer said, "for I think your speech produced it."

"My speech did?"

"I was affected by what you said. It took me out of one mood and put me in another."

"What sort of mood, Norman?"

"Well, maybe I was able to stop brooding over myself. I don't know, Cal, your speech really had a most amazing impact on me." Mailer drawled the last few words to drain any excessive sentimental infection, but Lowell seemed hardly to mind.

"Well, Norman, I'm delighted," he said, taking Mailer's arm for a moment as if, God and kingdom willing, Mailer had finally become a Harvard dean and could be addressed by the appropriate limb. "I'm delighted because I liked *your* speech so much."

These repetitions would have been ludicrous if not for the simplicity of feeling they obviously aroused in so complex a man as Lowell. Through the drinks and the evening at dinner, he kept coming back to the same conversation, kept repeating his pleasure in Mailer's speech in order to hear Mailer doggedly reaffirm his more than equal pleasure in Lowell's good words. Mailer was particularly graceless at these ceremonious repetitions by which presumably New England mandarins (like old Chinese) ring the stately gong of a new friendship forming.

In fact the dinner was what delivered Lowell's decision to remain for the March on the Pentagon. On the whole, he had come down for the event at the Department of Justice, he had in fact a dinner party at his home in New York on Saturday night, and he did not wish to miss it. That was obvious. For whatever reason Lowell had evidently been looking forward for days to Saturday evening.

"I wonder if I could get the plane back by six tomorrow," he kept asking aloud. "If we're arrested, I don't suppose there's much chance of that at all."

Mailer had not forgotten the party to which he was, in his turn, invited. Repeat: it had every promise of being wicked, tasty, and rich. "I think if we get arrested early," he said, "we can probably be released among the first."

"By six?"

"No, Cal," said Mailer, the honest soul, "if you get arrested, you had better plan on not making dinner before nine."

"Well, should we get arrested? What do you think of the merits?"

They talked about it for a while. It was Mailer's firm conclusion that this was probably the way they could best serve the occasion. "If the three of us are arrested," he said, "the papers can't claim that hippies and hoodlums were the only ones guilty."

No conclusion was reached that night. Over breakfast they were ready to take it up again. It was evident that none had thought about it too much; also obvious there was nothing particularly to think about. Over the years they had all been bored by speeches, polemics and political programmings which invariably detailed the sound-as-brickwork logic of the next step in some hard new Left program. Existentially, it hardly mattered whether the logic came from a Communist, Trotskyist, Splinter Marxist, union organizer, or plain Social Democrat. While the ideals of such speakers were sometimes as separated as a flush in one hand is from a full house in the other, there was dependably a false but uxorious confidence in the adenoidal whine of the speaker as he shifted gears in his larynx the better to drive the certain efficacy of the program into the ears of his audience. Thus, at their worst, had Communist speakers used these gears of the larynx to defend the Moscow-Berlin pact in 1939. So had Trotskyists worked in and out of the knots of the thesis of the degenerated worker's state—a thesis which seemed less absurd to Mailer in 1967 than to Sidney Hook in 1947, but the Trotskyists had been as full of the unbreakable logic of the next step as the Communists, so they had succeeded in smashing the bones of their own movement into the hundred final slivers of American Marxism, miniscule radical sects complete each with their own special martyred genius of a Marxicologist. There had been the enlightened polemics of the cultivated socialism of the Committee for Cultural Freedom which had been brought by

the sound-as-brickwork-logic-of-the-next-step in good Socialist *Anti*-Communism to so incisive an infestation by
the CIA that it now called up pictures of the cockroaches
in a slum sink; not all the wines of the Waldorf could
wash out a drop of that! Yes, and the labor movement,
and the confidence once held by Communists and Trotskyists, Splinterites, and Reutherites, that the labor union
would prove the strong back to jack the country up from
the Depression to that luminous plane where Peace and
Justice, Equality and Freedom would reign. The labor
movement lifted the country and carried it to a field of
plenty, but it was a football field where professionals
played, and America watched on Sunday full of Peace before the rainbow of the color set, feeling Justice when
their side won, knowing Equality since everyone presumably had an unimpeded view of his own set, and Freedom
in abundance for a man could always turn his set off, yes,
the labor unions now sat closer to the Mafia than to
Marx.

Well, Macdonald, Lowell, and Mailer knew all this,
they did not have to talk or argue, they had learned what
politics they had, each in his own separate way, and so
they did not need to discuss the sound-as-brickwork-logic-of-the-next-step. The March tomorrow would more or
less work or not work. If it didn't, the Left would always
find a new step—the Left never left itself unemployed
(that much must be said for the conservative dictum that
a man who wants to, can always find work) if the March
did more or less succeed, one knew it would be as a result of episodes one had never anticipated, and the results
might lead you in directions altogether unforeseen. And
indeed how could one measure success or failure in a
venture so odd and unprecedented as this? One did not
march on the Pentagon and look to get arrested as a link
in a master scheme to take over the bastions of the Republic step by step, no, that sort of sound-as-brickwork-
logic was left to the FBI. Rather, one marched on the
Pentagon because . . . because . . . and here the reasons
became so many and so curious and so vague, so political
and so primitive, that there was no need, or perhaps no
possibility to talk about it yet, one could only ruminate

over the morning coffee. What possibly they shared now between them at the morning table of the Hay-Adams was the unspoken happy confidence that politics had again become mysterious, had begun to partake of Mystery; that gave life to a thought the gods were back in human affairs. A generation of the American young had come along different from five previous generations of the middle class. The new generation believed in technology more than any before it, but the generation also believed in LSD, in witches, in tribal knowledge, in orgy, and revolution. It had no respect whatsoever for the unassailable logic of the next step: belief was reserved for the revelatory mystery of the happening where you did not know what was going to happen next; that was what was good about it. Their radicalism was in their hate for the authority—the authority was manifest of evil to this generation. It was the authority who had covered the land with those suburbs where they stifled as children while watching the adventures of the West in the movies, while looking at the guardians of dull genial celebrity on television; they had had their minds jabbed and poked and twitched and probed and finally galvanized into surrealistic modes of response by commercials cutting into dramatic narratives, and parents flipping from network to network—they were forced willy-nilly to build their idea of the space-time continuum (and therefore their nervous system) on the jumps and cracks and leaps and breaks which every phenomenon from the media seemed to contain within it.

The authority had operated on their brain with commercials, and washed their brain with packaged education, packaged politics. The authority had presented itself as honorable, and it was corrupt, corrupt as payola on television, and scandals concerning the safety of automobiles, and scandals concerning the leasing of aviation contracts—the real scandals as everyone was beginning to sense were more intimate and could be found in all the products in all the suburban homes which did not work so well as they should have worked, and broke down too soon for mysterious reasons. The shoddiness was buried in the package, buried somewhere in the undiscoverable root of all those modern factories with their sanitized

103

aisles and automated machines; perhaps one place the shoddiness was buried was in the hangovers of a working class finally alienated from any remote interest or attention in the process of the work itself. Work was shoddy everywhere. Even in the Warren Commission.

Finally, this new generation of the Left hated the authority, because the authority lied. It lied through the teeth of corporation executives as Cabinet officials and police enforcement officers and newspaper editors and advertising agencies, and in its mass magazines, where the subtlest apologies for the disasters of the authority (and the neatest deformations of the news) were grafted in the best possible style into the ever-open mind of the walking American lobotomy: the corporation office worker and his high school son.

The New Left was drawing its political aesthetic from Cuba. The revolutionary idea which the followers of Castro had induced from their experience in the hills was that you created the revolution first and learned from it, learned of what your revolution might consist and where it might go out of the intimate truth of the way it presented itself to your experience. Just as the truth of his material was revealed to a good writer by the cutting edge of his style (he could thus hope his style was in each case the most appropriate tool for the material of the experience) so a revolutionary began to uncover the nature of his true situation by trying to ride the beast of his revolution. The idea behind these ideas was then obviously that the future of the revolution existed in the nerves and cells of the people who created it and lived with it, rather than in the sanctity of the original idea.

Castro's Cuba was of course a mystery to Mailer. He had heard much in its favor, much he could hardly enjoy. That was not necessarily to the point. Revolutions could fail as well by Castro's method as by the most inflexible Comintern program; what seemed significant here, was the idea of a revolution which preceded ideology; the New Left had obviously adopted the idea for this March.

The aesthetic of the New Left now therefore began with the notion that the authority could not comprehend nor contain nor finally manage to control any political action whose end was unknown. They could attack it, beat it, jail it, misrepresent it, and finally abuse it, but they could not feel a sense of victory because they could not understand a movement which inspired thousands and hundreds of thousands to march without a coordinated plan. The bureaucrats of the Old Left had not been alone in their adoration of the solid-as-brickwork-logic-of-the-next-step; no, the bureaucrats of the American Center, now liked it as much, and were as aghast at any political activity which ignored it.

These Leviathan ruminations and meditations on the nature of the March coming up, and the reasons for their participation without much discussion now completed, ch-ch-ch-click! in the touch of the tea cup on Mailer's lip, let us move on to the event concerning us—that first major battle of a war which may go on for twenty years; let us even consider there is one interesting chance (one chance of a thousand) that in fifty years the day may loom in our history large as the ghosts of the Union dead.

2: THE ARMIES OF THE DEAD

Now who would be certain the shades of those Union dead were not ready to come on Lowell and Mailer as they strode through the grass up the long flat breast of hill at the base of Washington Monument and looked down the length of the reflecting pool to Lincoln Memorial perhaps one-half mile away, "then to step off like green Union Army recruits for the first Bull Run, sped by photographers . . ." was what Lowell was to write about events a bit later that day, but although they said hardly a word now, Lowell and Mailer were thinking of the Civil War: it was hard not to.

Walking over together from the hotel this Saturday

morning Lowell had again invoked the repetitions of the night before. "Your speech yesterday was awfully good, Norman."

"Yes, Cal, but I thought yours was simply fine."

"Did you really?"

So covering old historic ground, they enjoyed the stroll past the White House, the old State Department—now looking not unlike the largest mansion ever not quite built at Newport—on to the approaches of the Ellipse. Macdonald was following later, they were to meet him at the Washington Monument's end of the reflecting pool in an hour, but for now they were impatient to set out early.

The flat breast of the hill at the foot of the monument had that agreeable curve one finds on an athletic field graded for drainage. Here, the curve was more pronounced, but the effect was similar: the groups and couples walking down from Washington Monument toward the round pool and the long reflecting pool which led to Lincoln Memorial, were revealed by degrees—one saw their hats bobbing on the horizon of the ridge before you saw their faces; perhaps this contributed to a high sense of focus; the eye studied the act of walking as if one were looking at the gait of a troop of horses; some of the same pleasure was there: the people seemed to be prancing. It was similar to the way men and women are caught in the films of very good directors; the eye watching the film knows it has not been properly employed before. These people were animated; the act of stepping along seemed to loosen little springs in their joints, the action was rollicking, something was grave. Perhaps this etching of focus had to do with no more than the physical fact that Mailer, approaching somewhat lower on the swell of the hill, was therefore watching with his eyes on a line with those rollicking feet. That could not however be all of it. A thin high breath of pleasure, like a child's anticipation of the first rocket to be fired on Fourth of July, hung over the sweet grass of the hill on Washington Monument. They were prancing past this hill, they were streaming to battle. Going to battle! He realized that he had not taken in precisely this thin high sensuous breath of pleasure in close to twenty-four years, not since the first time he had

106

gone into combat, and found to his surprise that the walk toward the fire fight was one of the more agreeable—if stricken—moments of his life. Later, in the skirmish itself it was less agreeable—he had perspired so profusely he had hardly been able to see through his sweat—much later, months later, combat was disagreeable; it managed to consist of large doses of fatigue, the intestinal agitations of the tropics, endless promenades through mud, and general apathy toward whether one lived or not. But the first breath had left a feather on his memory; it was in the wind now; he realized that an odd, yes a *zany* part of him had been expecting quietly and confidently for years, that before he was done, he would lead an army. (The lives of Leon Trotsky and Ernest Hemingway had done nothing to dispel this expectation.) No, the sweetness of war came back. Probably there were very few good wars (good wars being free of excessive exhaustion, raddled bowels, miserable food, and computerized methods) but if you were in as good shape for war as for football, there was very little which was better for the senses. They would be executing Ernest Hemingway in effigy every ten years for having insisted upon this recognition, they would even be executing him in Utope City on the moon, but Mailer now sent him a novelist's blessing (which is to say, well-intended but stingy) because Hemingway after all had put the key on the table. *If it made you feel good, it was good.* That, and Saint Thomas Aquinas' "Trust the authority of your senses," were enough to enable a man to become a good working amateur philosopher, an indispensable vocation for the ambitious novelist since otherwise he is naught but an embittered entertainer, a storyteller, a John O'Hara! (Born January 31, same birthday as Mailer.)

These playful ruminations of high brass on the morning of battle came out of the intoxication of the day, the place, the event, the troops who were splendidly dressed (description later) and the music. As Lowell and Mailer reached the ridge and took a turn to the right to come down from Washington Monument toward the length of the long reflecting pool which led between two long groves of trees near the banks to the steps of Lincoln Memorial, out from that direction came the clear bitter-sweet excitation of a military trumpet resounding in the near distance, one peal which seemed to go all the way back through a galaxy of bugles to the cries of the Civil War and the first trumpet note to blow the attack. The ghosts of old battles were wheeling like clouds over Washington today.

The trumpet sounded again. It was calling the troops. "Come here," it called from the steps of Lincoln Memorial over the two furlongs of the long reflecting pool, out to the swell of the hill at the base of Washington Monument, "come here, come here, come here. The rally is on!" And from the north and the east, from the direction of the White House and the Smithsonian and the Capitol, from Union Station and the Department of Justice the troops were coming in, the volunteers were answering the call. They came walking up in all sizes, a citizens' army not ranked yet by height, an army of both sexes in numbers almost equal, and of all ages, although most were young. Some were well-dressed, some were poor, many were conventional in appearance, as often were not. The hippies were there in great number, perambulating down the hill, many dressed like the legions of Sgt. Pepper's Band, some were gotten up like Arab shieks, or in Park Avenue's doormen's greatcoats, others like Rogers and Clark of the West, Wyatt Earp, Kit Carson, Daniel Boone in buckskin, some had grown mustaches to look like *Have Gun, Will Travel*—Paladin's surrogate was here!— and wild Indians with feathers, a hippie gotten up like Batman, another like Claude Rains in *The Invisible Man* —his face wrapped in a turban of bandages and he wore a black satin top hat. A host of these troops wore capes, beat-up khaki capes, slept on, used as blankets, towels, improvised duffel bags; or fine capes, orange linings, or luminous rose linings, the edges ragged, near a tatter, the threads ready to feather, but a musketeer's hat on their head. One hippie may have been dressed like Charles Chaplin; Buster Keaton and W. C. Fields could have come to the ball; there were Martians and Moon-men and a knight unhorsed who stalked about in the weight of real armor. There were to be seen a hundred soldiers in

108

Confederate gray, and maybe there were two or three hundred hippies in officer's coats of Union dark-blue. They had picked up their costumes where they could, in surplus stores, and Blow-your-mind shops, Digger free emporiums, and psychedelic caches of Hindu junk. There were soldiers in Foreign Legion uniforms, and tropical bush jackets, San Quentin and Chino, California striped shirt and pants, British copies of Eisenhower jackets, hippies dressed like Turkish shepherds and Roman senators, gurus, and samurai in dirty smocks. They were close to being assembled from all the intersections between history and the comic books, between legend and television, the Biblical archetypes and the movies. The sight of these troops, this army with a thousand costumes, fulfilled to the hilt our General's oldest idea of war which is that every man should dress as he pleases if he is going into battle, for that is his right, and variety never hurts the zest of the hardiest workers in every battalion (here today by thousands in plaid hunting jackets, corduroys or dungarees, ready for assault!) if the sight of such masquerade lost its usual happy connotation of masked ladies and starving children outside the ball, it was not only because of the shabbiness of the costumes (up close half of them must have been used by hippies for everyday wear) but also because the aesthetic at last was in the politics —the dress ball was going into battle. Still, there were nightmares beneath the gaiety of these middle-class runaways, these Crusaders, going out to attack the hard core of technology land with less training than armies were once offered by a medieval assembly ground. The nightmare was in the echo of those trips which had fractured their sense of past and present. If nature was a veil whose tissue had been ripped by static, screams of jet motors, the highway grid of the suburbs, smog, defoliation, pollution of streams, overfertilization of earth, anti-fertilization of women, and the radiation of two decades of near blind atom busting, then perhaps the history of the past was another tissue, spiritual, no doubt, without physical embodiment, unless its embodiment was in the cuneiform hieroglyphics of the chromosome (so much like primitive writing!) but that tissue of past history, whether traceable in the flesh, or merely palpable in the collective underworld of the dream, was nonetheless being bombed by the use of LSD as outrageously as the atoll of Eniwetok, Hiroshima, Nagasaki, and the scorched foliage of Vietnam. The history of the past was being exploded right into the present: perhaps there were now lacunae in the firmament of the past, holes where once had been the psychic reality of an era which was gone. Mailer was haunted by the nightmare that the evils of the present not only exploited the present, but consumed the past, and gave every promise of demolishing whole territories of the future. The same villains who, promiscuously, wantonly, heedlessly, had gorged on LSD and consumed God knows what essential marrows of history, wearing indeed the history of all eras on their back as trophies of this gluttony, were now going forth (conscience-struck?) to make war on those other villains, corporation-land villains, who were destroying the promise of the present in their self-righteousness and greed and secret lust (often unknown to themselves) for some sexo-technological variety of neo-fascism.

Mailer's final allegiance, however, was with the villains who were hippies. They would never have looked to blow their minds and destroy some part of the past if the authority had not brainwashed the mood of the present until it smelled like deodorant. (To cover the odor of burning flesh in Vietnam?) So he continued to enjoy the play of costumes, but his pleasure was now edged with a hint of the sinister. Not inappropriate for battle. He and Lowell were still in the best of moods. The morning was so splendid—it spoke of a vitality in nature which no number of bombings in space nor inner-space might ever subdue; the rustle of costumes warming up for the war spoke of future redemptions as quickly as they reminded of hog-swillings from the past, and the thin air! wine of Civil War apples in the October air! edge of excitement and awe—how would this day end? No one could know. Incredible spectacle now gathering—tens of thousands traveling hundreds of miles to attend a symbolic battle. In the capital of technology land beat a primitive drum. New drum of the Left! And the Left had been until this year

110

the secret unwitting accomplice of every increase in the power of the technicians, bureaucrats, and labor leaders who ran the governmental military-industrial complex of super-technology land.

3: IN THE RHETORIC

Lowell and Mailer walked along the edge of the reflecting pool toward the Lincoln Memorial passing sometimes on the grass, often along the path, being recognized frequently—warm smiles, timid questions, or conversations which went on thirty seconds too long. Yaws. Small abysses. If it had been the hippies who made the first impression on the eye, there were now visible legions of protesters with banners and signs, men wearing blue garrison caps which carried the legend Veterans Against the War in Vietnam—what was curious about these veterans is how many had faces which could have sat as easily beneath an American Legion or VFW cap.

On the grass some people were picnicking, others were assembling. Large white streamers of painted cloth, ten or twenty feet long, were being fitted on the grass to their carrying sticks. A respectable horde of respectable professionals, lawyers, accountants, men in hats wearing eyeglasses, were evident. Reform Democrats some of them, members of SANE, or Women Strike for Peace—looking about, there were signs enough: American Friends Service Committee, CORE, W.E.B. DuBois Clubs, Inter-University Christian Movement, Catholic Peace Fellowship, Jewish Peace Fellowship, Southern Christian Leadership Conference, Students for a Democratic Society, SNCC, National Lawyers' Guild, The Resistance, National Conference for a New Politics—Mailer walked not too happily past such signs. In the apocalyptic garden of *his* revolution these sects and groups and clubs and committees were like rusty tin cans. He had the impression from previous days—now so much as fifteen years ago, for he had not gone near a sect in years; as quickly would he breed mosquitoes!—that the best to be said was that they were probably like vitamins, injurious to a healthy stomach, smelling like the storeroom of a pharmacology company's warehouse, doubtless productive of cancer over the long haul, but essential perhaps, perhaps! to a Left forever suffering from malnutrition. Mailer knew this attitude had nothing to do with reality—if names like SANE or Women Strike for Peace sounded like brand names which could have been used as happily to sell aspirin, he could hardly think the same of SNCC or SDS or one or two of the others; now and again, remarkable young men sprang out of these alphabet soups. No, it was more that the Novelist begrudged the dimming of what was remarkable in the best of these young men because some part of their nervous system would have to attach vision and lust and dreams of power, glory, justice, sacrifice, and future purchases on heaven to these deadening letters. As soon call political parties by the number of their telephone. Mailer thought the new parties of the Left ought to have names like motorcycle gangs and block athletic clubs had on their jackets: George Street Jumpers, and Green Dolphins, Orange Sparrows, Gasoline Ghosts, Paragon A.C., Purple Raiders, Silver Dragons, Bughouse Beasts—he had known immediately that neither Stokely Carmichael nor Black Power were insignificant phenomena on the day he heard that in Lowndes County, Alabama, Negroes were organizing into the Black Panther Party. Mailer, while a dilettante in Left Wing politics, was nonetheless free with his surgery; left to him, he would have cut out all middle-class protest movements like SANE and Women Strike for Peace because they derived, not genealogically he was certain, but spiritually, from the worst aspects of the American Communist Party, that old dull calculation that the apathetic middle class organizations with middle-class leaders and abstract Everyman names like Women, Students, Artists, Professionals, Mothers, Veterans, Grandmothers, yea why not Babes? Yes, had reasoned the Communists, large bloc names could bring large even gross increases in recruitment among the middle class. Vulgar gross increases were the result. It is one thing to call a factory hand a worker —that is good for his sense of reality—he is married to his machine more than to anything else, the name helps to remind him. But for a middle-class married woman to think of herself politically as a Mother, or worse, a Woman, could only indulge a sense of self-pity. Mediocrities flock to any movement which will indulge their self-pity and their self-righteousness, for without a Movement the mediocrity is on the slide into terminal melancholia. Most such political movements served as piping systems for the brain, and flushing systems for the heart, bringing in subsistence rations of ego and do-it-yourself compassion, all very well as social plumbing to keep mass man alive, but the Participant wasn't so certain that there weren't too many people alive already, certainly in America, that hog's trough of Paradise. The horror of mediocrities in a Left Wing movement was that cadres of the best young people used too much breath trying to illumine one glint of the ideal in material mediocre hearts. The Ruminant was by now convinced that technology land was the real capitalist bastion, and the mediocre middle-class middle-aged masses of the Left were—we have visited this station already—the first real champions of technology land: they could not conceive of a revolution without hospitals, lawyers, mass meetings, and leaflets to pass out at the polls.

Mailer and Lowell continued to walk around the reflecting pool, then back of the speaker's stand (which was in front of the steps of Lincoln Memorial) and took a promenade back on the other side to the circular pool near the Washington Monument, there—after wait, delay and confusion about place—to pick up Macdonald and stroll back again down the now crowding banks and path, each of them stopping in turn to greet or chat with any one of a dozen different people each hundred yards, and at last reach the line of police behind the speaker's stand, there to wait and be recognized by one of the young men with an armband who was serving as a Monitor, and so were admitted to the roped-in area on the lower steps of the Memorial which contained perhaps a thousand people, groups, committees, press, gangs of media, combos of entertainment, notables, and honored noncommunicative Black Power groups looking somehow blacker in skin than they had looked in the old coffee-and-cream days of liberal integration. Having reached this sinecure which surrounded the new solid carpentering of the speaker's stand with the baker's dozen of microphones, they stood and chatted with other—the word was undeniable—"notables," flunkies, ushers, monitors, cameramen, and expediters of the March, and felt, at least so Mailer felt, the slow sweet filling of long unused reservoirs, and intimations of all the armies of the past which had gathered on a field like this believing their cause to be grand and just and heroic, and therefore amazingly sweet—the long promenade sweeping the circle of the long reflecting pool and the gathering thousands on its banks had seemed to capture that sense of long-gone armies, that fine strain of love which hovers like some last lavender in the dying echo of a superbly played string, there was a love of evening in the warm morning air, a violet of late shadows, a ghost of Gettysburg and the knowledge that a sense of danger had finally come to the American Left, not to the brave students who had gone South years ago to hunt for Negro rights, but to the damnable mediocre middle of the Left, and that stirred a tenderness which lifted like a thin smoke of battle, tinted rose-color in legend, to honor the light in the blood welling from the fallen brave. Yes, the presence of those endless newspaper reports of thousands of paratroops and MPs and police and U. S. Marshals waiting for them at the Pentagon—that novel sense of mass collective danger —had fifty or a hundred thousand civilians ever assembled before in America for a purpose remotely like this: a symbolic battle which might have real broken heads?— had brought the roll of old thunders, old loves, and old patriotic drums to the sterile heart of the American Left.

"Yes, we have to get arrested today," Mailer thought, "no alternative for it." If technology land had built Global Village, well shank it up technology land, let Global Village hear today that America's best poet? and best novelist?? and best critic???? had been arrested in

114

protest of Uncle Sam's Whorehouse War. And if Paul Goodman had been here, Mailer supposed he could have been ranked as America's best inspiration to the young?????? But Goodman had worked all week in the most honorable causes, first for draft resisters in New York, then in Washington to give a worthy, humorless, incontrovertible, and not uncourageous speech before the National Security Industrial Association which had four hundred members of the military-industrial complex. Goodman having analyzed, vivisected, and scolded the assembled corporate magnates ("you are . . . the most dangerous body of men at the present in the world")—a spring-cleaning operation of the soul so to tell them off —had fairly had enough of *the cause* after the Ambassador, and was obliged to go back to New York. (Mailer, not knowing about Goodman's speech to the military-industrial complex, had—we may suppose—given a secret sneer, "Those guys who don't drink miss all the fun!")

Waiting for the literal March to the Pentagon to begin, there were no drinks being served. Only speeches. Perhaps it was the shadow caused by Paul Goodman's absence—the full sentence from which we quoted above had gone: "You are the military industrial of the United States, the most dangerous body of men at the present in the world, for you not only implement our disastrous policies but are an overwhelmingly lobby for them, and you expand and rigidify the wrong use of brains, resources, and labor, so that change becomes difficult." Only Goodman could say "at the present in the world," "implement," "disastrous policies," "overwhelming lobby," "expand and rigidify"—everything he said was right, so naturally it had to be said in a style which read like LBJ's exercises in Upper Rhetoric (the Rhetoric, Mailer now decided, being located three inches below and back of Erogenous Zone Clitoric).

Thoughts like these ran like Huns and Vandals through Mailer's mind whenever he had to listen to speeches. The run of the rhetoric now booming through the loudspeakers was not quite down there grabbing for the marbles with the worst of Goodman's dishmop prose, but was nonetheless inspirative of that mood which he had come to name the Great Left Pall. Of course, Mailer had an instinct for missing good speeches—at the Civil Rights March in Washington in 1963 he had gone for a stroll just a little while before Martin Luther King began, "I have a dream," so Mailer—trusting no one else in these matters, certainly not the columnists and the commentators— would never know whether the Reverend King had given a great speech that day, or revealed an inch of his hambone. It was agreeable to have one's own impression on such matters. Today, for instance, neither Mailer nor Lowell had known that the featured speaker Clive Jenkins of the British Labor party had been attacked by a member of the American Nazi party who had managed to knock over the podium and the twelve or more mikes, before the Nazi was in turn wrestled to the ground by William Sloane Coffin, Jr., Yale Chaplain—the hero of Friday's occasion at the Department of Justice (and doubtless once captain of the Yale wrestling team). No, Mailer and Lowell had been at the other end of the reflecting pool looking for Macdonald. So one could give a record of the speeches but they were not heard, nor even listened to. Dr. Spock gave for example a perfectly decent speech, simply and saliently worded. He and his wife were a most attractive young elderly couple, his wife in fact not elderly—she was often introduced as Janey Spock, they looked like the sort of wealthy Republicans who might have waited in the lobby of the Roosevelt for the Dewey victory party on Election Night in 1948, but Mailer had an animus against Spock. Three of Mailer's four wives had used Spock's book on infant and baby care as their bible. Mailer had put his nose in the book once in a while, and outside of Spock's occasional faith in medicine, the book did not seem unsound. In fact, it even seemed possessed of common sense. Nonetheless, Mailer did not like Spock too much. A marriage is never so ready to show where it is weak as when a baby is ill, and Spock was therefore associated in Mailer's mind more with squalling wives than babies. Dr. Spock's speech, as the Historian subsequently read it quoted in part in the newspapers, said:

We are convinced that this war which Lyndon Johnson is waging is disastrous to our country in every way, and that we, the protesters, are the ones who may help to save our country if we can persuade enough of our fellow citizens to think and vote as we do.

That was nice and about par for the speeches. They said almost nothing one had not heard before, but the sentiments were incontestable, and the words went out over the loudspeakers and dropped in dull echoes on the reflecting pool and in the trees, and occasionally a whistle or a rattle of applause would come back like a crisp fluttering of leaves (or a rattle of rifle fire) from one or another area in that huge audience. There were not, however, any large demonstrations in answer to the speakers. Mailer sitting off to one side and behind them could hardly hear a word, but he suspected the acoustics were poor out by the reflecting pool, for the applause and cheers were like the bored sounds a baseball crowd makes when their side gets a walk and it no longer matters very much because the team is far ahead. So was everyone here now far ahead on Rhetoric.

Mailer began to count the house. It seemed to him that if the Washington March in 1963 had brought in a quarter of a million people, then there were half as many here today; if the crowd four years ago had been one hundred thousand, then fifty thousand now had showed. Mailer's computations were rudimentary. The crowd today filled about as much space as the crowd on that other day, but were dispersed a degree more loosely. It was one of the little inconveniences, one of the sewed-up pockets of modern history that no one was capable of counting the crowd. Each newspaper and government bureau and Left Wing organizing committee released the count which made the most sense from their own point of view; so the mob today would be numbered everywhere from twenty-five thousand to two hundred twenty-five thousand. The Novelist thought that if his estimate of a crowd half the size of the 1963 attendance was correct, then a huge number had turned out. In '63 everything had been well-organized, everybody had been for the March, everybody from SNCC to *Life* magazine. A U. S. Senator had given a party in the evening for leaders of the March. Today one came with the invitation to look paratroopers in the eye.

On went the speeches. Mailer had no particular idea of their order or what they said. Lincoln Lynch of CORE spoke and Dagmar Wilson of Women Strike for Peace, Nguyen Van Luy, a Vietnamese-born American citizen, and Coffin, who introduced a group of Californians who had carried a peace torch to the rally, walking twenty-four miles a day. John Wilson of SNCC told the crowd that "white people are just beginning to find out what it's like to have grievances and not be able to influence the government," and one wondered which young white Wasp girls had been the innocents to give him such impression. "Welcome to the club," said Wilson. Then he accused Johnson, McNamara, and Rusk of being the "biggest war criminals in the country."

"We must resist," Wilson shouted, "we must resist, resist, resist, and resist." Later he bellowed, "Hell, no—we won't go," and the crowd picked it up. He was a good speaker and so was Ella Collins, sister of Malcolm X.

"Do you want peace?" she asked the crowd.

"Yes," they roared back.

"Well, let's go get it."

The comedy of the New Left, its Achilles' heel, black as tar, was now being displayed. Ella Collins still talked to Whites as if one could conceive of a society where they might all parade down the same street, but most of the Blacks in this roped-off section had moved into the future, into that Black Twenty-first Century when Black Power had succeeded in rendering the white man invisible at will for the black; so these Blacks moved among the eager ingratiating smiles of young New Leftists or the wounded silence of the older ones with an exquisite disdain which left the Whites next to invisible, washed-out. It had been (until the recognition of such continued black disdain) a happier day on this occasion than back on these same steps in August 1963. On that day all Negroes and Whites had been polite to each other. A well-controlled but slightly hysterical propensity to laugh too much had hung over every dialogue between Negro liberals and White, there had been discomfort in the air, a bleak air of oppression back of all good humor as if the sun of a bright summer day were racing unseen clouds over the horizon to get to evening before the storm, discipline had lain like a net over the audience in the meadow and around the pool. Everyone had celebrated the day as happy—it had at best succeeded in not being morose—it was like a grand fiftieth wedding anniversary in which fifty years of family feuds were swept under those grave formal manners whose real content is depression. Nobody quite understood in those days the dark somewhat incoherent warnings of Jimmy Baldwin being true to his own, yet trying to warn his old white friends.

Now there was no room for the sore beneath the skin. A new sore, Vietnam, had pushed the old sore into the light. What a sore! The best of the Whites recoiled in horror from what was now seen, for the evil they had visited on the Blacks was either indescribably worse than they had ever conceived, or the Black had made a Faustian pact with Mephisto, and the Devil was now here to collect.

Not for little humor had Negroes developed that odd humorless crack in their personality which cracked each other into laughter, playing on one side an odd mad practical black man who could be anything, wise chauffeur, drunken butler, young money-mad Pullman porter, Negro college graduate selling insurance—the other half was sheer psychopath, rocks in the ice-cube, pocket oiled for the switchblade, I'll kill you, Whitey, burn baby, all tuned to a cool. These Blacks moved through the New Left with a physical indifference to the bodies about them, as if ten Blacks could handle any hundreds of these flaccid Whites, and they signaled to each other across the aisles, and talked in quick idioms and out, an English not comprehensible to any ear which knew nothing of the separate meanings of the same word at separate pitch (Maoists not for nothing these Blacks!) their hair carefully brushed out in every direction like African guerrillas or huge radar stations on some lonely isle, they seemed to communicate with one another in ten dozen modes, with fingers like deaf and dumb, with feet, with their stance, by the flick of their long wrist, with the radar of their hair, the smoke of their will, the glide of their passage, by a laugh, a nod, a disembodied gesture, through mediums, seeming to speak through silent mediums among them who never gave hint to a sign. In the apathy which had begun to lie over the crowd as the speeches went on and on (and the huge army gathered by music, now was ground down by words, and the hollow absurd imprecatory thunder of the loudspeakers with their reductive echo —you must FIGHT . . . *fight* . . . fight . . . fite . . . ite . . . , in the soul-killing repetition of political jargon which reminded people that the day was well past one o'clock and they still had not started) the Blacks in the roped-in area about the speaker's stand were the only sign of active conspiracy, they were up to some collective expression of disdain, something to symbolize their detestation of the White Left—yes, Mailer was to brood on it much of the next day when he learned without great surprise that almost all of the Negroes had left to make their own demonstration in another part of Washington, their announcement to the press underlining their reluctance to use their bodies in a White War. That was comprehensible enough. If the Negroes were at the Pentagon and did not preempt the front rank, they would lose face as fighters; if they were too numerous on the line, they would be beaten half to death. That was the ostensible reason they did not go, but Mailer wondered if he saw a better.

Dellinger was finishing his speech. "We said we would disrupt the Pentagon, and I believe it is already being disrupted . . . We will go to the Pentagon and we will face the troops. We will turn it into a teach-in for the troops." Dellinger was a man of middle height and middle build, sturdy in appearance, solid, half-bald, professional, genial, with a redeeming smile of shy diffidence—a hint less of the Quaker's moral substance, and he could easily have been taken for Class Agent of his fellow graduates at Yale—he had the hard-working, modestly gregarious, and absolutely devoted sense of how mission and detail interlock which is so necessary to good Class Agents, that rare vintage mixture of New England incorruptibility and good fellowship. Of course, Mailer hardly knew him. They had met once or twice at rallies and done no more than smile good greetings to one another. Years ago in 1959 when Dellinger was already an editor on *Liberation* (then an anarchist-pacifist magazine, of worthy but not very readable articles in more or less vegetarian prose) Mailer had submitted a piece, after some solicitation, on the contrast between real obscenity in advertising, and alleged obscenity in four-letter words. The piece was no irreplaceable work of prose, and in fact was eventually inserted quietly into his book, *Advertisements for Myself*, but it created difficulty for the editorial board at *Liberation*, since there was a four-letter word he had used to make his point, the palpable four-letter word which signifies a woman's most definitive organ: these editorial anarchists were decorous; they were ready to overthrow society and replace it with a communion of pacifistic men free of all laws, but they were not ready to print cunt. Dellinger had been caught in the middle—he had wanted to publish an article by Norman Mailer, and had no objection to the language, but was finally unable to convince the rest of the board. So the piece had been returned. But Dellinger, caught in a ludicrous editorial posture, had nonetheless handled himself with dignity, so Mailer always liked him after that. Since then, eight years of literary apocalypse had gone on in editorial offices. Today a Left Wing editor who would not print **** or **** was in danger of being beaten to death at Berkeley with stones on which was painted: Fuck!

This facet of the Left might offer much amusement to any heart so cynical as our Participant, but there had been a moment of exceptional consequence for radical activities in just that period. The late Reverend A. J. Muste, the austere impeccable dean of American anarchists (a man so pure in motive that in comparison to him Norman Thomas was as Sadie Thompson) had come to the deep and much searched conclusion of his soul that he, personally, would no longer eschew participation in radical activities which contained Communists. Since this decision came at a time when the Communists were

121

themselves breaking up under the knockdown combinations of Hungary's revolt, and Polish and Czechoslovakian riots and/or uprisings by Communist students and workers, plus the denigration of Stalin by Khrushchev—the American Communist was finally down! he was down! poor American Communist who had taken the most lethal mauling in the history of political club fighters. Consider a countdown of the punches: famine in the Ukraine; Moscow trials; Hitler-Stalin pact; slave-labor camps; Cold War; political burial of the Progressive party; the hounding of the Hollywood Ten; the infiltration of the Party ranks by the FBI; the loss of all bridgeheads in the labor unions; great tensions between Russia and China—those poor Communists had been beaten near to death (it was their secret cure for cancer) but had never been knocked down until the new hierophant said the old dead idol was there to be dismantled. So the monolithic ideology of Stalin went down, and with him went a stable of stout-hearted, brain-deadened, punch-drunk pugs. The American Communist Party, already dissolved politically by the Smith Act, now divided, broke up, segmented into pieces of shell like Trotskyist sects—the American Left was finally free of its unendurable overweight punch-drunk pug of a mother-in-law, and Muste had an instinct to end the old hopeless Left Wing war, extend a Christian anarchist's hand to the fallen, and go out to do battle, not together—but not apart. Let the future, not parties, determine the shape of revolutionary ideas. It was an historic moment, and the all-but-dead Left prospered, the New Left was to a degree born of Muste's decision, and a generation of college students came along who were finally indifferent to the blockhouse polemics of the past, and the real nature of the Soviet. It was the real injustice in America which attracted their attention—poverty, civil rights, an end to censorship—their attention was toward an American Revolution; of what it might consist, was another matter—one's idea of a better existence would be found or not found in the context of the revolution. To the New Left, commissars, like FBI men, had taken on the lineaments of pop art—they were pop villains—to be drawn in poster paint. And indeed one speculates at the breakdown in the cognitive process of the FBI analyst as he tried to comprehend the workings of the couriers in SNCC and the hippie fringe of the SDS.

At any rate, Dellinger was Muste's man, he had worked for him, under him, with him. When Muste died, Dellinger had been his natural successor. Like Muste, he had never joined a political party. So, he was a natural coordinator of all such Mobilizations as this March on the Pentagon.

That was finally beginning. After hours of waiting, after the military exuberance of listening to a rallying trumpet had faded into hours of speeches, and the blanked-out unavoidable apathy of the Great Left Pall (troops up for battle, troops dropped down) now at last, two hours after the yeast of a happy beginning had been punched in (it was to rise again)—the order to form into ranks was passed around the roped enclosure, and Lowell, Macdonald, and Mailer were requested to get up in the front row, where the notables were to lead the March, a row obviously to be consecrated for the mass media. Newsreel, still, and television cameras were clicking and rounding and snapping and zooming before the first rank was even formed.

4: A HALF-MILE TO VIRGINIA

It had been a particularly oncrous wait for the Critic, the Poet, and the Novelist. They had talked to people, met people, chatted with other notables like Sidney Lens and Monsignor Rice of Pittsburgh (to whom Lowell had confessed with an enigmatic smile that he was now a "lapsed Catholic," a remark which brought no rush of sympathy from the priest, more a thoughtful non-approving grunt) they had lolled about in the sun, watched the

Black contingent drift off on an Oriental scramble of secret signals, had passed around chocolate bars in lieu of lunch, Mailer refusing a bite (he had the uncharacteristic conviction he must not eat or drink until the March was over, or he would spoil the now undeniable clarity and sweet anticipation of his nerves) and had finally contented each other with wry twists of the eyebrow at the interminable tedium of the speeches. No use to tell oneself that the people who spoke had worked hard to prepare this March, and so were entitled to their reward. Bugger all reward. Half the troops would desert if the speeches went on. (And in fact half the troops did—no telling how many more would have set out if the invitation to move to the Pentagon had followed the noontime exhilaration of the music.) Mailer, of course, had been preparing an extempore speech for the odd chance they might call on him; he would have liked to address fifty or one hundred thousand people: the beginning of a twenty year war is here today in our March, he might have said, rising to the occasion—but the call never came, which did little to improve his impatience.

Well, finally they were now set to go. The March was to begin on a road which separated the upper and lower levels of steps at Lincoln Memorial, and debauched in about two hundred feet onto the Arlington Memorial Bridge, a span some half-mile long which was to lead to a traffic circle on the Virginia side—how better to know one has crossed the border from one state to another than by encountering a traffic circle? Then they would strike out to the Pentagon. Mailer, of course, knew little of this yet—he was certainly too nearsighted to see that far ahead, and much too vain to wear his eyeglasses before hundreds of Leicas and Nikons and Exactas in the hands of professional photographers. No, rather he stood in the makings of the front line of notables (which was having as much trouble being formed as the markings in a cigarette put together by an amateur cowboy). Notables kept being crowded into the second rank by notables less notable than themselves, so they made great efforts to get back to the front rank which promptly buckled. Then upstarts and arrivistes tried to infiltrate the flanks of this front line which naturally created a tangle. At least sixty people were trying to get into a front line which was not wide enough for forty. It was not unlike the squeeze at a football game—whoever cheers most and sits down last has no seat. Next the order was passed—still impossible to move out—to link arms. Mailer's arm was promptly taken by Sid Lens, an old radical leader from the Fellowship of Reconciliation, who had the red meaty face and cunning look of a man who has been in many a trade union harangue, war, stampede, and squeeze-out over the years, and has lasted, sir, has lasted like one of those tough-skinned balloons with a lead bottom which always spring up when you strike them. If a Committee from the Feature Formers Guild of Heaven had been given instructions to design a face which was halfway in appearance between Sidney Lens and Robert Lowell, they might have come up with Norman Mailer; stationed between Lens and Lowell he felt the separate halves of his nature well-represented, which gave little pleasure, for no American citizen likes to link arms at once with the two ends of his practical working-day good American schizophrenia. So Mailer managed in the general wrestling, buckling, and staggering of the line to work around to the other side of Lowell, and leave to Lens the cartel of being stationed between Lowell and Macdonald—which is probably what Lens had wanted from the beginning, and was why, old pirate of union negotiations, he had chosen to begin in the first place with Mailer. (Modern politics may be built on the art of attaining specific small ends by requesting others.)

At any rate, despite all strainings and waverings, the ranks began to form behind the first rank, and a hollow square of young Mobilization monitors formed up ahead of the leading rank of notables in order to sweep like a plug or a piston along the bridge, thus keeping infiltrators from passing the flanks and destroying the front of the March, but the notables in consequence were shifted down from the forwardmost line to what was now no more than the third line, to Mailer's disappointment, for he had been pleased to be in the front rank, in fact had fought doggedly to keep position there, anticipating at the end of the March a confrontation face to face with the eyes of soldiers guarding an entrance to the Pentagon, and thought if his head was to be busted this day, let it be before the eyes of America's TV viewers tonight.

Besides, back in the third row, the danger from behind was no longer to be disregarded. After fifteen minutes of pushing, eddying, compressing and decompressing from ranks, the March at last started up in a circus-full of performers, an ABC or CBS open convertible with a built-on camera platform was riding in privileged position five yards in front of them with TV executives, cameramen, and technicians hanging on, leaning out, off on their own crisis run as they crawled along in front. Two monitors kept working like cheerleaders through portable loudspeakers to dress the front rank, which kept billowing and shearing under the pulses of inertia and momentum from the ranks behind, and a troop of helicopters, maybe as many as eight or ten, went into action overhead, while ten to twenty cameramen, movie and still, walking backward, wheeling, swinging from flank to flank, danced in the hollow square.

Picture then this mass, bored for hours by speeches, now elated at the beginning of the March, now made irritable by delay, now compressed, all old latent pips of claustrophobia popping out of the crush, and picture them as they stepped out toward the bridge, monitors in the lead, hollow square behind, next the line of notables with tens, then hundreds of lines squeezing up behind, helicopters overhead, police gunning motorcycles, cameras spinning their gears like the winging of horseflies, TV car bursting seams with hysterically overworked technicians, sun beating overhead—this huge avalanche of people rumbled forward thirty feet and came to a stop in disorder, the lines behind breaking and warping and melding into themselves to make a crowd not a parade, and some jam-up at the front, just what no one knew, now they were moving again. Forty more feet. They stopped. At this rate it would take six hours to reach the Pentagon. And a murmur came up from behind of huge discontent, not huge yet, huge in the potential of its discontent. "Let's get going," people in the front lines were calling out.

The monitors reformed the hollow square, maneuvering interlopers to the side with a maximum of politeness for the circumstances. Now again, the procession inched forward. The problem was at last apparent—it was to keep everybody from engorging the entrance to the bridge before the first ranks of the March were actually upon it.

During this delay, the notables came to be familiar with one monitor, a young pale Negro with a small portable battery-pack loudspeaker who kept dressing the line with sharp little commands, "Move up here, please; move back there now, will you now! Come on! Let's get it going. Follow me, keep my pace. No, stop! Stop right there!" The notables were getting raw recruit training: Dr. Spock and Janey Spock, Lens, Lowell, Mailer, Macdonald, Dellinger, Jerry Rubin—if the Negroes had left the March en masse, the exception here left behind was obviously embodying any desire for total representation of his people. A pale dirty cream in color, nobody could ever say he had lost his black—Mailer wasn't there to speak for the other notables, but *he* hadn't been ordered about so continuously since his first day in the Army. In fact, it was like old times on the Left when you took any Negro into the club that you could get. The white monitors for the Mobilization looked in the main to be college students, not unathletic, chosen where possible for their ability to handle the March with a minimum of force. (Such at least was their function for the March—later some were to be active at the Pentagon, some to be arrested.) But the pale Negro was no heroic paradigm of a noble African; rather he had a screeching birdlike voice which cut to the marrow of all good nerve, and the sort of conniving pimp's face which Midwestern bellboys used to develop by the habit of taking an extra dollar from the hotel whore. "Dress up that line, there, dress it up, what's the matter with all of you? Come on, cooperate with me. Help me keep this thing moving right," he drilled through the loudspeaker like an angry hospital nurse dealing with some well-whipped orphans. But, in fact, they were not moving at this moment, just milling and filing. He had gone too far.

"Look here," said Lowell to the monitor in a no-nonsense voice, "we're perfectly willing to cooperate with you, but there's no need to yell and get officious. Be sensible."

This emptied the pale Negro's balloon. He was sensible for the rest of the March. Mailer was now admiring again the banker manqué in Lowell—no mean banker had been lost to Boston when Lowell put his hand to the poem.

Once again they began to move, once again the cameras whirred, the television convertible crawled ahead, the helicopters hung above, motors chopping, motorcycles gargled in low gear, the hollow square stepped out on the bridge, and the line of notables, and the first ranks behind. For a hundred yards they moved in a slow uneven step, arms locked, advancing for ten paces, halting for five seconds, moving again, the shock and release of the stop, then the start, traveling in waves down the thick close-packed ranks—from above, from the helicopters, it must have looked like the pulsations in the progression of a caterpillar.

Then came a long halt. It went on for ten minutes. They were now a third of the way across the bridge with hundreds of tanks massed solidly behind them all the way back to the entrance of the bridge. There, a fearful congestion like a crowd trying to push out of a stadium exit and not succeeding, rather pressing in on people ahead, produced an urgency at the rear which began to make itself felt up front; underneath the tension of secretly wondering what they would do when they reached the Pentagon was now added the frustration of being unable to move! Full of excitement, not without fear, the crowd jammed upon the bridge was in danger of turning unruly. "Why don't we move? Why don't we just move ahead?" said a boy behind Mailer. He literally pushed against the line of notables, thus jamming into a professor named Donald Kalish, one of the leaders of the Mobilization. "I came here to get to the Pentagon," said the boy, "not to wait in line like this."

Something was wrong, Mailer decided. It would make sense to send provocateurs to start violence within the ranks on the bridge—the entire March could be lost, or spoiled, before it reached the Pentagon. "Let's get going,"

shouted the boy, "let's go. I don't want to be held up
. . . I want to get to those soldiers at the Pentagon."

Yes, his voice had no real ring, Mailer decided, his dialogue was wrong. And to the mix of adrenaline in circulation, came another, one he did not like to feel arriving,
for it left him tense if he could not use it: he was getting
ready for a fight. He would of course not throw the first
punch, not ever! that would be just what he would need
for his reputation. To throw the punch which started the
rumble which wrecked the March on the Pentagon! And
every camera in town to pick up the action. No, Mailer
was merely getting prepared for the kid to swing, and so
covertly studying him. The kid was probably no fighter—
his nose was too long and pointed for that; he had never
caught anything on the nose, that was obvious, but still he
had some kind of snap in him, he was confident of pos-
sessing something. Possibly he had a good left hook,
probably good enough to drop a man if he caught him by
surprise; then he would drive a kick into the ear—that
might be his style. Mailer was full of adrenaline now—
how fortunate his hangover was modest, or his brain
would be left smoking like an electric hot plate.

"They're not going to hold me here," said the kid,
looking ugly, again shoving into Kalish.

"Now, son, take it easy," said Kalish.

"What are they all, yellow?" screamed the kid. "Let's
get going. That's what we're here for."

"Hey, let's not lose our cool," said Mailer in his imitation of Marlon Brando's voice in *The Wild One*. It was a
fair imitation and often came to his larynx on the rip tide
of adrenaline. But that was not the key to lock this kid up
today.

"I want to move," said the boy.

"Why don't you join the monitors," said Kalish. It was
a simple suggestion. The boy could hardly refuse. He left
his spot and sauntered up ahead; soon he was in the line
of sweepers. But the nascent general in Mailer was much
annoyed, as if somehow he had been derelict in not holding the agent provocateur where he belonged, back at his
own rank.

"It was the only thing to do," said Kalish. "The monitors will be able to handle him better than we can." Mailer felt a too generous portion of middle age in the communality Kalish had just granted him.

But now the order came for them all to sit down. That helped. Sitting down, no one could push. The sense of a mounting oppression from the rear began to ease. But there was still much impatience.

An older monitor with a microphone attached to a big portable loudspeaker came up to Mailer, "Will you talk to them?" he asked. "I think you might be able to quiet them."

"Give me a minute to think of something." At the look of doubt in the monitor's face, Mailer added, "They're quiet now. Save me for when I'm really needed." He was telling the truth. It seemed to him that once he spoke, his ability to quiet a crowd would be considerably less the second time. Yet what could he say? It would have to be basic.

"Distrust those who are impatient with you. A riot only aids the Pentagon and the power of LBJ. We are engaged in a war which may go on for twenty years. Nothing less is involved than whether America becomes a great nation or a totalitarian tyranny. For now, be patient—the delay is nothing against twenty years." Yea, good speech. A part of him must now hope the crowd would grow a hint unruly again, so that he might pacify them with his oratory. (Still, he didn't like his speech—it was too moderate.) "I'm ready now," he said to the monitor.

"Thank you." But they were on the move again. It was never, however, to become a routine parade. The majority of demonstrators, if one counted the women, had never marched in ranks; there were no leaders sufficiently well-known to command order easily; indeed it was impossible to keep physical contact with a majority of the demonstrators while they were on the bridge, for the bridge was too crowded to pass back and forth. Communication depended on the portable loudspeakers; order on the good will and wit of the speaker employing them. In the center of that March across the bridge, buried in the middle of that half mile, the crush of marchers must have surged back and forth like a wash of waves caught by the change of tides in a channel, there was the promise of chaos everywhere, but order was saved from disorder as the mob, good-humored, then evil, then good-humored again, inched its way across the bridge, waiting in place, sitting down, marching again, singing songs, "We Shall Overcome"—blue bruise of misery among the voices, genuine sorrow for happier days on the Left Plantation with the old Civil Rights Negroes, not these new Deep Purple Blacks, still—shouting their slogans, "Hell, no, We Won't Go," "LBJ, how many kids did you kill today?"—it is possible any other group so large, so leaderless, so infused with anxiety for the unknown situation ahead, and so packed upon the bridge would have erupted, but finally it was a pacifist crowd: that was the obvious gamble on which the move across the bridge had been chosen; if not for the underlying composition of these gentle troops, there would have been no way to assemble on Washington's side of the Potomac. The rally would have had to be at the Pentagon itself—which indeed was where many would argue later it should most certainly have been in the first place. In any event, up at the front of this March, in the first line, back of that hollow square of monitors, Mailer and Lowell walked in this barrage of cameras, helicopters, TV cars, monitors, loudspeakers, and wavering buckling twisting line of notables, arms linked (line twisting so much that at times the movement was in file, one arm locked ahead, one behind, then the line would undulate about and the other arm would be ahead) speeding up a few steps, slowing down while a great happiness came back into the day as if finally one stood under some mythical arch in the great vault of history, helicopters buzzing about, chop-chop, and the sense of America divided on this day now liberated some undiscovered patriotism in Mailer so that he felt a sharp searing love for his country in this moment and on this day, crossing some divide in his own mind wider than the Potomac, a love so lacerated he felt as if a marriage were being torn and children lost—never does one love so much as then, obviously, then—and an odor of wood smoke, from where you knew not, was also in the air, a smoke of dignity and some calm heroism, not

131

unlike the sense of freedom which also comes when a
marriage is burst—Mailer knew for the first time why
men in the front line of a battle are almost always ready to
die: there is a promise of some swift transit—one's soul
feels clean; as we have gathered, he was not used much
more than any other American politician, litterateur, or
racketeer to the sentiment that his soul was not unclean, but
here, walking with Lowell and Macdonald, he felt as if he
stepped through some crossing in the reaches of space between this moment, the French Revolution, and the Civil
War, as if the ghosts of the Union Dead accompanied
them now to the Bastille, he was not drunk at all, merely
illumined by hunger, the sense of danger to the front,
sense of danger to the rear—he was in fact in love with
himself for having less fear than he had thought he might
have—he knew suddenly then he had less fear now than
when he was a young man; in some part of himself at
least, he had grown; if less innocent, less timid—the cold
flame of a perfectly contained exaltation warmed old
asthmas of gravel in the heart, and the sense that they
were going to face the symbol, the embodiment, no, call
it the true and high church of the military-industrial complex, the Pentagon, blind five-sided eye of a subtle
oppression which had come to America out of the very
air of the century (this evil twentieth century with its
curse on the species, its oppressive Faustian lusts, its
technological excrement all over the conduits of nature,
its entrapment of the innocence of the best—for which
young American soldiers hot out of high school and in
love with a hot rod and his Marine buddies in his platoon
in Vietnam could begin to know the devil of the oppression which would steal his soul before he knew he had
one) yes, Mailer felt a confirmation of the contests of his
own life on this March to the eye of the oppressor, greedy
stingy dumb valve of the worst of the Wasp heart, chalice
and anus of corporation land, smug, enclosed, morally
blind Pentagon, destroying the future of its own nation
with each day it augmented in strength, and the Novelist
induced on the consequence some dim unawakened
knowledge of the mysteries of America buried in these

132

liberties to dissent— What a mysterious country it was. The older he became, the more interesting he found her. Awful deadening programmatic inhuman dowager of a nation, corporation, and press—tender mysterious bitch whom no one would ever know, not even her future unfeeling Communist doctors if she died of the disease of her dowager, deadly pompous dowager who had trapped the sweet bitch. (Perhaps this near excess of patriotism in poetic dose came from locking arms with Lowell; it was not Mailer's fortune to cross from the Capital to Virginia every day in the company of a grand poet!) He was, in fact, by now even virtually in love with the helicopters, not because the metaphors of his mind had swollen large enough to embrace even them! no! he loved the helicopters because they were the nearest manifestation of the enemy, and he now loved his enemy for the thundering justification they gave to his legitimate—so he would term it—sentiments of pride in himself on this proud day, yes, the helicopters, ugliest flying bird of them all, dragon in the shape of an insect, new vanity of combat, unutterable conceit, holy hunting pleasure, spills and thrills of combat on a quick hump and jump from the down-home Vietnam country club, symbol of tyranny to a city man, for only high officials and generals and police officers flitted into cities on helicopters this small in size—Mailer, General Mailer, now had a vision of another battle, the next big battle, and these helicopters, press, television and assorted media helicopters hovering overhead with CIA-FBI-all others of the alphabet in helicopters—and into the swarm of the choppers would come a Rebel Chopper in black, or in Kustom-Kar Red, leave it to the talent of the West Coast to prepare the wild helicopter; it would be loaded with guns to shoot pellets of paint at the enemy helicopters, smearing and daubing, dripping them, dropping cans of paint from overhead to smash on the blades of the chopper like early air combat in World War I, and Fourth of July rockets to fire past their Plexiglass canopies. That was the way, Mailer told himself, that was the way. The media would scream at the violence of those dissenters who attacked innocent helicopters with paint, and America—if it still had a humor—would laugh. Until then—insufferable arrogance of these helicopters swinging and hovering and wheeling overhead, as if to remind everyone below of their sufferance, their possession, and the secret of who owned the air—corporation land.

They had one more long wait at the end of the bridge, not twenty yards from the exit, and sat down, near to safety (from the dangers of a stampede) but not safe yet for they were still on the bridge. At last they moved on, continued along a road for a while, passed under a culvert. On the railing of this culvert, fifteen feet above, stood a handsome young Negro carrying a placard. "NO VIETNAMESE EVER CALLED ME A NIGGER," and the marchers cheered as they passed beneath, and Mailer was impressed—not so easy to stand on the edge of a parapet while thousands marched beneath—confident must be such a stance against the evil eye. Was a mad genius buried in every Negro? How fantastic they were at their best—how dim at their worst.

Now the March was leaving the road, was crossing open fields marked off for their route, and the demand to lock arms became more and more difficult to maintain for the demonstrators in the lead were all in a rush to be first to the Pentagon, now visible in the distance—thin tinge of lead to the silver of the mood. Marchers coming up from behind began to circle forward around the sides of the hollow square which had narrowed to a rectangle going through the culvert, but then widened into a fan as they spread across the field. Some marchers being fatigued, others impatient, the ranks deteriorated at last, and everybody strolled over the grass at his own rate for the last quarter mile. They were now passing fences with high barbed wire—cause to wonder if they were open pens to hold the masses soon to go under arrest—that was Mailer's idea. (Invariably his sound perceptions were as quickly replaced by wild estimates; he should have divined that the government was not going to pen people in full view of others who were free, nor give fields of such photographs to European papers with any faint reminders implicit of when last civilians had been seen behind barbed wire.) Looking at those pens, Mailer's steps passed from grass to concrete. They were in the North Parking Area of the Pentagon. The March was ended. They had come to their goal.

5: THE WITCHES AND THE FUGS

Since the parking lot was huge as five football fields, and just about empty, for they were the first arrivals, the terminus of the March was without drama. Nor was the Pentagon even altogether visible from the parking lot. Perhaps for that reason, a recollection returned to Mailer of that instant (alive as an open nerve) when they had seen it first, walking through the field, just after the March had left the road on the Virginia side of the Potomac; there, topping a rise, it appeared, huge in the near distance, not attractive. Somehow, Mailer had been anticipating it would look more impressive than its pictures, he was always expecting corporation land to surprise him with a bit of wit, an unexpected turn of architectural grace—it never did. The Pentagon rose like an anomaly of the sea from the soft Virginia fields (they were crossing a park), its pale yellow walls reminiscent of some plastic plug coming out of the hole made in flesh by an unmentionable operation. There, it sat, geometrical aura complete, isolated from anything in nature surrounding it. Eras ago had corporation land begun by putting billboards on the old post roads?—now they worked to clean them up—just as the populace had finally succeeded in depositing comfortable amounts of libido on highway signs, gasoline exhaust, and oil-stained Jersey macadam —now corporation land, here named Government, took over state preserves, straightened crooked narrow roads, put up government buildings, removed unwelcome signs till the young Pop eye of Art wept for unwelcome signs —where are our old friends?—and corporation land would succeed, if it hadn't yet, in making nature look like an outdoor hospital, and the streets of U.S. cities, grace of Urban Renewal, would be difficult to distinguish when drunk from pyramids of packaged foods in the aisles of a supermarket.

For years he had been writing about the nature of totalitarianism, its need to render populations apathetic, its instrument—the destruction of mood. Mood was forever being sliced, cut, stamped, ground, excised, or obliterated; mood was a scent which rose from the acts and calms of nature, and totalitarianism was a deodorant to nature. Yes, and by the logic of this metaphor, the Pentagon looked like the five-sided tip on the spout of a spray can to be used under the arm, yes, the Pentagon was spraying the deodorant of its presence all over the fields of Virginia.

The North Parking Lot was physically separated from the Pentagon by a wide four-lane highway. Corporate wisdom had been at work—they might have been rattling about in the vast and empty parking lot of a modern stadium when no game is being played. Being among the first hundred to arrive, they found themselves in a state of confusion. No enemy was visible, nor much organization. In the reaches of the parking lot where they had entered was some sort of crane, with what appeared to be a speaker's platform on the end of its arm, and that was apparently being gotten ready for more speeches. Lowell, Macdonald, and Mailer discussed whether to remain there. They were hardly in the mood for further addresses, but on the other hand, combat was getting nearer —one could tell by the slow contractions of the gut. It was not that they would lose their courage, so much as that it would begin to seep away; so the idea of listening to speeches was not intolerable. There would be at least company.

But a pleasant young woman accompanied by her child had come up to greet Lowell, and she now mentioned that the hippies were going to have a play at the other

136

end of the parking lot and music seemed by far the better preparation for all battle, and music was indeed coming from that direction. So they set out, a modest group in the paved empty desert of the North Parking Area, and strolled toward the sounds of the band which were somehow medieval in sound, leaving behind the panorama of marchers slowly flowing in. On the way, they agreed again that they would be arrested early. That seemed the best way to satisfy present demands and still get back to New York in time for their dinners, parties, weekend parts. The desire to get back early is not dishonorable in Lowell and Macdonald; they had stayed on today, and indeed probably had come this far because Mailer had helped to urge them, but Mailer! with his apocalyptic visions at Lincoln Memorial and again on the March, his readiness to throw himself, breast against breast, in any charge on the foe, why now in such a rush? Did he not respect his visions?

Well the party that night looked to be the best coming up in some time; he simply hated to miss it. Besides, he had no position here; it was not his March on the Pentagon in conception or execution; he was hardly required to remain for days or even hours on the scene. His function was to be arrested—his name was expendable for the cause. He did not like the idea of milling about for hours while the fine line of earlier perception (and Vision!) got mucked in the general confusion. Besides, he was a novelist, and there is no procurer, gambler, adventurer or romantic lover more greedy for experience in great gouts— a part of the novelist wished to take the cumulative rising memories of the last three days and bring them whole, intact, in sum, as they stood now, to cast, nay—shades of Henry James—to *fling* on the gaming tables of life resumed in New York, and there amass a doubling and tripling again. He was in fact afraid that within the yawning mute concrete of the parking lot this day which had begun with such exultation would dissipate into leaderless armies wandering about, acting like clowns and fools before the face of the authority; or worse, raw massacres, something more than bones broken: actual disasters—that was also in the air. He did not know if he was secretly afraid too

137

much would happen or too little, but one thing he knew he hated—that would be to wait, and wait again, and nerve up to the point of being arrested, and get diverted and wait again while the light of the vision went out of the day and out of his head until hungry and cold they would all shamble off shamefacedly to New York on a late plane, too late for everything all around. One could not do that to this day. Great days demanded as much respect as great nights—Victorian, no Edwardian, were Mailer's more courtly sentiments.

And in his defense, one decent motive. He had the conviction that his early arrest might excite others to further effort: the early battles of a war wheel on the hinge of their first legends—perhaps his imagination, in lockstep to many a montage in many an old movie, saw the word going out from mouth to ear to mouth to ear, linking the troops—in fact cold assessment would say that was not an inaccurate expectation. Details later.

Yes, Mailer had an egotism of curious disproportions. With the possible exception of John F. Kennedy, there had not been a President of the United States nor even a candidate since the Second World War whom Mailer secretly considered more suitable than himself, and yet on the first day of a war which he thought might go on for twenty years, his real desire was to be back in New York for a party. Such men are either monumental fools or excruciatingly practical since it may be wise to go to every party you can if the war is to continue for two decades. Of course, the likelihood is that the government—old corporation land—knew very well how wise it was to forge an agreement in negotiation to stage (dump) the marchers on arrival in the North Area's parking—coming off the March and into the face of a line of troops at the Pentagon, Mailer along with a good many others would not have been diverted with thoughts of New York whereas the parking area was so large and so empty that any army would have felt small in its expanse.

Well, let us move on to hear the music. It was being played by the Fugs, or rather—to be scrupulously phenomenological—Mailer heard the music first, then noticed the musicians and their costumes, then recognized two of them as Ed Sanders and Tuli Kupferberg and knew it was the Fugs. Great joy! They were much better than the last time he had heard them in a grind-it-out theater on Macdougal Street. Now they were dressed in orange and yellow and rose colored capes and looked at once like Hindu gurus, French musketeers, and Southern cavalry captains, and the girls watching them, indeed sharing the platform with them were wearing love beads and leather bells—sandals, blossoms, and little steel-rimmed spectacles abounded, and the music, no rather the play, had begun, almost Shakespearean in its sinister announcement of great pleasures to come. Now the Participant recognized that this was the beginning of the exorcism of the Pentagon, yes the papers had made much of the permit requested by a hippie leader named Abbie Hoffman to encircle the Pentagon with twelve hundred men in order to form a ring of exorcism sufficiently powerful to raise the Pentagon three hundred feet. In the air the Pentagon would then, went the presumption, turn orange and vibrate until all evil emissions had fled this levitation. At that point the war in Vietnam would end.

The General Services Administrator who ruled on the permit consented to let an attempt be made to raise the building ten feet, but he could not go so far as to allow the encirclement. Of course, exorcism without encirclement was like culinary art without a fire—no one could properly expect a meal. Nonetheless the exorcism would proceed, and the Fugs were to serve as a theatrical medium and would play their music on the rear bed of the truck they had driven in here at the end of the parking lot nearest to the Pentagon some hundreds of yards from the speaker's stand where the rally was to take place.

Now, while an Indian triangle was repeatedly struck, and a cymbal was clanged, a mimeographed paper was passed around to the Marchers watching. It had a legend which went something like this:

October 21, 1967, Washington, D.C., U.S.A., Planet Earth
    We Freemen, of all colors of the spectrum, in the name of God, Ra, Jehovah, Anubis, Osiris, Tlaloc,

139

Quetzalcoatl, Thoth, Ptah, Allah, Krishna, Chango, Chimeke, Chukwu, Olisa-Bulu-Uwa, Imales, Orisasu, Odudua, Kali, Shiva-Shakra, Great Spirit, Dionysus, Yahweh, Thor, Bacchus, Isis, Jesus Christ, Maitreya, Buddha, Rama do exorcise and cast out the EVIL which has walled and captured the pentacle of power and perverted its use to the need of the total machine and its child the hydrogen bomb and has suffered the people of the planet earth, the American people and creatures of the mountains, woods, streams, and oceans grievous mental and physical torture and the constant torment of the imminent threat of utter destruction.

We are demanding that the pentacle of power once again be used to serve the interests of GOD manifest in the world as man. We are embarking on a motion which is millennial in scope. Let this day, October 21, 1967, mark the beginning of suprapolitics.

By act of reading this paper you are engaged in the Holy Ritual of Exorcism. To further participate focus your thought on the casting out of evil through the grace of GOD which is all (ours). A billion stars in a billion galaxies of space and time is the form of your power, and limitless is your name.

Now while the Indian triangle and the cymbal sounded, while a trumpet offered a mournful subterranean wail, full of sobs, and mahogany shadows of sorrow, and all sour groans from hell's dungeon, while finger bells tinkled and drums beat, so did a solemn voice speak something approximate to this: "In the name of the amulets of touching, seeing, groping, hearing and loving, we call upon the powers of the cosmos to protect our ceremonies in the name of Zeus, in the name of Anubis, god of the dead, in the name of all those killed because they do not comprehend, in the name of the lives of the soldiers in Vietnam who were killed because of a bad karma, in the name of sea-born Aphrodite, in the name of Magna Mater, in the name of Dionysus, Zagreus, Jesus, Yahweh, the unnamable, the quintessent finality of the Zoroastrian fire, in the name of Hermes, in the name of the Beak of Sok, in the name of scarab, in the name, in the name, in the name of the Tyrone Power Pound Cake Society in the Sky, in the name of Rah, Osiris, Horus, Nepta, Isis, in the name of the flowing living universe, in the name of the mouth of the river, we call upon the spirit . . . to raise the Pentagon from its destiny and preserve it."

Now spoke another voice. "In the name, and all the names, it is you."

Now the voice intoned a new chant, leaving the echo of the harsh invocation of all giants and thunders in the beat of cymbals, triangles, drums, leather bells, the sour anguish of a trumpet reaching for evil scurried through the tents of a medieval carnival.

Then all the musicians suddenly cried out: "Out, demons, out—back to darkness, ye servants of Satan—out, demons, out! Out, demons, out!"

Voices from the back cried: "Out! . . . Out! . . . Out! . . . Out!" mournful as the wind of a cave. Now the music went up louder and louder, and voices chanting, "Out, demons, out! Out, demons, out! Out, demons, out!"

He detested community sing—an old violation of his childhood had been the bouncing ball on the movie screen; he had wanted to watch a movie, not sing—but the invocation delivered some message to his throat. "Out, demons, out," he whispered, "out, demons, out." And his foot—simple American foot—was, of course, tapping. "Out, demons, out." Were any of the experts in the Pentagon now shuddering, or glory of partial unringed exorcism—even vibrating? Vibrating experts? "Out, demons, out! Out, demons, out!" He could hear Ed Sanders' voice, Ed of the red-gold head and red-gold beard, editor and publisher of a poetry magazine called *Fuck You,* renaissance conductor, composer, instrumentalist and vocalist of the Fugs, old protégé of Allen Ginsberg, what mighty protégés was Allen amassing. Sanders spoke: "For the first time in the history of the Pentagon there will be a grope-in within a hundred feet of this place, within two hundred feet. Seminal culmination in the spirit of peace and brotherhood, a real grope for

141

peace. All of you who want to protect this rite of love may form a circle of protection around the lovers."

"Circle of protection," intoned another voice.

"These are the magic eyes of victory," Sanders went on. "Victory, victory for peace. Money made the Pentagon—melt it. Money made the Pentagon, melt it for love."

Now came other voices, "Burn the money, burn the money, burn it, burn it."

Sanders: "In the name of the generative power of Priapus, in the name of the totality, we call upon the demons of the Pentagon to rid themselves of the cancerous tumors of the war generals, all the secretaries and soldiers who don't know what they're doing, all the intrigue bureaucracy and hatred, all the spewing, coupled with prostate cancer in the deathbed. Every Pentagon general lying alone at night with a tortured psyche and an image of death in his brain, every general, every general lying alone, every general lying alone."

Wild cries followed, chants: "Out, demons, out! Out, demons, out! Out! out! out! Out, demons, out."

Sanders: "In the name of the most sacred of sacred names Xabrax Phresxner."

He was accompanied now by chants of, "hari, hari, hari, hari, rama, rama, rama, rama, Krishna, hari Krishna, hari, hari, rama, Krishna."

"Out, demons, out."

They all chanted: "End the fire and war, and war, end the plague of death. End the fire and war, and war, end the plague of death." In the background was the sound of a long sustained Ommmm.

On which acidic journeys had the hippies met the witches and the devils and the cutting edge of all primitive awe, the savage's sense of explosion—the fuse of blasphemy, the cap of taboo now struck, the answering roar of the Gods—for what was explosion but connections made at the rate of 10 to the 10th exponent of the average rate of a dialogue and its habitual answer—had all the TNT and nuclear transcendencies of TNT exploded some devil's cauldron from the past?—was the past being consumed by the present? by nuclear blasts, and blasts into the collective living brain by way of all exploding acids, opiums, whiskies, speeds, and dopes?— the past was palpable to him, a tissue living in the tangible mansions of death, and death was disappearing, death was wasting of some incurable ill. When death disappeared, there would be no life.

Morbid thoughts for the edge of battle, thoughts out alone without wings of whiskey to bring them back, but Mailer had made his lonely odyssey into the land of the witches, it had taken him through three divorces and four wives to decide that some female phenomena could be explained by no hypothesis less thoroughgoing than the absolute existence of witches. A lonely journey, taken without help from his old drugs, no, rather a distillate of his most difficult experience, and he had arrived at it in great secrecy, for quondam Marxist, nonactive editor of a Socialist magazine, where and how could he explain or justify a striking force of witches—difficult enough to force a Socialist eye to focus on what was existential. Now, here, after several years of the blandest reports from the religious explorers of LSD, vague Tibetan lama goody-goodness auras of religiosity being the only publicly announced or even rumored fruit from all trips back from the buried Atlantis of LSD, now suddenly an entire generation of acid-heads seemed to have said goodbye to easy visions of heaven, no, now the witches were here, and rites of exorcism, and black terrors of the night— hippies being murdered. Yes, the hippies had gone from Tibet to Christ to the Middle Ages, now they were Revolutionary Alchemists. Well, thought Mailer, that was all right, he was a Left Conservative himself. "Out, demons, out! Out, demons, out!"

"You know I like this," he said to Lowell.

Lowell shook his head. He looked not untroubled. "It was all right for a while," he said, "but it's so damn repetitious."

And Macdonald had a harsh glee in his pale eye as if he were half furious but half diverted by the meaninglessness of the repetitions. Macdonald hated meaninglessness even more than the war in Vietnam; on the other hand, he lived for a new critical stimulation: here it might be.

But to Lowell it was probably not meaningless. No, probably Lowell reacted against everything which was hypnotic in that music. Even if much of his poetry could be seen as formal incantations, halfway houses on the road to hypnosis and the oceans of contemplation beyond,

> O to break loose, like the chinook
> salmon jumping and falling back,
> nosing up the impossible
> stone and bone-crushing waterfall—

yes, even if Lowell's remarkable sense of rhythm drew one deep into the poems, nonetheless hypnotic they resolutely were not, for the language was particular, with a wicked sense of names, details, and places.

> . . . Remember playing
> Marian Anderson, Mozart's *Shepherd King,*
> *il re pastore?* Hammerheaded shark,
> the rainbow salmon of the world—your hand
> a rose . . . And at the Mittersill, you topped
> the ski-run . . .

Lowell's poetry gave one the sense of living in a well, the echoes were deep, and sound was finally lost in moss on stone; down there the light had the light of velvet, and the ripples were imperceptible. But one lay on one's back in this well, looking up at the sky, and stars were determinedly there at night, fixed points of reference; nothing in the poems ever permitted you to turn on your face and try to look down into the depths of the well, it was enough you were in the well—now, look up! The world dazzled with its detail.

Lowell, drawn to hypnosis, would resist it, resist particularly these abstract clackety sounds like wooden gears in a noisemaker, "Hari, hari, hari, hari, rama, rama, Krishna, hari, rama, Krishna," and the whoop of wild Indians in "out, demons, out!" Nothing was more dangerous to the poet than hypnosis, for the *style* of one's entrance to that plain of sleep where all ideas coalesced into one, was critical—enter by any indiscriminate route, "Om, Om, Om," and who knows what finely articulated bones of future prosody might be melted in those undifferentiated pots—no, Lowell's good poetry was a reconnaissance into the deep, and for that, pirate's patrols were the best—one went down with the idea one would come back with more, but one did not immerse oneself with open guru Ginsberg arms crying, "Baa, baa, slay this sheep or enrich it, Great Deep," no, one tiptoed in and made a raid and ideally got out good. Besides, the Fugs and Hindu bells and exorcisms via LSD were all indeed Allen Ginsberg's patch; poets respected each others' squatter's rights like Grenadiers before the unrolled carpet of the King.

But of course Lowell's final distaste was for the attraction itself of these sounds (which were incidentally lifting Mailer into the happiest sense of comradeship). Without a drink in him, he was nonetheless cheering up again at the thought of combat, and deciding it would be delightful to whack a barricade in the company of Ed Sanders with the red-gold beard who had brought grope-freak talk to the Village and always seemed to Mailer a little overliberated, but now suitable, yes, the Novelist was working up all steam in the "Out, demons, out."

But now these meanderings were interrupted by a sight to the rear of them and a battle cry, except there was not really a cry at all, just the unheard sense of a cry in the silent rush, the intent silence of a group of near a few hundred men, some wearing motorcycle helmets or fencing jackets or football shoulder pads, who were walking very rapidly, in fact almost at an odd run, in a long wedge perhaps two hundred feet long, forty or fifty wide at the base, and at the front, at the point, in the vanguard two or three carried standards, two or three blue and gold flags of the N.L.F., yes the American branch of the Vietcong was rushing across the parking lot for a first assault on the unseen Pentagon at a point not fifty yards from where the Fugs were playing.

On came the rush, the men carrying the standard running at an odd angle, as if the weight of the flag and pole brought their bodies and arms out too far ahead of their

145

legs, so that they gave the impression, like Groucho Marx, of having torsos too large and too humped over for their limbs, (or perhaps this image came from the protection and stuffing they wore) and behind them were men carrying other standards and posters, a sea of slogans, (which could later be used for weapons—sticks and shards of broken masonite) nearly all the men at that odd incline forward from the vertical as if keening at the wind, and Mailer knew where he had seen this before, this posture of men running in a charge, yes it had been in the photographs by Mathew Brady of Union soldiers on the attack across a field, and on they came now, rolled up in some collective wave of purpose, their individual bodies seeming so much larger than their limbs, because their bodies were part of a mass, and one became aware of their feet as something more fragile and separated from them. The attack came on, The Wedge ran forward, this was a bona fide attack, a prepared attack, yes, and it jammed forward into some narrow exit out of the parking lot, some neck of road and fence and embankment and small pines and the body of troops in this attack, flags in the lead, charged by, went out of sight, and the rear of The Wedge galloping behind, rushed into a jam of bodies on the embankment, heaved to, pushed them forward, heaved, succeeded, pushed again, and ground finally to a straining equilibrium, then a halt.

For a few minutes, nothing happened. It was impossible to see what was going on at the head of the column, and the Fugs continued to play, "Out, demons, out!" From all over the parking lot, people were now streaming toward them to see what the attack had developed, many more people had arrived while they were listening to the music, and a man who knew Lowell or Macdonald came up to Mailer and said with a smile, "They're looking for you to speak at the other end."

But the other end was hundreds of yards away, far away from this unresolved action at their elbow. "Yes," said the man with a grin, "they said, 'will the real Norman Mailer stand up?'" It was a reference to two photographs he had used on the jacket of *Why Are We In Vietnam?*

"I'll get over in a while," said Mailer. It was mildly fatiguing to one specialized portion of the brain to keep preparing these variations on an extempore speech he still had not made. In fact, he had about decided he really did not wish to speak. It seemed a suggestion absurd in the face of the action now building, exactly the sort of thing to expect of a literary man. But his vanity was tempted. In a day or so many speeches, they ought to hear one piece of unorthodoxy.

Still, he did not want to leave. That sense of thin air and exaltation burning in the lungs, that intimation of living at high altitude had come back. "Let's try to see what's going on with that attack," he suggested.

They now left the Fugs and walked to the rear of the column jammed at that unseen exit. The men above were obviously packed too tightly for any late arrival to work himself up high enough to comprehend what was happening. It seemed foolish somehow to stand at the rear and ask questions, and they walked a few feet away and debated whether to go to the far end of the parking lot and hear speeches. The day was hovering again on anticlimax.

Abruptly—no warning—the men at the base of the stairs, the very troops who had carried the N.L.F. flags, were running toward the rear in a panic. Mailer had then that superimposition of vision which makes descriptions of combat so contradictory when one compares eyewitness reports—he did not literally see any uniformed soldiers or marshals chasing this civilian army down the embankment, there was nothing but demonstrators flying down toward them now, panic on their faces, but Mailer's imagination so clearly conceived MPs chasing them with bayonets that for an instant he did literally see fixed bayonets and knew in some other part of himself he didn't, like two transparent images almost superimposed. Then he saw nothing but the look of terror on the faces coming toward him and he turned to run in order not to be run down by them, conceiving for one instant MPs squirting Mace in everybody's eyes. Then panic was on him too. He didn't want Mace. He sprinted a few steps, looked over his shoulder, stepped in a drainage trough where the parking lot concrete was hollowed, almost fell with a

147

nasty wrench of his back and abruptly stopped running, sheepishly, recognizing that some large fund of fear he had not even felt for a minute these three days had nonetheless lived in him like an abscess quick to burst now at the first mean threat. He was furious, furious at himself for fleeing and this shame was not balmed by the quick sight he had over one shoulder of Dwight Macdonald standing calm and still, while tens of people scrambled around him in panic. Macdonald had the quiet look on his face of a man who had lived his life, and had learned what he learned, and was not going to run from anyone.

They reassembled. It was confusing. Nobody knew why the men on the stairs had suddenly begun to flee. An attack had been mounted, had been stopped, and a retreat had gone off in their faces, partly swept them up in the terror and now had dissipated itself. His worst perspectives were being fulfilled. The one sequence he did not wish to follow on this late afternoon was in full prospect now—they would wander unattached to any troop or effort, always on the fringe, always ignorant of the next move, always confused. Then it would be dark. He had a picture again of three notables, silly to themselves, walking about with a candle, looking to be copped.

"Listen," Mailer said, "let's get arrested now." Stating the desire created it, and put a ligature across the rent in his nerve.

"Look, Norman," said Lowell, "if we're going to, shall we get away from here? I don't see any good that's accomplished if we're all picked up right next to a Vietcong flag."

This was not to be contested. Mailer had never understood how demonstrating with an N.L.F. flag was going to spark a mass movement to end the war. He could not argue with Lowell. The remark was sensible, and yet he felt uneasy, as if one should never be too sensible in war. Still—it was difficult enough for people to take him seriously without standing next to *that* flag!

So they moved on, looking for a line to cross, or a border, or a fence at the extremity of the parking lot, and came upon one in no time at all. To their left, perhaps fifty yards from where the attack had jammed, was a grassy field with United States MPs stationed in it. To their front was a low rope, not a foot off the ground. Protestors from the parking lot were standing behind this rope, two or three deep. Lowell, Mailer, and Macdonald worked into position until they had nothing in front of them but the rope, and the MPs.

6: A CONFRONTATION BY THE RIVER

It was not much of a situation to study. The MPs stood in two widely spaced ranks. The first rank was ten yards behind the rope, and each MP in that row was close to twenty feet from the next man. The second rank, similarly spaced, was ten yards behind the first rank and perhaps thirty yards behind them a cluster appeared, every fifty yards or so, of two or three U. S. Marshals in white helmets and dark blue suits. They were out there waiting. Two moods confronted one another, two separate senses of a private silence.

It was not unlike being a boy about to jump from one garage roof to an adjoining garage roof. The one thing not to do was wait. Mailer looked at Macdonald and Lowell. "Let's go," he said. Not looking again at them, not pausing to gather or dissipate resolve, he made a point of stepping neatly and decisively over the low rope. Then he headed across the grass to the nearest MP he saw.

It was as if the air had changed, or light had altered; he felt immediately much more alive—yes, bathed in air —and yet disembodied from himself, as if indeed he were watching himself in a film where this action was taking place. He could feel the eyes of the people behind the rope watching him, could feel the intensity of their existence as spectators. And as he walked forward, he and the MP looked at one another with the naked stricken lucid-ity which comes when absolute strangers are for the moment absolutely locked together.

The MP lifted his club to his chest as if to bar all passage. To Mailer's great surprise—he had secretly expected the enemy to be calm and strong, why should they not? they had every power, all the guns—to his great surprise, the MP was trembling. He was a young Negro, part white, who looked to have come from some small town where perhaps there were not many other Negroes; he had at any rate no Harlem smoke, no devil swish, no black, no black power for him, just a simple boy in an Army suit with a look of horror in his eye, "Why, why did it have to happen to me?" was the message of the petrified marbles in his face.

"Go back," he said hoarsely to Mailer.

"If you don't arrest me, I'm going to the Pentagon."

"No. Go back."

The thought of a return—"since they won't arrest me, what can I do?"—over these same ten yards was not at all suitable.

As the MP spoke, the raised club quivered. He did not know if it quivered from the desire of the MP to strike him, or secret military wonder was he now possessed of a moral force which implanted terror in the arms of young soldiers? Some unfamiliar current, now gyroscopic, now a sluggish whirlpool, was evolving from that quiver of the club, and the MP seemed to turn slowly away from his position confronting the rope, and the novelist turned with him, each still facing the other until the axis of their shoulders was now perpendicular to the rope, and still they kept turning in this psychic field, not touching, the club quivering, and then Mailer was behind the MP, he was free of him, and he wheeled around and kept going in a half run to the next line of MPs and then on the push of a sudden instinct, sprinted suddenly around the nearest MP in the second line, much as if he were a back cutting around the nearest man in the secondary to break free—that was actually his precise thought—and had a passing perception of how simple it was to get past the MPs. They looked petrified. Stricken faces as he went by. They did not know what to do. It was his dark pinstripe suit, his vest, the maroon and blue regimental tie, the part in his hair, the barrel chest, the early paunch—he must have looked like a banker himself, a banker, gone ape! And then he saw the Pentagon to his right across the field, not a hundred yards away, and a little to his left, the marshals, and he ran on a jog toward them, and came up, and they glared at him and shouted, "Go back."

He had a quick impression of hard-faced men with gray eyes burning some transparent fuel for flame, and said, "I won't go back. If you don't arrest me, I'm going on to the Pentagon," and knew he meant it, some absolute certainty had come to him, and then two of them leaped on him at once in the cold clammy murderous fury of all cops at the existential moment of making their bust—all cops who secretly expect to be struck at that instant for their sins—and a supervising force came to his voice, and he roared, to his own distant pleasure in new achievement and new authority—"Take your hands off me, can't you see? I'm not resisting arrest," and one then let go of him, and the other stopped trying to pry his arm into a lock, and contented himself with a hard hand under his armpit, and they set off walking across the field at a rabid intent quick rate, walking parallel to the wall of the Pentagon, fully visible on his right at last, and he was arrested, he had succeeded in that, and without a club on his head, the mountain air in his lungs as thin and fierce as smoke, yes, the livid air of tension on this livid side promised a few events of more interest than the routine wait to be free, yes he was more than a visitor, he was in the land of the enemy now, he would get to see their face.

PART IV:

Saturday Night and All of Sunday

1: BUST 80 BEYOND THE LAW

One of the oldest devices of the novelist—some would call it a vice—is to bring his narrative (after many an excursion) to a pitch of excitement where the reader no matter how cultivated is reduced to a beast who can pant no faster than to ask, "And then what? Then what happens?" At which point the novelist, consummate cruel lover, introduces a digression, aware that delay at this point helps to deepen the addiction of his audience.

This, of course, was Victorian practice. Modern audiences, accustomed to superhighways, put aside their reading at the first annoyance and turn to the television set. So a modern novelist must apologize, even apologize profusely, for daring to leave his narrative, he must in fact absolve himself of the charge of employing a device, he must plead necessity.

So the Novelist now pleads necessity. He will take a momentary delay in the proceedings—because in fact he must—to introduce a further element to our history which will accompany us intermittenly to the end. It must now be admitted—the reader does well to expect a forthright shock—that the Participant was not only a witness and actor in these proceedings, but was being photographed as well! Mailer had—in what he considered an inexcusable weak moment—agreed to the request of a young English filmmaker named Dick Fontaine to have a documentary made of him for British television. Once before he had had such a documentary filmed and the experience had been finally not pleasant because it seemed to consist of sitting in a chair and cerebrating for the camera. Mailer, when all was said, was no Arnold Toynbee, no Bertrand Russell (perhaps not even an Eric Goldman) no, with all granted, Mailer as an intellectual always had something of the usurper about him—something in his voice revealed that he likely knew less than he pretended. Watching himself talk on camera for this earlier documentary, he was not pleased with himself as a subject. For a warrior, presumptive general, ex-political candidate, embattled aging enfant terrible of the literary world, wise father of six children, radical intellectual, existential philosopher, hard-working author, champion of obscenity, husband of four battling sweet wives, amiable bar drinker, and much exaggerated street fighter, party giver, hostess insulter—he had on screen in this first documentary a fatal taint, a last remaining speck of the one personality he found absolutely insupportable—the nice Jewish boy from Brooklyn. Something in his adenoids gave it away—he had the softness of a man early accustomed to mother-love. So Mailer stayed away from further documentaries of himself. Talented cinematographers like the Maysles brothers approached him—he had no interest. Fontaine who had been introduced with the best of credentials by a young English lady in whose personality the novelist took delight, succeeded through sheer bull British perseverance in extracting a promise that Fontaine and his crew could be present at a few of the novelist's more active projects. No speeches.

Therefore, witness the first fulfillment of this promise. It was on the initial night of shooting Mailer's second film (which was most tentatively entitled *Bust 80* and was later to be called *Beyond the Law*) a study of detectives and suspects in a police precinct. Mailer had theories on how to make films. He liked to take people who were able to talk themselves in and out of trouble, and cast them in situations which he tried to make sufficiently intense so that they would not be too aware of the camera. Whether they had ever acted before, did not often concern him. It was his theory—not too novel an hypothesis —that many people who had never acted, and could never begin to act on stage without training, still had several extraordinary characterizations they could bring to a

153

film provided they spoke their own words and had no script to remember. It can be seen this is a lively theory which leaves much to the director and takes much away from him; Mailer boosted the ante on the first night of shooting by having three camera crews and several interrogations going on in several rooms at once—the cries or shouts of one interrogation affected the quiet dialogue of another. The intensity of this process, cameras, actors, and scenes working simultaneously on the same floor (which is about the way matters proceed in a police station) conceivably worked a magic on the actors—Mailer's opinion of the film as it began to come together in the early rushes is that it was not impossible he had divined and/or blundered onto the making of the best American movie about police he had ever seen. It was certainly the first film which had ever bypassed altogether the formal morality of Hollywood crime and punishment. His film brought forth instead the incredible—which is to say existential—life buried in all passing relations between cops and criminals: his police were the most interesting police he had come across in films, his suspects were as vivid as the best faces one sees on a strange street.

But the first night's shooting was chaos, and promised disaster. The director had picked some of his most bullheaded friends to play cops; some of his most complicated buddies to play crooks—action abounded everywhere: confusion kept up with it: cameras, sound men, and still photographers often collided, the tail of one film crew being run into by the lens of another. To this disorder was added a fourth camera, the BBC crew working for Fontaine—more than once that night the Director came close to barring the fourth crew for inevitably they were an active part of the confusion. Yet, at a given moment when an exciting scene was still full of action, the first camera ran out of film. "Get another camera," Mailer bawled into the corridor. But the second camera was being loaded; so was the third. "Well, who's that over there," roared the Director, "who's that over there whose camera is going now?"

"Oh, that's the BBC."

Technological crews generate little élan until their working process has delivered the first joke. "Oh, that's the BBC," carried the night, and left Mailer with an impression of a cameraman who loaded so fast he seemed never to run out of film. The next time he saw that cameraman was in the dressing room of a small television studio in New York. Mailer, soon to be interviewed on the approaching March on the Pentagon, was having television cosmetics applied to his face, and looked into the mirror to see the lens of the camera on him. Now he did order the cameraman and his sound man out. "Do you think I've reached the age of forty-four in order to have movies taken of myself while I'm being made up?"

The next time he saw them was in Washington. As Mailer came off the stage of the Ambassador Theater, Fontaine and the cameraman, Leiterman, were beaming. "We got wonderful stuff of you tonight," said Fontaine. They were there the next day at the Department of Justice, and Mailer had the opportunity to watch Leiterman work. There were long periods when nothing was occurring which he thought appropriate to photograph, but he never put his camera down, yet it must have weighed twenty pounds. All during that long afternoon, Leiterman kept it cradled in his arms, ready to photograph the first target of opportunity. The next day, out on the March, walking backward over Arlington Memorial Bridge in the center of the hollow square, Leiterman was photographing the line of notables. Whenever he saw Mailer, he would smile. This seemed part of his photographic technique: He always smiled encouragingly at his subject. After a while, one was glad to see him—even while listening to the Fugs, Mailer had felt Leiterman's camera on him; as Lowell, Macdonald, and Mailer had approached the rope they were going to cross in order to be arrested, Leiterman and Fontaine had been with them.

But now, perambulating around the Pentagon in the first ten seconds of his arrest, with the U. S. Marshal's hand still full of tremors on his arm, what pleasant shock to see Leiterman suddenly dart in front of them, give his great smile of encouragement to Mailer—it had the spark of something most special now—and with his eye to the optical finder, start filming the progress of the Marshal and himself from five feet in front, Leiterman walking backward at the same great rate they were walking forward, so that he performed a small athletic prodigy since their path was uneven, they walked up small slopes, down them, crossed a concrete path, stepped over grass, were on the walks again, climbed up a ramp without breaking pace, and all the while, five feet ahead, ten feet ahead, unaware of what was behind him, Leiterman walking backward at a very fast rate, staggering occasionally and recovering with his heavy camera on his shoulder nonetheless seemed never to let go of the grip of his lens on his subject, all the while mustering a beatific encouraging grin, as if he were saying, "Go man, you are making it for a touchdown."

Mailer's arm was being held in the trembling grip of a U. S. Marshal—this trembling a characteristic physical reaction of the police whenever they lay hands on an arrest, or at least so Mailer would claim after noticing police in such a precise state for three out of the four times he had in his life been arrested—yes they had trembled almost uncontrollably. Whether this was due to a sudden onrush—quote Freud from a letter to Fliess—of "unruly latent homosexuality," or whether from a terror before God that they judged other men sufficiently to make arrest, or whether simply they were cowards, or if to the contrary they trembled from the effort it cost them to keep from assaulting the prisoner, whatever, Mailer could not quite decide—he had sometimes even wondered if it had to do with the incongruities of his own person, whether it was possible he offended some deeps in the police, no matter, the fact, incontrovertible, was that policemen quivered uncontrollably as they laid hands on him. This observation taken and confirmed in the first few steps he made in company with the Marshal after his successful arrest, it had been to his great surprise and pleasure, for there is a certain loneliness in these first few steps—that he had looked up to see Leiterman.

And now a reporter darted up on the flank of this procession to ask a question of Mailer with that friendly, intimate, solicitous attention reporters project into the

156

dramatic work of getting a quote; done well enough the subject feels sufficiently important to believe his immortal initials are being carved on a buttock of history. "Why were you arrested, Mr. Mailer?"

The subject was not absolutely calm. To his own excitement was added the tense quivering grip of the Marshal—the sense of breathing mountain air had hardly abated; his lungs seemed to take in oxygen with a thin edge, his throat burned. But his voice, to his surprise, was calmer than himself—for once it came out about the way he wanted it to, quiet and even. "I was arrested for transgressing a police line." ("Of course, he was misquoted," said Mailer's sister later. "He wouldn't use a word like transgress." She did not anticipate the solemnity men bring to these matters.) "I am guilty," Mailer went on. "It was done as an act of protest to the war in Vietnam."

"Are you hurt in any way?" asked the reporter.

"No. The arrest was correct."

He felt as if he were being confirmed. (After twenty years of radical opinions, he was finally under arrest for a real cause.) Mailer always supposed he had felt important and unimportant in about as many ways as a man could feel; now he felt important in a new way. He felt his own age, forty-four, felt it as if he were finally one age, not seven, felt as if he were a solid embodiment of bone, muscle, flesh, and vested substance, rather than the will, heart, mind, and sentiment to be a man, as if he had arrived, as if this picayune arrest had been his Rubicon. He was secretly altogether pleased with himself at how well he had managed his bust—no cracks on the head, no silly scenes—he was damned if he was going to spoil it with an over-intense speech now, no, just the dry salient statement. (Of course, he did not know that one of the first two reports to go out would have him saying: "I am guilty, I transgressed a police line," so that some of the follow-up stories would have him arrested by accident. But for that matter, he had been inaccurate himself—it was a *Military* Police line he had crossed.)

They were walking along now on a path roughly parallel to a side of the Pentagon he learned later was the River Entrance, and to his left he could see water which

157

he assumed was the Potomac—in fact, it was a basin of the Potomac called Boundary Channel, and pleasure craft were anchored at a marina within it.

The grip of the Marshal's hand had lightened. Perhaps it was the attention paid to him by the reporters, but the Marshal's features had gone through a small metamorphosis. As his rage and agitation subsided, his face converted back into an intelligent, clean-featured American face, not let us say unlike the pleasant modest appearance of Mr. Fran Tarkenton, quarterback for the New York Giants. Mailer and the Marshal began to descend from their peak of mountain air. About now, a man in plain clothes halted Leiterman. "You can't come with us," said the man. So Leiterman signed off with a short wave and a smile and Mailer now alone again in his mind, crossed a ramp over a dual highway below and came onto an asphalt reception area of the Pentagon, seeing objects now with the kind of filtered vision which sometimes comes to a man on drugs in the bleak hour when he is coming down—a glimpse is had of everyday things in their negative aspect, the truth of the object (even the beloved is then an object) stripped of all love, sentiment, or libido. They were coming into a reception area adjacent to the wall; paved in gray asphalt, the air itself in these shadows looked gray, and the soldiers and Marshals standing about had a cold professional studied indifference Mailer had not seen in twenty-three years, not since he had come to Leyte as a replacement, and had been apparently invisible to the eyes of the veterans, cavalrymen from Texas overseas thirty months and more. The soldiers here had such a look. Even the indifference of the faces one sees in a New York subway have more reaction, as if the air along this sheltered wall of the Pentagon had been injected with Novocain. A pall covered the tension.

2: THE MARSHAL AND THE NAZI

They put him in the rear seat of a Volkswagen camper and he welcomed the opportunity to relax. Soon they would drive him, he guessed, to some nearby place where he would be arraigned, fined, and released. He kept searching the distance for sight of Lowell and Macdonald whom he assumed would be following any minute. The thought that they might not have been picked up was depressing, for he could only guess at the depths of Lowell's dejection if he had botched his arrest, and now, with each twenty seconds, he became more gloomily certain that Lowell and Macdonald had been turned back, had failed to get arrested, and blamed himself now for the rush with which he had set out—he should have warned them the arrest might not be automatic, that one might have to steal it—he felt somehow incompetent at not having properly prepared them.

Now a new man entered the Volkswagen. Mailer took him at first for a Marshal or an official, since he was wearing a dark suit and a white motorcycle helmet, and had a clean-cut stubborn face with short features. But he was carrying something which looked like a rolled-up movie screen over five feet long, and he smiled in the friendliest fashion, sat down next to Mailer, and took off his helmet. Mailer thought he was about to be interrogated and he looked forward to that with this friendly man, no less! (of course the prisoner often looks forward to his interrogation) but then another man carrying a clipboard came up to them, and leaning through the wide double door of the camper, asked questions of them both. When Mailer gave his name, the man with the clipboard acted as if he had never heard of him, or at least pretended never to have heard of him, the second possibility seeming possible since word traveled quickly from reporters.

"How do you spell it?"

"M.A.I.L.E.R."

"Why were you arrested, Mr. Miller?"

"For transgressing a police line as a protest against the war in Vietnam."

The Clipboard then asked a question of the man sitting next to him. "And why were *you* arrested?"

"As an act of solidarity with oppressed forces fighting for liberty against this country in Southeast Asia."

The Clipboard nodded drily, as if to say, "Yeah, we're all crazy here." Then he asked, pointing to the object which looked like a rolled-up movie screen. "You want that with you?"

"Yessir," said the man next to Mailer. "I'd like to take it along."

The Clipboard gave a short nod, and walked off. Mailer would never see him again. If the History has therefore spent a pointless exchange with him, it is to emphasize that the first few minutes of an arrest such as this are without particular precedent, and so Mailer, like a visitor from Mars, or an adolescent entering polite society, had no idea of what might be important next and what might not. This condition of innocence was not, however, particularly disagreeable since it forced him to watch everything with the attention, let us say, of a man like William Buckley spending his first hour in a Harlem bar—no, come! things are far safer for Mailer at the Pentagon.

He chatted with his fellow prisoner, Teague, Walter Teague was the name, who had been in the vanguard of the charge Mailer had seen from the parking lot. But before any confused impressions were to be sorted, they were interrupted by the insertion of the next prisoner put into the Volkswagen, a young man with straight blond hair and a Nazi armband on his sleeve. He was installed in the rear, with a table between, but Mailer was not happy, for his eyes and the Nazi's bounced off each other like two heads colliding—the novelist discovered he was

160

now in a hurry for them to get this stage of the booking completed. He was also privately indignant at the U. S. Army (like a private citiezn, let us say, who writes a letter to his small-town newspaper) at the incredible stupidity of putting a Nazi in the same Volkswagen camper with Pentagon demonstrators—there were two or three other cars available, at least!—next came the suspicion that this was not an accident, but a provocation in the making. If the Nazi started trouble, and there was a fight, the newspaper accounts would doubtless state that Norman Mailer had gotten into an altercation five minutes after his arrest. (Of course, they would not say with whom.) This is all doubtless most paranoid of Mailer, but then he had had nearly twenty years of misreporting about himself, and the seed of paranoia is the arrival of the conviction that the truth about oneself is never told. (Mailer might have done better to pity the American populace—receiving misinformation in systematic form tends to create mass schizophrenia: poor America—Eddie and Debbie are True Love.)

Now they were moved out of the camper and over to an Army truck. There was Teague, and the novelist, and another arrestee—a tall Hungarian who quickly told Mailer how much he liked his books and in much the same breath that he was Freedom Fighter—there was also a new U. S. Marshal, and the Nazi. The prisoners climbed one by one over the high tailgate, Mailer finding it a touch awkward for he did not wish to dirty his dark blue pinstripe suit, and then they stood in the rear of the truck, a still familiar 2½ ton 6-by of a sort which the novelist hadn't been in for twenty-one years, not since his Army discharge.

Standing in the truck, a few feet apart from each other, all prisoners regarding one another, the Nazi fixed on Mailer. Their eyes locked like magnets coming into line, and for perhaps twenty seconds they stared at each other. Mailer looked into a pair of yellow eyes so compressed with hate that back of his own eyes he could feel the echo of such hatred ringing. The Nazi was taller than Mailer, well-knit, and with neatly formed features and a shock of blond hair, would have been handsome but for the ferocity of his yellow eyes which were sunk deep in their sockets. Those eyes made him look like an eagle.

Yet Mailer had first advantage in this eye-staring contest. Because he had been prepared for it. He had been getting into such confrontations for years, and rarely lost them, even though he sometimes thought they were costing him eyesight. Still, some developed instinct had made him ready an instant before the Nazi. Every bit of intensity he possessed—with the tremors of the March and the Marshal's arm still pent in him—glared forth into the other's eyes: he was nonetheless aghast at what he saw. The American Nazis were all fanatics, yes, poor mad tormented fanatics, their psyches twisted like burning leaves in the fire of their hatreds, yes, indeed! but this man's conviction stood in his eyes as if his soul had been focused to a single point of light. Mailer could feel violence behind violence rocking through his head. If the two of them were ever alone in an alley, one of them might kill the other in a fight—it was not unlike holding an electric wire in the hand. And the worst of it was that he was not even feeling violent himself—whatever violence he possessed had gone to his eyes—by that route had he projected himself on the Nazi.

After the first five seconds of the shock had passed, he realized he might be able to win—the Nazi must have taken too many easy contests, and had been too complacent in the first moment, yes it was like wrestlers throwing themselves on each other: one knuckle of one finger a little better able to be worked on a grip could make the difference—now he could feel the hint of force ebbing in the other's eyes, and could wonder at his own necessity to win. He did not hate the Nazi nearly so much as he was curious about him, yet the thought of losing had been intolerable as if he had been *obliged* not to lose, as if the duty of his life at this particular moment must have been to look into that Nazi's eye, and say with his own, "You claim you have a philosophical system which comprehends all—you know nothing! My eyes encompass yours. My philosophy contains yours. You have met the wrong man!" And the Nazi looked away, and was hysterical with fury on the instant.

"You Jew bastard," he shouted. "Dirty Jew with kinky hair."

They didn't speak that way. It was too corny. Yet he could only answer, "You filthy Kraut."

"Dirty Jew."

"Kraut pig."

A part of his mind could actually be amused at this choice—he didn't even hate Germans any more. Indeed Germans fascinated him now. Why they liked his books more than Americans did. Yet here he could think of nothing better to return than "Kraut pig."

"I'm not a Kraut," said the Nazi, "I'm a Norwegian." And then as if the pride of his birth had tricked him into communication with an infidel, thus into sacrilege, the Nazi added quickly, "Jew bastard red," then cocked his fists. "Come here, you coward," he said to Mailer, "I'll kill you."

"Throw the first punch, baby," said Mailer, "you'll get it all."

They were both absolutely right. They had a perfect sense of the other. Mailer was certainly not brave enough to advance on the Nazi—it would be like springing an avalanche on himself. But he also knew that if the Nazi jumped him, one blond youth was very likely to get massacred. In retrospect, it would appear not uncomic—two philosophical monomaniacs with the same flaw—they could not help it, they were counterpunchers.

"Jew coward! Red bastard!"

"Go fuck yourself, Nazi baby."

But now a tall U. S. Marshal who had the body and insane look of a very good rangy defensive end in professional football—that same hard high-muscled build, same coiled spring of wrath, same livid conviction that everything opposing the team must be wrecked, sod, turf, grass, uniforms, helmets, bodies, yes even bite the football if it will help—now leaped into the truck and jumped between them. "Shut up," he said, "or I'll wreck both of you." He had a long craggy face somewhere in the physiognomical land between Steve McQueen and Robert Mitchum, but he would never have made Hollywood, for his skin was pocked with the big boiling craters of a red lunar acne, and his eyes in Cinemascope would have blazed an audience off their seat for such gray-green flame could only have issued from a blowtorch. Under his white Marshal's helmet, he was one impressive piece of gathered wrath.

Speaking to the Marshal at this point would have been dangerous. The Marshal's emotions had obviously been marinating for a week in the very special bile waters American Patriotism reserves for its need. His feelings were now caustic as a whip—too gentle the simile!—he was in agonies of frustration because the honor of his profession kept him from battering every prisoner's head to a Communist pulp. Mailer looked him over covertly to see what he could try if the Marshal went to work on him. All reports: negative. He would not stand a chance with this Marshal—there seemed no place to hit him where he'd be vulnerable; stone larynx, leather testicles, ice cubes for eyes. And he had his Marshal's club in his hand as well. Brother! Bring back the Nazi!

Whether the Marshal had been once in the Marine Corps, or in Vietnam, or if half his family were now in Vietnam, or if he just hated the sheer New York presumption of that slovenly, drug-ridden weak contaminating America-hating army of termites outside this fortress' walls, he was certainly any upstanding demonstrator's nightmare. Because he was full of American rectitude and was fearless, and savage, savage as the exhaust left in the wake of a motorcycle club, gasoline and cheap perfume were one end of his spectrum, yeah, this Marshal loved action, but he was also in that no man's land between the old frontier and the new ranch home—as they, yes *they* —the enemies of the Marshal—tried to pass bills to limit the purchase of hunting rifles, so did *they* try to kill America, inch by inch, all the forces of evil, disorder, mess and chaos in the world, and *cowardice!* and city ways, and slick shit, and despoliation of national resources, all the subtle invisible creeping paralyses of Communism which were changing America from a land where blood was red to a land where water was foul—yes in this Marshal's mind—no lesser explanation could suffice for the Kinight of God light in the flame of his eye—

the evil was without, America was threatened by a foreign disease and the Marshal was threatened to the core of his sanity by any one of the first fifty of Mailer's ideas which would insist that the evil was within, that the best in America was being destroyed by what in itself seemed next best, yes American heroism corrupted by American know-how—no wonder murder stood out in his face as he looked at the novelist—for the Marshal to lose his sanity was no passing psychiatric affair: think rather of a rifleman on a tower in Texas and a score of his dead on the street.

But now the Nazi began to play out the deepest of ceremonies. The truck standing still, another Marshal at the other end of the van (the one indeed who had arrested Mailer) and Teague and the Hungarian to different sides, everyone had their eyes on the Norwegian. He now glared again at Mailer, but then whipped away his eyes before a second contest could begin, and said, "All right, Jew, come over here if you want a fight."

The Marshal took the Nazi and threw him against the side-wall of the truck. As he bounced off, the Marshal gave him a rap below the collarbone with the butt of his club. "I told you to shut up. Now, just shut up." His rage was intense. The Nazi looked back at him sullenly, leaned on the butt of the club almost defiantly as if the Marshal didn't know what foolish danger he was in to treat the Nazi so, the Nazi had a proud curved hint of a smile, as if he were recording the features of this Marshal forever in the history of his mind, the Nazi's eyes seemed to say to the Marshal, "You are really on my side although you do not admit it—you would like to beat me now because in the future you know you will yet kiss my boots!" And the Marshal traveling a high edge of temper began to slam the Nazi against the wall of the truck with moderate force, but rhythmically, as if he would pacify them both by this act, bang, and bang, step by step, the imaginary dialogue of the Marshal to the Nazi now sounding in Mailer's ear somewhat like this, "Listen, Nazi, you're nothing but a rat fart who makes my job harder, and gives the scum around me room to breathe, cause they look at you and feel righteous. You just keep me diverted from the real danger."

And the Nazi looked back with a full sullen pouting defiance as if from deep in himself he was all unconsciously saying to the Marshal, "You know I am beautiful, and you are frightened of me. I have a cause and I am ready to die for it, and you are just ready to die for a uniform. Join me where the real war is. Already the strongest and wildest men in America wear our symbol on their motorcycle helmets."

And the Marshal, glaring back at the Nazi, butt of his club transfixing him against the wall of the van, gave a contemptuous look, as if to drop him with the final unspoken word. "Next to strong wild men, you're nothing but a bitch."

Then the truck began to move, and the Marshal calmer now, stood silently between Mailer and the Nazi; and the Nazi also quiet now, stood in place looking neither at the Marshal nor Mailer. Some small storm of hysteria seemed to have worked itself out of the van.

3: GRANDMA WITH ORANGE HAIR

There was not much to see through the canvas arch of the vehicle. A view of a service road they passed along, a little bumping, a bit of swaying—in two minutes they arrived at the next stop. It was the southwest wall of the Pentagon, so much was obvious, for the sun shone brightly here.

Probably they were at the rear of a large mess hall or cafeteria, since a loading platform extended for a considerable distance to either side of where the truck had come in. There were MPs and Marshals on the platform, maybe twenty or thirty, as many again in the back-up area where they had come in. At a long desk at the base of the loading platform, the prisoners were being booked. Each had a Marshal beside him. It was quiet and orderly. The Nazi was standing next to Mailer, but now neither looked at the other. It was indeed all over. The Nazi looked quietly spent, almost gentle—as if the outbursts had been his duty, but duty done, he was just a man again—no need to fight.

They took Mailer's name, having trouble with the spelling again. He was now certain it was not trivial harassment but simple unfamiliarity. The clerk, a stout Marshal with the sort of face that belonged to a cigar, worked carefully at his sheets. The questions were routine—name, address, why arrested—but he entered them with a slow-moving pen which spoke of bureaucratic sacraments taken up, and records set down in perpetuity.

When this was over, Mailer was led by the Marshal who had first arrested him, over to the open door of a sort of school bus painted olive-drab. There was, however, a delay in boarding it, and the Marshal said, "I'm sorry, Mr. Mailer, we have to wait here for a minute to get your number."

"I don't mind."

They were being particularly polite with each other. Mailer had a clear opportunity to look again at this Marshal's face; the *vibrations* of the arrest now utterly discharged, he had an agreeable face indeed, quiet, honest, not unintelligent, not unhumorous. And he talked with the pleasant clipped integrity of a West Virginia accent. Mailer was going to ask him if he came from West Virginia, then out of some random modesty about putting too intensive a question and being wrong, he said instead, "May I ask your name?" It was as one might have expected, a name like Tompkins or Hudkins. "May I ask which state you're from, Marshal?"

"It's West Virginia, Mr. Mailer."

"My wife and I had a young lady work for us once who came from West Virginia. Your accent is similar to hers."

"Is that a fact?"

"Yes, I was wondering if you might be related. There's

a suggestion of family resemblance." He mentioned the name. No relation.

Now the necessary paper was delivered to the Marshal. He signed it, and Mailer could board the bus. He had been given the number 10. He was the tenth man arrested at the Pentagon.

"Well, goodbye, Mr. Mailer. Nice talking to you."

"Yes."

Perhaps they were troubled partisans. Or did each wish to show the other that the enemy possessed good manners?

No, thought Mailer, it was ritual. At the moment of the arrest, cop and criminal knew each other better than mates, or at least knew some special *piece* of each other better than mates, yes an arrest was carnal. Not sexual, carnal—of the meat, strangers took purchase of each other's meat. Then came the reciprocal tendency to be pleasant. Beneath all those structures advertised as majestic in law and order there was this small carnal secret which the partners of a bust could share. It was tasty to chat afterward, all sly pleasures present that the secret was concealed. Mailer thought of a paragraph he had written once about police—it had probably acted upon him as much as anything else to first imagine his movie. Now his mind remembered the approximate sense of the paragraph, which actually (indulging Mailer's desire to be quoted) went exactly like this:

. . . they contain explosive contradictions within themselves. Supposed to be law-enforcers, they tend conceive of themselves as the law. They are more responsible than the average man, they are more infantile. They are attached umbilically to the concept of honesty, they are profoundly corrupt. They possess more physical courage than the average man, they are unconscionable bullies; they serve the truth, they are psychopathic liars . . . their work is authoritarian, they are cynical: and finally if something in their heart is deeply idealistic, they are also bloated with greed. There is no human creation so contradictory, so finally enigmatic, as the character of the average cop . . .

Yes, and without an arrest, he would never have known that this very nice Marshal from West Virginia with his good American face and pleasant manners and agreeable accent, had also a full quiver of sadism and a clammy sweat of possession as he put the arm on you. But indeed, what knowledge had the Marshal of him?

Inside the bus, at the rear of the aisle, was a locked cage and three or four protesters were enclosed there; jailed within their jailing. They greeted him with jeers, cat-calls, hellos, requests for cigarettes, water—after the first impact, it was not ill-spirited. "Hey, look," said one of the kids behind the bars, "they got older people in with us too."

"What time does this bus leave for Plainfield?" Mailer asked. The laughter came back. It was going to be all right. He could hear them whispering.

"You Norman Mailer?" asked one.

"Yes."

"Hey, great. Listen, man, we got to talk."

"I hope we don't have too much time." More laughter. He was beginning to feel good for the first time since his arrest. "What did you gentlemen do to be given such honor?" asked Mailer with a wave at their cage.

"We're the ones who were resisting arrest."

"Did you resist it much?"

"Are you kidding?" said one dark-haired gloomy thin young pirate with a large Armenian mustache and a bloodied handkerchief on his head, "if we put our hands in front of our face to keep from being beaten to death, they said we were resisting." Hoots and jeers at the fell accuracy of this.

"Well, did you all just sit there and take it?"

"I got in a couple of good shots at my Marshal," said one of the kids. It was hard to tell if he was lying. Something about their incarceration in the cage made it difficult to separate them, or perhaps it was that they seemed part of a team, of a musical group—the Monsters, or the Freaks, or the Caged Kissers—they had not known each

169

other an hour ago, but the cage did the work of making them an ensemble.

The rest of the bus was slowly filling. Mailer had first taken a seat next to a young minister wearing his collar, and they chatted not unhappily for a few minutes, and then both crossed the aisle to sit on the side of the bus which looked out on the loading platform and the table where they had been booked. From these seats, Mailer had a view of the Marshals and MPs outside, of new arrests arriving in trucks, and of the prisoners coming into the bus, one by one, every couple of minutes. After a while, he realized the bus would not move until it was filled, and this, short of massive new arrests, would take at least an hour.

It was not disagreeable waiting. Each new prisoner was obliged to make an entrance like an actor coming on stage for his first appearance: since prisoners in transit are an enforced audience, new entrance automatically becomes theater. Some new men sauntered on the bus, some bowed to the faces in the aisle, some grinned, some scowled and sat down immediately; one or two principled pacifists practicing total noncooperation were dragged off the 2½-ton trucks, bumped along the ground, tugged over to the bus, and thrown in by the Marshals. Bleeding a little, looking dazed, the three or four young men who arrived by this route were applauded with something not unlike the enthusiasm a good turn gets in a music hall. Handsome young boys got on the bus, and slovenly oafs, hippies, and walking wounded. One boy had a pant leg soaked in blood. A fat sad fellow with a huge black beard now boarded; a trim and skinny kid who looked like he played minor league shortstop took a seat, a Japanese boy, androgynous in appearance, told a few prisoners around him that none of the Marshals had been able to decide if he was a boy or a girl, so they had not known—for he would not tell them—whether a Marshal or a Matron should search him. This was quickly taken up with pleasure and repeated down the bus.

Outside, a truck would arrive every five or ten minutes and some boys and girls would dismount and go to the base of the loading platform to be booked, the boys to

170

enter the bus, the girls to go off to another bus. Still no sign of Lowell or Macdonald. Mailer kept hoping they would appear in the next haul of prisoners. After a while he began to study the Marshals.

Their faces were considerably worse than he had expected. He had had the fortune to be arrested by a man who was incontestably one of the pleasanter Marshals on duty at the Pentagon, he had next met what must be the toughest Marshal in the place—the two had given him a false spectrum. The gang of Marshals now studied outside the bus were enough to firm up any fading loyalty to his own cause: they had the kind of faces which belong to the bad guys in a Western. Some were fat, some were too thin, but nearly all seemed to have those subtle anomalies of the body which come often to men from small towns who have inherited strong features, but end up, by their own measure, in failure. Some would have powerful chests, but abrupt paunches, the skinny ones would have a knob in the shoulder, or a hitch in their gait, their foreheads would have odd cleaving wrinkles, so that one man might look as if an ax had struck him between the eyes, another paid tithe to ten parallel deep lines rising in ridges above his eye brows. The faces of all too many had a low cunning mixed with a stroke of rectitude: if the mouth was slack, the nose was straight and severe; should the lips be tight, the nostrils showed an outsize greed. Many of them looked to be ex-First Sergeants, for they liked to stand with the heels of their hands on the top of their hips, or they had that way of walking, belly forward, which a man will promote when he is in comfortable circumstances with himself and packing a revolver in a belt holster. The toes turn out; the belly struts. They were older men than he might have expected, some in their late thirties, more in their forties, a few looked to be over fifty, but then that may have been why they were here to receive prisoners rather than out on the line—in any case they emitted a collective spirit which, to his mind, spoke of little which was good, for their eyes were blank and dull, that familiar small-town cast of eye which speaks of apathy rising to fanaticism only to subside in apathy again. (Mailer had wondered more than once at that cu-

171

rious demand of small-town life which leaves something good and bright in the eyes of some, is so deadening for others—it was his impression that people in small towns had eyes which were generally livelier or emptier than the more concentrated look of city vision.) These Marshals had the dead eye and sour cigar, that sly shuffle of propriety and rut which so often comes out in a small-town sheriff as patriotism and the sweet stink of a crooked dollar. Small-town sheriffs sidled over to a crooked collar like a High Episcopalian hooked on a closet queen. If one could find the irredeemable madness of America (for we are a nation where weeds will breed in the gilding tank) it was in those late afternoon race track faces coming into the neon lights of the parimutuel windows, or those early morning hollows in the eye of the soul in places like Vegas where the fevers of America go livid in the hum of the night, and Grandmother, the church-goer, orange hair burning bright now crooned over the One-Arm Bandit, pocketbook open, driving those half-dollars home, home to the slot.

"Madame, we are burning children in Vietnam."

"Boy, you just go get yourself lost. Grandma's about ready for a kiss from the jackpot."

The burned child is brought into the gaming hall on her hospital bed.

"Madame, regard our act in Vietnam."

"I hit! I hit! Hot deedy, I hit. Why, you poor burned child—you just brought me luck. Here, honey, here's a lucky half-dollar in reward. And listen sugar, tell the nurse to change your sheets. Those sheets sure do stink. I hope you ain't got gangrene. Hee hee, hee hee. I get a supreme pleasure mixing with gooks in Vegas."

One did not have to look for who would work in the concentration camps and the liquidation centers—the garrison would be filled with applicants from the pages of a hundred American novels, from *Day of the Locust* and *Naked Lunch* and *The Magic Christian,* one could enlist half the Marshals outside this bus, simple, honest, hard-working government law-enforcement agents, yeah! There was something at loose now in American life, the poet's beast slinking to the marketplace. The country had al-

172

ways been wild. It had always been harsh and hard, it had always had a fever—when life in one American town grew insupportable, one could travel, the fever to travel was in the American blood, so said all, but now the fever had left the blood, it was in the cells, the cells traveled, and the cells were as insane as Grandma with orange hair. The small towns were disappearing in the bypasses and the supermarkets and the shopping centers, the small town in America was losing its sense of the knuckle, the herb, and the root, the walking sticks were no longer cut from trees, nor were they cured, the schools did not have crazy old teachers now but teaching aids, and in the libraries, *National Geographic* gave way to *TV Guide*. Enough of the old walled town had once remained in the American small town for gnomes and dwarfs and knaves and churls (yes, and owls and elves and crickets) to live in the constellated cities of the spiders below the eaves in the old leaning barn which—for all one knew—had been a secret ear to the fevers of the small town, message center for the inhuman dreams which passed through the town at night in sleep and came to tell their insane tale of the old barbarian lust to slaughter villages and drink their blood, yes who knew which ghosts, and which crickets, with which spider would commune—which prayers and whose witch's curses would travel those subterranean trails of the natural kingdom about the town, who knows which fevers were forged in such communion and returned on the blood to the seed, it was an era when the message came by the wind and not by the wire (for the town gossip began to go mad when the telephone tuned its buds to the tip of her tongue) the American small town grew out of itself, and grew out of itself again and again, harmony between communication and the wind, between lives and ghosts, insanity, the solemn reaches of nature where insanity could learn melancholy (and madness some measure of modesty) had all been lost now, lost to the American small town. It had grown out of itself again and again, its cells traveled, worked for government, found security through wars in foreign lands, and the nightmares which passed on the winds in the old small towns now traveled on the nozzle tip of the flame thrower, no dreams now of barbarian lusts, slaughtered villages, battles of blood, no, nor any need for them— technology had driven insanity out of the wind and out of the attic, and out of all the lost primitive places: one had to find it now wherever fever, force, and machines could come together, in Vegas, at the race track, in pro football, race riots for the Negro, suburban orgies—none of it was enough—one had to find it in Vietnam; that was where the small town had gone to get its kicks.

That was on the faces of the Marshals. It was a great deal to read on the limited evidence before him, but he had known these faces before—they were not so different from the cramped, mean, stern, brave, florid, bestial, brutish, narrow, calculating, incurious, hardy, wily, leathery, simple, good, stingy, small-town faces he had once been familiar with in his outfit overseas, all those Texans from all those small towns, it was if he could tell—as at a college reunion—the difference these more than twenty years had made. If it were legitimate to read the change in American character by the change in the faces of one's classmates, then he could look at these Marshals like men he had known in the Army, but now revisited, and something had gone out of them, something had come in. If there was a common unattractive element to the Southern small-town face, it was in that painful pinch between their stinginess and their greed. No excess of love seemed ever to come off a poor white Southerner, no fats, no riches, no sweets, just the avidity for such wealth. But there had been sadness attached to this in the old days, a sorrow; in the pinch of their cheeks was the kind of abnegation and loneliness which spoke of what was tender and what was lost forever. So they had dignity. Now the hollows in their faces spoke of men who were rabid and toothless, the tenderness had turned corrosive, the abnegation had been replaced by hate, dull hate, cloud banks of hate, the hatred of failures who had not lost their greed. So he was reminded of a probability he had encountered before: that, nuclear bombs all at hand, the true war party of America was in all the small towns, even as the peace parties had to collect in the cities and the suburbs. Nuclear warfare was dividing the nation. The day of power for the small-town mind was approaching—who else would be left when atomic war was done would reason the small-town mind, and in measure to the depth of their personal failure, would love Vietnam, for Vietnam was the secret hope of a bigger war, and that bigger war might yet clear the air of races, faces, in fact—technologies—all that alienation they could not try to comprehend.

It was not a happy meditation. Among the soldiers he had known, there was the chance to talk. He did not see many faces here who would ever talk. Cheers. They were dragging a girl out of one of the trucks now. Pale-skinned, with light brown hair, no lipstick, dungarees, she had that unhappy color which came from too many trips to marijuana garden. Nonetheless, she waved to her boyfriend while being dragged along the ground. He was eventually dragged into their bus.

Mailer began to chat with the young clergyman. His name was John Boyle, and he was Presbyterian Chaplain at Yale. The number of his arrest was nine. They joked about this—he had beaten Mailer to the Bench. Actually he had seen the Protagonist get arrested, had followed to see if he were being treated properly (a sign of Mailer's age, a proper sign of status!) was turned back with assurances, wandered behind Pentagon lines, and in the course of protesting the arrest of a demonstrator, was apprehended himself (although the Marshal had wanted to release him when he saw his collar).

"Well," said Mailer, "at least we have low numbers."

"Do you think that will mean much?"

"We should be the first to get out."

From where he sat in the bus, he could see square vertical columns back of the loading platform, columns reminiscent of Egyptian architecture: Mailer now had a rumination about the nature of Egyptian architecture and its relation to the Pentagon, those ultra-excremental forms of ancient Egyptian architecture, those petrified excrements of the tomb and the underground chambers here

175

at the Pentagon, but he was not an Egyptologist, no sir, and the connection eluded him. He must pursue it later. Something there. But the rumination running down, we may quickly leave his thoughts.

4: A BUSLOAD OF SLOGANS

In fact, the bus is getting ready to leave the Pentagon. A driver has gotten on—to many cheers—and a wire gate is closed across the front to protect the chauffeur from attack by any prisoners while he is driving. There are also bars across each window. (Obviously Mailer has had the fantasy of bending the bars and making his escape, and has decided not to—it would certainly make him famous for too little.) The sun has been beating on the bus and it is as uncomfortably warm as a small Southern bus depot on an Indian summer afternoon, which is what the faces outside might suggest, if not for the Pentagon walls. And a battle has been taking place, even if no sign of it seems to be reaching here—except, gloomy thought, the battle cannot be going too well, for there is not the remotest sign of panic in this rear area. Except there also seems less air of self-congratulation. It is frustrating not to know.

The motor started. They backed up, turned around, pulled away. Now, their hands were out the window with their fingers extended in the V for Victory sign. They passed MPs standing at attention on the open end of the loading area, looking not unlike buoys in a channel as you pull out to sea. To a man, the prisoners in the bus began to yell, "Hell, no, we won't go; hell, no, we won't go!" and at the subtle shift of expression in each MPs face, other slogans were quickly fed: "End the war in

Vietnam. Bring the boys home! End the war in Vietnam. Bring the boys home." There was a rollicking solidarity now on the bus, somewhere between young coal miners under arrest for a strike, and a high school team riding back from a successful game. In fact, the MPs had the look of substitutes on a high school football bench when the team is behind or the game is worrisome, they stood erectly at the highest pitch of attention—tweak them and they would have twanged like a bow—their chins jammed up under their upper jaws, jaws under their head, head in helmet, line of vision cut off six feet from the ground— that classic military attention which says: It don't matter how bad I am, when I stand like this, sir, I am being good.

"Hey, hey, LBJ! How many kids did you slay today?" shouted the prisoners in the bus to the MPs and waved their fingers in V for Victory. It felt like a victory, one hardly knew over what, perhaps over the lack of imagination (and so the secret consternation) of those young MPs, same age as so many of the prisoners, but utterly uncomprehending of why anyone their age would wish for this purpose to get arrested.

They sang much of the way. Shouting their slogans to high school adolescents at the few intersections where they stopped for traffic lights in the small suburban shopping streets on their route, the kids looking surprisingly like high school kids in Hollywood and TV, the long pants, sweaters, sneakers; the girls in variations on middie blouses and mini-skirts, saddle shoes. A part of him had always tried to believe that the America he saw in family television dramas did not exist, had no power—as of course he knew it did—to direct the styles and the manners and therefore the ideas of America (for in a country where everyone lived so close to their senses, then style, precisely, and manner, precisely, carved ideas into the senses) ideas like conformity, cleanliness, America-is-always-right. They did not have to know too much about the endless reverberations of chic, no, clean American kids could end up giving lollipops (shaped like Grandma's half-dollar) to their favorite Vietnamese cripple— "Hey, Hank, was this little girl burned by VC or us?"

Now the kids on the street looked at them with blank faces. They had no idea of what the V for Victory sign meant, nor even the slogans, "Hey, hey LBJ." There was that dim look which must come toward teachers from the bigger boys in the rear row—by the use of cajolery and some sizable intimidation, not to mention soul-suffocating uses of repetition, yes, a passing grade of seventy lurks in those dim eyes. So these high school kids watching them pass had that same dim look. "Yes, Sally, yes, there's something I heard was going on at the Pentagon." No, if their bus made all the noise of a high school bus after winning a game, the game had taken place on Mars, Mars where all the bright kids went. Which is maybe why they made so much noise now. Because they had never traveled on a high school victory bus.

It offered its wry perspective. All the dull kids, too stupid to study, ovulating turgid fantasies in the back row, all liveliness sunk in premature sapience of burgeoning young meats, and up front, the bright middle-class children, little intellectual drills, their mental voracity driving them to further, better, higher critiques of the public material before them until—Vietnam! Would America have to end by taking all its bright children and packing them off in buses to the Muzak Run? (For they might offer music in the gas chambers in the new totalitarianism.) He still could not believe such a day would come, but it was sometimes harder to keep this faith intact at night. Recall him to: "That long dark night of the soul when it is always three o'clock in the morning."

Ah, yes, thought Mailer, as the shopping street flickered past the bus window at a rate not faster than a good horse's trot, yes, bless Fitzgerald for his clear line—and why that long dark night, yes, why, when all was said? and Wolfe dead too early and Hemingway a suicide—how much guilt lay on the back of a good writer—it grew worse and worse. As the power of communication grew larger, so the responsibility to educate a nation lapped at the feet, new tide of a new responsibility, and one had become a writer after all to find a warm place where one was safe—responsibility was for the pompous, and the public servants; writers were born to discover wine. It

178

was an old argument and he was worn with it—he had written a good essay once about the failure of any major American novelist to write a major novel which would reach out past the best-seller lists to a major part of that American audience brainwashed by Hollywood, TV, and *Time*. Yes, how much of Fitzgerald's long dark night may have come from that fine winnowing sense in the very fine hair of his nose that the two halves of America were not coming together, and when they failed to touch, all of history might be lost in the divide. Yes, there was a dark night if you had the illusion you could do something about it, and the conviction that not enough had been done. Or was it simply impossible—had the two worlds of America drifted irretrievably apart? Marooned on these unhappy and somewhat fruitless questions, he nonetheless enjoyed the ride through the late afternoon sunlight on these streets in Virginia (was there any other state with so sweet a name?) eddying through a melancholy which was not without its private flavor, for he felt remarkably disembodied from all proceedings—yes, he had a glint of the emotion; doubtless, he felt shriven. Did religious sentiments arrive thus often to men with as much meat on their bones as himself, wondered Mailer?

So it went. Lots of song, all the slogans. "Hell, no, we won't go." "Bring the troops home now." "Hey, hey, LBJ." He yelled with the rest. That was the advantage of being shriven—you could join the Communist Sing. And this fine young clergyman from Yale for companion.

Then his thoughts began to meander again—down a long broad slow river of thought. He turned a bend—he had it. Delight. He had made the grand connection between Egyptian architecture and the Pentagon. Yes. The Egyptian forms, slab-like, excremental, thick walls, secret caverns, had come from the mud of the Nile, mud was the medium out of which the Egyptians built their civilization, abstract ubiquitous mud equaled in modern times only by abstract ubiquitous money, filthy lucre (thoughts of Norman O. Brown). And American Civilization had moved from the existential sanction of the frontier to the abstract ubiquitous sanction of the dollar bill. Nowhere had so much of the dollar bill collected as at the Pentagon, giant mudpie on the banks of America's Nile, our Potomac! Well, decided Mailer, now much cheered, the secret in prison was to have a view out the window—but thoughts of Jack Ruby growing cancer in a windowless air-conditioned cell came to depress him.

Now they reached their prison. It was the U. S. Post Office in Alexandria. A square stolid red-brick building of that pale lusterless (abstract ubiquitous) brick (as opposed to the old wine-red, clay-red brick of the Smithsonian) was there on a street off the main shopping street to receive them.

5: THE POST OFFICE

They passed in single file out of the bus, and walked under guard through the empty downstairs floor of the Post Office, normally closed on this late Saturday afternoon, and were met by a couple of police, state troopers perhaps, who counted them off, and marched them to an elevator. They ascended slowly, the elevator making the deliberate unctuous sounds of a heavy piece of government machinery well-oiled and inspected for years. They stopped on what seemed the third floor, and walked down the corridor of what could have been a typical small-town office building, took a left turn into a narrower hall and found their quarters off this hall, two cells, about fifteen feet deep, twelve feet wide, equipped with sink, toilet, and a couple of benches along the two long walls.

Perhaps fifteen men shared the cell in which he now found himself, and they immediately characterized themselves by their first action, a social process he had noticed in new schools, in hospital wards, in the army, and in prison. Long before you knew someone's name, you knew their attitude to the institutional world you shared with them. Some of the men sat down on the benches and waited patiently, or held their heads in depression. One or two held their heads in pain where they had been clubbed by the Marshals, others stood by the bars that gave on the hall in order to catch every bit of news or rumor from the turnkey, and later, the lawyers; one or two did isometric exercises against the bars. Some kept going to the sink for a handful of water. Walter Teague, the first man Mailer had met after his arrest, lay down immediately on the floor with his white motorcycle helmet for a pillow, and went to sleep. On the bus, he had chatted just enough with Teague to recognize the other man's philosophy probably began with Lenin's remark that the revolution needed people who would work, sleep, think, and eat revolution twenty-four hours a day. Teague was a professional—there was something in the way he went immediately to sleep, as if experience had confirmed him in the opinion that nothing was going to happen for an hour or two at least which depressed Mailer's expectations altogether of being out of this jail in thirty minutes and on his way to New York. He was still in an indecent hurry to be arraigned, fined, lectured no doubt, and released—it was as if the cumulative excitements of these few days had become precious. Like an emotional connoisseur, let us say even like Huysmans' Des Esseintes, he wished now to steep essences of this experience at his leisure, and knew—looking at Teague—that if he were to hold on to the value of what had happened to him (and he knew by the unfamiliar variety of happiness he now felt that much indeed had happened to him—perhaps he knew, if no more, that he would now make a good soldier) he must take the next step and give up any quick idea of savoring, installing, banking the value of the experience by way of some enjoyable revery on the trip home tonight. No, something was wrong in the air. He felt no stir in the hall outside the prison, no sense of officials bending to a large administrative task—to the contrary, there was a definite impression of inactivity, of pall again.

He did not know why he had assumed the government would be quick, efficient, executive—he had probably supposed they would be in haste to process men in order not to strain their prison facilities which must be limited, and then reminded himself that the government could serve its punitive intentions best by not making their passage through jail too simple. How could he have assumed anything but petty harassment would be their due? Why had he expected the government to be crisp, modest, and pleasantly efficient in their processing of Pentagon prisoners? "Because ass," he said to himself, "they have brainwashed you as well." And it was true. The only reason he had expected to be out of jail in half an hour was the covert impression he had of government as brotherly; dull but brotherly; ten thousand hours of television, ten million words of newsprint added up to one thundering misapprehension of all the little details of institutional life.

But just about the time he began to settle in for a long wait, the turnkey told them the U.S. Commissioners had arrived, and a young law student, serving (in the field) for the Civil Liberties Union, gave them a short orientation lecture on their rights, the lecture most notable for his hesitation (as a student) to make any remark he could not defend altogether, so that the orientation quickly degenerated into a series of questions more vibrant than their answers.

"How soon will we be out?"

"It's possible they're making every effort to get you out fast."

"But you don't know the answer?"

The young man answering their questions had the tall bland pleasant slightly schizophrenic look of a student who would yet make a good corporation lawyer, but would not necessarily ever understand where the law was buried.

"As of this moment, I do not know."

"What do they want us to plead?"

"As of this moment, the choice of pleas has not yet been specified."

"Oh, Christ," muttered a prisoner in disgust.

They were all pegging their questions, and the law student stood outside the bars in the hall, and ducked the answers to the best of his ability.

"I gave a John Doe," said one prisoner. "Will they let me out?"

"It's possible this could affect the processing of your case."

"How do I change the John Doe?"

"No procedure has yet, so far as I know, been established."

That went on for a few minutes, then they were left alone. Then another lawyer came. He was older and from the Civil Liberties Union, and he had more information although not very much more. Teague was still sleeping.

Then a couple of prisoners were actually called, and came back in ten minutes to say their fine was $25, and they were being released on a promise not to return to the Pentagon. That shattered any small idea Mailer had held of paying a second visit. He had already calculated a time table. If he were out by eight o'clock, he would get back to his hotel, change, and catch a ten o'clock plane to New York, still make the party—if it were later, he might go by the Pentagon—there had been pleasure at the thought of returning to the battle. But not if he were to be arrested. The value of the first arrest would be spoiled altogether. There was an aesthetic economy to symbolic gestures—you must not repeat yourself. Arrested once, TV land would accept him (conceivably) as a man willing to stand up for his ideas: get busted twice on the same day, and they would view him as a freak-out panting for arrest. (Mailer's habit of living—no matter how unsuccessfully—with his image, was so engrained by now, that like a dutiful spouse he was forever consulting his better half.)

Yet, after these two prisoners were released, there was a long wait. Then one more was called. Then a wait. Mailer was still more or less confident, however, in the value of his low number. When John Boyle, the Presbyterian Chaplain at Yale went out, he expected to be next, but Boyle came back with a $25 fine, a thirty-day suspended sentence and no news for him. "They're going very slowly in there," he said. The turnkey, a mild looking grandfatherly southerner with steel-rimmed bifocal glasses, pale blue eyes, thin white hair, thin mouth, and gums much receded, teeth perhaps gone, was standing next to Boyle in the hall, and gave him a card to fill out. Then wishing to move the Chaplain to the next office, the turnkey reached for Boyle's sleeve, and tugged at it, as if to say, "You may be wearing the Collar, but you're just Sonny-boy to me." Like a shot the Chaplain's hand flew out and knocked the turnkey's fingers away, as if Boyle was replying, "Get those guilty hands off this Cloth." It was done. Not a further word passed between them. First Coffin, now Boyle. They obviously raised their reverends to be men at Yale! Where, wondered Mailer, were the Chaplains from Harvard?

Now he took his first drink of water. He had not had anything to eat or drink since breakfast, and the mild abstention had traveled with him through the day, consuming in some minute oven of his metabolism the fuel for a small sustaining fire intense enough to give its whispered suggestion of what extraordinarily developed spiritual states real hunger, real thirst, and real abstention might provide. He had felt, despite every petty motive, or low calculation on how to get back to New York for the party, a mild exaltation on which he had traveled through the day, a sense of cohering in himself which was he supposed the opposite of those more familiar states of alienation he could always describe so well: so, the hunger and thirst now gave their promise that years were coming when he, first spoiled son of an age of affluence, might have to live with hunger, with thirst, or more unendurable than both together, the monotonies of life in a prison cell. How fortunate was this run-through, this preparation for years ahead—how good to know that a little hunger and a little thirst were tonic for a day of battle, and discipline for dull hours in jail.

Yet, on these thoughts, he took a drink of water. It was characteristic of him to make such a move, and he hardly knew if he did it for the best or worst of reasons, did it because in recognizing the value of thirst he had a small panic to destroy the temptation to search such a moral adventure further, or did he do it precisely because he was now aware of the value of thirst, and so thirst by such consciousness had lost its value since the ability to

184

suffer drought was, by this logic, valuable only if water were not available. Or did he take a drink because he wished to study his new state after satisfying thirst? He noticed only that he was a trifle sad on the first sip, and couldn't stop going to the sink for more and more water afterward, which declared the result of the experiment: between the saint and the debauchee, no middle ground seemed tenable for his appetites. If he had now not had a cigarette in three years, it was because he had once been obliged to smoke as many as three packs in a day, and knew he would be smoking three packs again if ever he lit a single one.

The processing of prisoners started up again, the processing lapsed. Lawyers came by to talk through the bars, lawyers left, rumors flew. Many prisoners had been arrested on the charge of assaulting an officer—one rumor would have it that their offense was not inconsequential: sentences could go for thirty days, for ninety days or more. "But I didn't assault the Marshal—he assaulted me," was the predictable cry. Now prisoners needed money for their fines.

He had over two hundred dollars in cash in his wallet. Situated in the middle of a dozen young men who were probably without money, who had hitched to Washington and slept on a floor, this sum seemed inappropriate. Like a man who smiles at a cop to indicate he has no criminal activity whatsoever in his brain, so Mailer began to hand out money for fines as if to demonstrate that his wallet was normally empty. (A considerable misrepresentation!) It was his intention to keep fifty dollars for himself, and he managed to succeed in this, but it was not so easy as he thought. In the beginning, he loaned money to prisoners he liked, or to prisoners who had been injured by the Marshals and were therefore presumably in need of their liberty, but after a while, he became a visible feature in this small cell of the living presence of the theory of the bondsman, and prisoners he did not like, two particularly, were there to beseech him. He gave them money as well —some vague principle of man's equality before the law seemed here to apply, but he handed over $25 to one hirsute obese fellow—hirsute and obese, no less!—who had

185

been ready to go to his knees or even prostrate himself to get the loot and get out, whining all the while of his injuries, perspiring, swearing as profusely as his sweat that he would mail the money back in the next few days (which of course he did not) and Mailer set him free with great distaste. There was also a sly pale octaroon, hippest of the hip, hints of some sly jungle animal who would scavenge at the edge of camp, and he was another who would never pay back, and didn't, even taking Mailer's address with the slyest of smiles, "These formalities, man —they're a gas," said the smile. But there were others, he liked. One or two of the prisoners were proud, and did not ask for the money—he had to offer it. One kid, small, lithe, with the body moves of a superb athlete and the small bright snubbed features of a cat, took the money as if it were a detail—nice to get, but neither here nor there, simply his due. He had had the most spectacular arrest. Breaking through the line of MPs near to where Mailer had been arrested, he had dodged back and forth among the Marshals for many minutes, outrunning them, crossing field on them, doubling back, stopping short, sprinting, loping, teasing them, then outrunning them again— they had been too fatigued to hurt him when finally, fox to their hounds, he was caught by the river. He spoke in a stammer, great intensity behind his words, much intelligence. He gave Mailer a critique of the staging of his play *The Deer Park* which was about as incisive as his own. A remarkable boy, Mailer had decided—just the sort to have in your army.

Time went on. Promises arrived they would be out soon, word came to wait. Rumors slipped in that soon the Commissioner would start to process them in groups, only to be followed by other rumors that the Commissioner was feeling vindictive, and would drag out each single case. The memory of the last time he had been in prison was coming back to Mailer. The last time had been most unpleasant—he had been incarcerated in the prison hospital at Bellevue for assault upon his second wife. He had not known then if he would be inside for seven days or seven years. Finally it had been seventeen days. Released for trial, he received eventually a suspended sentence and probation for two years. They were not years he enjoyed to look back upon, but he had learned one lesson in prison then, and it came back to him now: in jail, a man who wished to keep his sanity, must never anticipate, never expect, never hope with such high focus of hope that disappointment would be painful. Because there was no place for disappointment to go in prison, except back into one's own cells. Prison was frustration. You had to be careful never to add to the vast vats of intrinsic prison frustration by having hopes which could be destroyed. For destroyed they would be. There was a psychic mechanism in prison which he had noted —somehow, hopeful rumors were always followed by cruel rumors, only to be replaced by hopeful rumors again. A prisoner was a yo-yo—so long as the essential mechanisms of prison could keep him going up and down, he was helpless to get out of his own self-concern. Self-absorption and apathy would be the poles of his emotion, and his resistance would have no spine. So he repeated to himself lessons learned on another day, and found them of use. Slowly, patiently, the idea of going to a party tonight was severed from his expectations, slowly the thought of seeing his wife and family this weekend was subdued. He would get out of jail in a half hour or he would not get out for thirty days (no, that was too much!) but whatever, he would not think of the immediate disposition of his future, and he would not hope. He would wait. A man was nothing in prison without his cool, for prison was the profoundest put-on of them all —it said, dig, man, you are here suffering for your crime. The put-on was nothing but an effect which pretended to be related to the cause, and had no relation to the cause —just as the feel of prison had nothing to do with the feel of the crime. So much for Existential Dynamics!

They were now being allowed to make their single telephone call. So Mailer soon got the opportunity to telephone his wife. The turnkey led him down the hall a few steps to an office where a lady clerical worker with tinted reddish hair and sequin-stubbed tortoise-shell eyeglasses was installed. Since the call had to be made collect she would put it through for him. She was obviously quite excited by the presence of all these prisoners; not simply because they were men—she had that high trilling gossipy Southern voice which speaks of long telephone calls with age-old girl friends, and no nonsense from men—but because, married or spinster (impossible to tell which), she had the livid curiosity of a small-town Southern woman. The fact that she was here to see these prisoners and talk to a few of them and study them—"Honey, you wouldn't believe their faces. Some you could talk to and never *know,* and some of the others looked *depraved*"—had given her a flush of power which put her in the nicest of moods. She talked to the novelist as if she were the receptionist in a particularly exclusive hospital. "And Mr. Mailer, tell me"—conspiratorial—"just how do you spell your name now?" Nod. "Uh-huh. And the telephone number is in Brooklyn, *New* York, is that correct?"

He felt a calm sweet pleasure at the sound of his wife's voice at the other end. She had a charming voice on the phone, crisp but soft, with a Southern flavor, and very clear. At this moment it had the open exposed tone of someone just awakened, or pulled from the shower, innocent but flustered—actually she had been on the phone the last hour, for word had been broadcast of his arrest, and friends had been calling, "Oh, golly," she said, "are you all right?"

"I'm fine."

"They didn't hurt you or anything?"

"I been around a little too long for that."

She laughed. "We're proud of you." A pause. "I love you."

"Yes, I love you too," he muttered into the phone under the beaming manic sequined spectacles of the lady clerical worker at his elbow. It was true. They had a marriage which had everything good in it and much that was very bad in it because finally they were strangers who happened to be in love with each other—before he had met her, he would not have believed this was necessarily possible. At any rate, they rarely felt so close to each other as when they were separated. Then at last they understood each other.

She was asking him when he would get out.

"I don't know. I don't think I'll get back tonight. Why don't you go to the party without me?"

"Don't be silly. I'm not going without you."

His last remark had been a gesture. He would have been in a state if she had gone to the party while he was languishing in the great lock-up. "Look," he said, "don't start worrying about when I get out. It's the quickest way to get unnerved." He gave a short lecture on the principle he had invoked two minutes before for himself.

"All right, but I still hope you get out early tomorrow. The girls will be very disappointed if they don't see you this weekend." He had four daughters from earlier marriages, and they came to visit on Friday and stayed through Sunday. Since his fourth marriage had given him two boys, they were a large and sometimes uproarious family on weekends.

"Brownie called," she said. Brownie was her stepfather.

"He did?"

"Brownie and Mom were very worried about you." She laughed. She had a fine laugh, much delicacy and much subtle vigor artfully combined. "Listen," she went on, "Brownie was one of the people working on getting some troops ready to fly up to Washington."

"He was?" Mailer said with delight. His stepfather-in-law was a retired Master Sergeant who worked in supply at Fort Benning in Georgia. "That's too good," he said.

"Isn't it. I said to Brownie, 'Damn you, it's all your fault!'" She laughed again. "You know Brownie. I bet he thinks I really am blaming him."

They laughed at this, and then she told him a quick story about a little thing his sons had done that day. Then their time was up. As he put down the phone, he was left with a picture of his two sons, painful in its clarity. He loved his daughters very much, he had had the best of love affairs with them, for the terminations of the marriages had been painful, and their love was therefore always touched with sorrow, but they were girls and he sometimes felt that because they loved him, he could not make a serious mistake with them. If he did something wrong, they being women would grow up around the mistake and somehow convert it to knowledge. But his sons! He had the feeling that because they were men, their egos were more fragile—a serious error might hurt them forever. So he never knew whether he was too strong or too soft with them.

Perhaps because of his sons, he saw everything in terms of football these days; he could see each of his boys in twenty years on a professional football team. The older one was wild and fierce and angelic and delicate, graceful as a young prince, sly as a thief—he would make a great running back, a superb pass receiver. He was competitive as a maniac when he wanted to win. The younger one was capable of taking tremendous punishment (at present from his older brother) he was going to play linebacker, no doubt (and with his sleeves rolled up). He would be enormous, and very powerful, and with the happiest disposition in the world, for his brain was keen, his eye was quick. When a back would come flying through a hole, he would grab him with one hand, hold him in the air and dump him down. Then he would pick him up. "Hope I didn't hurt you, fellow," he would say with a happy insane glint in his eye. Yes, the younger one had the broth and marrow of goodness; everyone in the family loved him (except his older brother who had to contemplate the day when his younger brother would be ready).

But these thoughts had broken right through any injunction to feel no hope about getting out. Now, for a moment, he had almost a disorderly desire to be back with his wife, his daughters and his sons, feeling the presence of prison with the same resentment a healthy man has for the first onslaught of an unfamiliar sickness—how did it dare to attack him? And he also felt something of the same panic. If one did not get rid of the disease in a hurry, it was going to get worse and worse. Perhaps the turnkey felt a suggestion of this, since he began to apologize to Mailer for the brevity of the call, "It's just that everybody wants to phone," he said sorrowfully, "so we have to hurry you fellows up."

He was more American than anyone had a right to be, that high worried forehead, narrow receded mouth, white hair, those innocent blue eyes so capable of watching an

190

execution (only to worry about it later) and the steel-rimmed spectacles. Narrowness, propriety, good-will, and that infernal American innocence which could not question one's leaders, for madness and the boils of a frustrated life resided beneath. No, he would not want to hear Mailer's arguments on why we should get out of Vietnam, no, he would shake his head and cluck his tongue and say, "It's an awful war, I know, but I guess all wars are awful, and it's a shame, but our boys have to fight them I suppose." Now the turnkey gave a rueful little grin, and said, "You know, I sure wish you fellows could have had this demonstration on a weekday. It makes us have to work all weekend through, and we don't get no time off."

Was this one reason the Marshals had been so furious? He could see the lost weekend in the turnkey's eyes. Would he have sat with his wife in some prefab ranch house built to module, watching his television set? Or would family have visited? There was something in his Southern accent, not of the deep South (what Mailer's wife called Down Home) but of the hills, something of that mournful, discommoded, fundamentally displaced tone which came to Southerners when they moved even from their own small town to the next. They were thus rooted that no one suffered so much as Southerners with uprooting. Mailer almost felt the turnkey's physical discomfort at what it cost not to be rooted now in his chair watching his favorite Saturday evening set of shows. America ripped itself apart and then dressed the wounds with television. Was that why Southerners usually made the best soldiers?—because they were still young enough to feel their uprooting with ferocity?

Back in the cell, he played chess for a while with a young prisoner who wore a surplus combat jacket. They drew the board on a piece of paper, marked little squares of torn paper for pieces; but the game was fragile. One good breath would end it, unless they were able to reconstruct their moves.

He had not played in years and might have been in difficulty if the other player had not been so bad. Finally the other confessed he was on a trip. "Man, you can't imagine what today has been like. What a trip!"

Yes, what a trip! On the March, odysseys to the moon; and at the Pentagon, Marshals with faces like gorgons. Mailer soon lost interest in the game which he was in no danger of losing. He was thinking about his wife. If one disclosed what one knew of a subject by the cutting edge of the style employed, so one appropriated a culture with a wife, at least so far as one loved a wife. He had had four wives, and some part of four cultures had been his, not enough, no doubt, but something he had learned, something, of Jewish genius and of revolutionaries and large indiscriminate love for the oppressed from his first wife; and a love of painting and sensuality and drama and Latin desperation, yes, and a sense of the tragic not so incomplete from his second wife; and he had had a love affair with England for his third, and the fine dialectic of propriety and wickedness. manner and the mode of social murder in well-established places, yes he had had a fair love affair with the third. And now he was married to an American girl, just as difficult as the rest, or more difficult —for he understood her the least. She was beautiful, she was blonde, with that stubbornness and delicacy of feature only American girls seemed able to develop, and she had had a childhood like a million others in America, growing up in Atlanta, and Tampa, and Sarasota, and Louisville, and a dozen smaller places between, and since she had studied acting in New York, and had been in some plays and many television shows, and had made television commercials, and had been once the star of an ill-fated mystery movie made in Spain, she had a professional voice now which was without an accent when she met new people, but at home his love affair with the South could have its day for she talked without thinking in a spectrum of Southern voices, everything from the faintest trace to the raucous ball-your-fists hollering of a Georgia jackass. There were times listening to her First Sergeant's tones in the middle of a quarrel when he had to dare a stroke in order to keep himself from beating up on her beautiful white Southern girl face.

They had had their marriage four years now, and they were still in love all evidence would declare. Separations made them painfully aware of each other—they each traveled then in the psyche of the other, they were rarely surprised by the mood of the other's voice on a long-distance call, and at best they had a cleanness of sentiment for each other which spoke of healthy families and sunlight on water, such excellences, but they were still strangers. She would never comprehend him—he sometimes thought she had no interest in that—and he wondered if he would ever know her. It infuriated him. Forget all pride as a husband, a lover, a man—the novelist in him was outraged. To live four years with a woman and not be able to decide if her final nature was good or evil? That might make for great interest in a marriage, much trickiness to love, large demands for manly discpline, but what was the novelist to think of himself?—especially when he (like all novelists) prided himself on his knowledge of women. Mailer finally came to decide that his love for his wife while not at all equal or congruent to his love for America was damnably parallel. It was not inconceivable to him that if he finally came to believe his wife was not nearly so magical as he would make her, but was in fact petty, stingy, small-minded, and evilly stubborn (which is what he told her in many a quarrel) why then he would finally lose some part of his love affair with America, he would have to, because there were too many times when thinking of his country and some new one of the unspeakable barbarities it invented with every corporation day, he would decide that no it could not be an altogether awful country because otherwise how would his wife, a Southerner and an Army brat, have come out so subtle, so supple, so mysterious, so fine-skinned, so tender and wise.

We will remember that Mailer had a complex mind of sorts. He would have considered it irretrievably heavy-handed to have made any direct correspondence between his feelings for his wife, and the change in his feelings toward America (which tended to change a little every minute from the truth he had detected in the last face he saw) but he would also have thought it cowardly to ignore the relation, and dishonest to assume that none of his wife's attractiveness (and unattractiveness) came from her presence so quintessentially American.

193

It was after all natural that he should have a love affair with America—how much worse if the grandsons of the immigrants did not. No, the trick was merely to never lose sight of his fourth wife's absolutely unquenchable even unendurable individuality. Let him treat her as a symbol, and he was out of it—which is why perhaps she was so American. At any rate, Mailer's relation to the Marshals, guards, turnkeys, and trustees along the route of his imprisonment and indeed to the occasional Southern demonstrator he met, had a relation which came in part from the flavor of seeing them next to his Southern in-laws. Mailer's wife was as opposed to the war in Vietnam as he was, except when she was very drunk and then she would talk of her brothers in Vietnam. She had two brothers who had served there—one of them, a Marine, had come back with a competence in Karate, the other was a career soldier in the Air Force—her stepfather had recently been cited. Mailer had always gotten along with his Southern in-laws; his time in the 112th Cavalry (out of San Antonio) and his periodic visits to Arkansas to see his best Army buddy had made him not too much of a stranger to them—so by the same token he got on well now with all the prison personnel. Some of them were nice enough to be his in-laws, some not, but he could not pretend he did not understand them, or that he must hate them because they were Southerners. Rather he brooded over them, as his in-laws were perhaps brooding now about him. It would prove a horror beyond measurable horror if the country slid into disaster with a hundred small civil wars, and an excess of internal good will.

Time passed. The Commissioner stopped proceedings to have dinner, which was much to the annoyance of the turnkey and the guards, who had hoped to process everyone and go home. The Civil Liberties lawyers collected small change, and hamburgers were brought back for the prisoners, classic American hamburgers, mustard, pickle, relish, ketchup, a gourd of cheap sweets and chemical sours on dull dough and shank bone meat—it tasted better if one pictured billboards and drive-in waitresses with tight silk pants and cowboy boots. Yes, America always lent itself to personification. One could munch a hamburger and carry the American highway along as a presence—the sharp jarring sights, the long dull spaces, the satisfying undemanding flavor of it all if you were bored —yes, the hamburger was three centuries from the Pilgrim.

Now, new word came. They were not to be processed here after all. They were to be shipped to Washington, D.C., workhouse in Occoquan, Virginia. And where was Occoquan?—why twenty miles down the road. Twenty out and twenty back—that would take an hour: hopes faded now of any release on Saturday evening. But the lawyer said they would be processed all through the night at Occoquan. They might still get out. So it went, slap and back, slap and back went the rumors, like water trapped between bulkheads.

But on the street, as they marched out to the bus, Fontaine, the documentary-maker, and Leiterman, the cameraman, and Heiss, the soundman, were waiting.

As a result he was merry, "How long have you been here?" They joked at the length of their durance. He was delighted to see them. He had found out from a Civil Liberties lawyer just before leaving, that the Commissioner in the Post Office had been saving him for last. That had not inspired happiness even if he was isolating himself from quick hope—but seeing the cameramen here was tonic. After he got in the bus, they tried to film him by the available light in the ceiling of the vehicle, and asked him questions which he answered with a pompousness he thought detectable only to himself. They would be showing this movie after all in Britain, he would be spokesman, yes envoy extraordinaire for his cause, so he had to try to speak like an American public figure for British consumption, very dry, very cheerful.

"Have they been treating you all right?"

"Yes, very correct. Americans are always correct except when they're burning babies in foreign countries they know nothing about." That would go down well with the British.

Other prisoners called out their remarks, held up their fingers in a V for Victory sign. How rousing this would all look in Europe.

"Want to hear our slogans?" asked Mailer.

"Oh, yes," said Fontaine.

"Let's sing them a song, boys," Mailer called out. He could not help it—the mountebank in him felt as if he were playing Winston Churchill. Ten minutes ago in the cell he had been mired in long slow thoughts of four wives—now he had a stage again and felt not unheroic. "Can it be," he wondered to himself, "that I have misspent twenty years as a novelist, and all along have been languishing as an actor?"

They started to sing "We Shall Overcome," but the bus driver, as if wishing to make the point that America was more totalitarian than ever, promptly turned off the lights, and they sang in darkness for the soundman. Then they shouted slogans. Finally, they took off, waving their fingers in V for Victory through the darkness. One last cry, "Hey, hey, LBJ. How many kids did you slay today?"

In a dark bus, through a dark night, they traveled. It was getting near to ten o'clock on Saturday night, the lights were out in many houses in the Virginia countryside. The drive took on pleasure as journeys at night in buses through unfamiliar country in America always take on pleasure, as if in all echo of Thomas Wolfe, it is the moment for which Americans live, the collective journey through the dark when strangers are brought close by the wind and the sound of the tires, the lights on the highway, the compass of the night. All the stale impatient resentful wastes of those hours they had spent in their cells were washed now in the night air which blew through the windows. A silence came over them—that restful silence of men traveling, that sense of security in their muscle and in their number, and in their patience, which he had not felt since old days in the Army moving in convoy along dark roads. He was almost glad he had not yet been released, for he would have missed this trip, and so have not been reminded that a night journey on a bus was one of the few times when everything ambitious, wild, overconceived, hopeless, garish, and suffocatingly technical in American life nonetheless came together long enough to give the citizens a little peace, for maybe it was only when they were on the move that Americans could feel anchored in their memories. Was anything more agreeable than these small hills moving by in the dark like animals? Yes, it was on a journey that the tender memories of the past (and the more sorrowful) shifted somewhere in the seat of their unconscious repose, and warmed the blood, warmed the heart, warmed something at best of that cold anxious center where was inspired so much of the American fever, yes, tender memories which did not have to rise to the mind, but drifted like lights (boudoir lights? harbor lights?) on the warm river of the journey.

6: A NIGHT AT OCCOQUAN

That night at Occoquan, Mailer had a long revery about the war in Vietnam before he fell asleep. It was not to be the most comfortable slumber, for the mattress had old stuffing and was not two inches thick (as well as dirty) and the springs on the cot had lost their tone so the bed curved like a hammock. He had a clean pillow-case and a thin dirty blanket for cover which would not have kept a small animal warm, but it did not matter, for the heat was turned high in the long dormitory room where he slept with more than a hundred other men, and since the lights were on, and the air was filled with smoke, the condition was comparable to dozing in the dim heated currents of the Smoking Car on an overnight train.

It had not been a particularly eventful evening once they arrived. It had of course not been uneventful either, since nearly everything is interesting about a prison in the first few hours (although such interest is similar to the scrutiny a patient will give a hospital when he enters for an operation) but the ebb and flow of rumor, if nothing else, kept everyone up.

There had been their arrival and their processing—neither without drama, for many guards were about now, more than they had seen all day, and the prisoners moved in file from dimly lit rooms and hallways to desks under bright lights, their health being ascertained—"Do you need medical care?"—their fingerprints taken. It seemed when all was done, a small haul of information for the time it took, the lines in which they had to stand, and the separate rooms and officials they were obliged to pass, but it had nonetheless the mild but salutary interest of a dry run, a preliminary to one's commitment to a concentration camp—the future officials' faces might show the same hard lean grasp of a competence in police work, even the lights and the hallways, even the pale institutional green paint of the walls would be the same. Perhaps even the prison would be not so dissimilar. At night, under the lights, and the rapt presence of forty or fifty guards in the corners and the corridors and the bus debarkation point, existed that stricken awareness of a dire event to which the air itself can seem to be sensitive. In combat, on patrol, there had been times when the air had altered, not in odor but in presence, and around a bend in the trail had been a dead man, two hours dead, one hour dead—yes, and in the air of this place now an excitation had arisen, like a nest disturbed, harbinger perhaps of years of crisis ahead when more of the citizenry would be arrested and sent in the beginning to just such places of modest incarceration. Occoquan was a minimum security prison; built around a quadrangle of red brick, it had small repetitive arches lining all four sides of the arcade around the quadrangle. It had even in the night that sad aspiring look, that pale imitation of cloisters, which is to be found occasionally in the architecture of state junior colleges. It spoke of, it emphasized its minimum security—this green quadrangle, these men's dormitories off the cloistered walk—doubtless the first concentration camps would belong to this model. He had written for years about American architecture and its functional disease—that one could not tell the new colleges from the new

198

prisons from the new hospitals from the new factories from the new airports. Separate institutions were being replaced by one institution. Yes, and the irony was that this workhouse at Occoquan happened to be more agreeable architecturally than many a state university he had seen, or junior college. There was probably no impotence in all the world like knowing you were right and the wave of the world was wrong, and yet the wave came on. Floods of totalitarian architecture, totalitarian superhighways, totalitarian smog, totalitarian food (yes, frozen), totalitarian communications—the terror to a man so conservative as Mailer, was that nihilism might be the only answer to totalitarianism. The machine would work, grinding out mass man and his surrealistic wars until the machine was broken. It would take nihilists for that. But on the other hand nothing was worse than a nihilism which failed to succeed—for totalitarianism would then be accelerated. The gloom of these alternatives was perfect for the gloom of the huge dormitory in which he found himself after processing. It was a room more than a hundred feet long, more than forty feet wide, shaped like an airplane hangar with a curved ceiling and it had four rows of beds running the length of it, more than thirty beds in each row. Here, except for breakfast, and interviews with lawyers in the adjoining room, the prisoners were to stay.

A new rumor mill was working its gears. The equivalent of a plaza in this enormous room (Mailer did not necessarily think once of e. e. cummings) was a table in the middle of the central aisle on which were heaped old paperbacks, apples, and ham sandwiches in wax paper on a tray, and a coffee urn. The ham in the sandwiches was surprisingly good—from local Virginia pigs might one hope? Impossible!—it was obliged to come from cans of tinned Virginia ham packed in Chicago.

At this impromptu town square set up about the table, news was passed. Here he learned that David Dellinger had been arrested and released just a short while before he had arrived, and word of others—Dagmar Wilson, leader of Women Strike for Peace, was under arrest, and Dr. Spock had tried to get arrested and the Marshals had refused. There was no word of Macdonald or Lowell—he was certain by now they were back in New York, and was, on the whole, relieved. Macdonald would have enjoyed every minute of prison, but something in the emptiness of these hours would be injurious to Lowell. The very deadness. Installed blindfold in a prison, one might still know before a sound was heard that the walls of a jail were about you, for the center of your breath was dead.

There were rumors of course. Rumors were like hypodermics injected into the numb corpus of prison time. They were all going to get out in a few hours went the rumor, because the lawyers would work through the night and the Commissioners would work through the night. It was hard not to be tempted by this prospect. His shirt collar was filthy by now, filthy to the point where he could feel the dirt chafing his neck. He was full of the odor of his own perspiration. That did not bother him yet —he had tolerance for his own—but by tomorrow things would be getting funky. He could take a shower, but not to put on this same shirt and pin-striped suit with the vest. Each hour in jail, the vest became more absurd. It was too late to get back to New York tonight, but how agreeable to sleep at the Hay-Adams instead of here. The latrine with its three thrones was reminiscent of that first universal week of constipation in the army.

Then came the counter-rumors. The Commissioners had gone home for the night. Nothing until morning. More rumors. Massive arrests going on. Prisoners would be coming in all night, so many that nobody would get out tomorrow. Tomorrow was Sunday. The Commissioners would not work on Sunday.

He decided to get a bunk, and settle in. He had friends in the place, and many acquaintances. People he had known for years in Greenwich Village were with him in this dormitory now. There was Bob Nichols for one, Robert Nichols, the architect, and designer of playground equipment—he and his wife had been friends of Mailer's sister for years. Now he had been arrested with Dave Dellinger. Tuli Kupferberg was there, editor of a pre-psychedelic magazine which came out with new titles for

200

each issue, *Birth, Death, Love,* so forth—an amusing magazine with the sharpest teeth in its bite. Then Tuli Kupferberg had become a member of the Fugs. The last time Mailer had seen him was today at the North Parking Lot in the exorcism of the Pentagon. How odd must Nichols and Kupferberg have looked to the Marshals. Kupferberg with his calm gentle face, long flowing black beard, long black hair which reached his shoulders and Nichols, thin, almost cadaverous, with that old-fashioned Wasp integrity in the eye, and the deep cavernous hollow of his cheeks—he looked like Lowell smelted down to the irreducible Puritan.

And there was Teague, the man with the white motorcycle helmet who had been put in the Volkswagen immediately after Mailer, and had then gone to sleep on the floor of the cell in the Post Office. He was wide awake now, he had slept for cause, had gathered his energies, and was now conducting a free school in the dormitory for whoever would listen. A crowd of fifteen or twenty prisoners were invariably around his bunk; his expositions of the value and demerits of the March on the Pentagon were the only active theater in the prison dormitory, and so prisoners gathered, students, hippies, young faculty instructors, even one short heavy-set Irish kid with small squashed features and a red face who looked exactly like a young policeman just finished with training. Probably he was exactly a young policeman assigned to this, his first job, for he never opened his mouth, never spoke to anyone, just listened to everything which was said with the same worried look he must once have had in school when he could not understand what the teacher's words were about. Teague was indubitably a Leninist. One worked for the Revolution twenty-four hours a day, one proselyted, one organized, one explained, one instructed, one inspired, one worked. One took advantage of prison and turned it into a free university for the prisoners where they could acquire revolutionary élan. One took the collective experience of the revolutionary activity (in this case, the assault on the Pentagon) and one analyzed the experience, one extracted the revolutionary content from the less-than-revolutionary chaos of mixed intents, compromised programs, and sell-outs.

Teague was now arguing that the entire assembly, rally, March, and attempted investiture of the Pentagon had been wrong from beginning to end, too ambitious in its promises, too timid in its execution, too mingled in its forces, too amorphous in its lack of control, too compromised in its collaboration with the government—Mailer found himself listening with interest. It was not that he agreed precisely or disagreed with Teague. Everything Teague said was probably true, and yet the indictment was too easy—it had all the hard firm impact of all the sound-as-brickwork-logic of the next step—he had heard Communists and Trotskyists expatiating on social problems and social actions for years with just this same militant, precise, executive command in analyzing the situation, the same compelling sense of structure, same satisfying almost happy dissection and mastication of the bone and tendons of the problem before them, and Mailer had in fact decided years ago, repelled by some bright implacable certainty in the voices of such fulltime Marxists, that Leninism finally was good for Leninists about the way psychoanalysis was good for psychoanalysts. It was a superb mental equivalent to weight-lifting—the brain worked, perspired, flushed itself, and came back with hard tangible increments in mental tone and vigor, but it had nothing to do with the real problem which was: how do you develop enough grace to capture a thief more graceful than yourself? Leninism was built to analyze a world in which all the structures were made of steel—now the sinews of society were founded on transistors so small Dragon Lady could hide them beneath her nail. But it was agreeable nonetheless to Listen-to-Teague, Teague was the happiest man now in this prison, the most active, the most awake, the most resplendent in his element. Mailer thought of arguing with him, but it seemed unfair. If he scored points in debate—which was highly unlikely—he would merely depress the one source of energy in the room.

Definitive word came through. The lawyers were gone, the Commissioners were gone: nobody out until morning.

So Mailer picked his bunk. It was next to Noam Chomsky, a slim sharp-featured man with an ascetic expression, and an air of gentle but absolute moral integrity. Friends at Wellfleet had wanted him to meet Chomsky at a party the summer before—he had been told that Chomsky, although barely thirty, was considered a genius at MIT for his new contributions to linguistics—but Mailer had arrived at the party too late. Now, as he bunked down next to Chomsky, Mailer looked for some way to open a discussion on linguistics—he had an amateur's interest in the subject, no, rather, he had a mad inventor's interest, with several wild theories in his pocket which he had never been able to exercise since he could not understand what he read in linguistics books. So he cleared his throat now once or twice, turned over in bed, looked for a preparatory question, and recognized that he and Chomsky might share a cell for months, and be the best and most civilized of cellmates, before the mood would be proper to strike the first note of inquiry into what was obviously the tightly packed conceptual coils of Chomsky's intellections. Instead they chatted mildly of the day, of the arrests (Chomsky had also been arrested with Dellinger), and of when they would get out. Chomsky—by all odds a dedicated teacher—seemed uneasy at the thought of missing class on Monday.

On that long unwinding passage from the contractions of the day into the deliberations of the dream, Mailer passed through a revery over much traveled and by now level ground where he thought once more of the war in Vietnam, the charges against it, the defenses for it, and his own final condemnation which had landed him here on this filthy blanket and lumpy bed, this smoke-filled barracks air, where he listened half asleep to the echoes of Teague's loud confident Leninist voice, he, Mailer, ex-revolutionary, now last of the small entrepreneurs, Left Conservative, that lonely flag—there was no one in America who had a position even remotely like his own, who else indeed could offer such a solution as he possessed to such a war, such a damnable war. Let us leave him as he passes into sleep. The argument in his brain can be submitted to the reader in the following pages with somewhat more order than Mailer possessed on his long voyage out into the unfamiliar dimensions of prison rest. Let us hope the argument is not too long, for then like most arguments it would merely be repeating a point already made, amassing new facts to shore polemical walls not buttressed sufficiently by the pouring of the first facts.

7: WHY ARE WE IN VIETNAM?

He knew the arguments for the war, and against the war—finally they bored him. The arguments in support of the war were founded on basic assumptions which had not been examined and were endlessly repeated—the arguments to withdraw never pursued the consequences.

He thought we were in the war as the culmination to a long sequence of events which had begun in some unrecorded fashion toward the end of World War II. A consensus of the most powerful middle-aged and elderly Wasps in America—statesmen, corporation executives, generals, admirals, newspaper editors, and legislators had pledged an intellectual troth: they had sworn with a faith worthy of medieval knights that Communism was the deadly foe of Christian culture. If it were not resisted in the postwar world, Christianity itself would perish. So had begun a Cold War with intervals of overt war, mixed with periods of modest collaboration. As Communist China grew in strength, and her antagonisms with the Soviet Union quickened their pace, the old troth of the Wasp knights had grown sophisticated and abstract. It was now a part of the technology of foreign affairs, a thesis to be called upon when needed. The latest focus of this thesis was of course to be found in Vietnam. The arguments presented by the parties of war suggested that if Vietnam fell to the Communists, soon then would Southeast Asia, Indonesia, the Philippines, Australia, Japan, and India fall also to the Chinese Communists. Since these Chinese Communists were in the act of developing a nuclear striking force, America would face eventually a united Asia (and Africa?) ready to engage America (and Russia?) in a suicidal atomic war which might level the earth, a condition to the advantage of the Chinese Communists, since their low level of subsistence would make it easier for them to recover from the near to unendurable privations of the post-atomic world.

Like most simple political theses, this fear of a total nuclear war was not uttered aloud by American statesmen, for the intimations of such a thesis are invariably more powerful than the thesis itself. It was sufficient that a paralysis of thought occurred in the average American at the covert question: should we therefore bomb the nuclear installations of the Chinese now? Obviously, public discussion preferred to move over to the intricate complexities of Vietnam. Of course, that was an ugly unattractive sometimes disgraceful war, murmured the superior apologists for the Hawks, perhaps the unhappiest war America had ever fought, but it was one of the most necessary, for (1) it demonstrated to China that she could not advance her guerrilla activities into Asia without paying a severe price; (2) it rallied the small Asian powers to confidence in America; (3) it underlined the depth of our promise to defend small nations; (4) it was an inexpensive means of containing a great power, far more inexpensive than fighting the power itself; and (5) it was probably superior to starting a nuclear war on China.

In answer, the debaters best armed for the Doves would reply that it was certainly an ugly disgraceful unattractive war but not necessary to our defense. If South Vietnam fell to the Vietcong, Communism would be then not 12,000 miles from our shores, but 11,000 miles. Moreover, we had not necessarily succeeded in demonstrating to China that guerrilla wars exacted too severe a price from the Communists. On the contrary, a few more guerrilla wars could certainly bankrupt America, since we now had 500,000 troops in South Vietnam to the 50,000 of the North Vietnamese, and our costs for this one small war had mounted to a figure between $25,000,000,000 and $30,000,000,000 a year, not so small an amount if one is reminded that the Second World War cost a total of $300,000,000,000 over four years, or less than three times as much on an average year as Vietnam! (Of course, there has been inflation since, but still! What incredible expense for so small a war—what scandals of procurement yet to be uncovered. How many more such inexpensive wars could the economy take?)

The Doves picked at the seed of each argument. Yes, they said, by fulfilling our commitments to South Vietnam, we have certainly inspired confidence in the other small Asian powers. But who has this confidence? Why the most reactionary profiteers of the small Asian nations now have the confidence; so the small Asian nations are polarized, for the best of their patriots, foreseeing a future plunder of Asia by Asian Capitalists under America's protection, are forced over to the Communists.

Yes, the Doves would answer, it is better to have a war in Vietnam than to bomb China, but then the war in Vietnam may serve as the only possible pretext to attack China. Besides the question of Chinese aggression has been begged. China is not, by its record, an aggressive nation, but a timid one, and suffers from internal contradictions which will leave her incapable for years of even conceiving of a major war.

This was not the least of the arguments of the Doves: they could go on to point out that North Vietnam had been occupied for centuries by China, and therefore was as hostile to China as Ireland was to England—our intervention had succeeded therefore in bringing North Vietnam and China closer together. This must eventually weaken the resistance of other small Asian powers to China.

Besides, said the Doves, part of the real damage of Vietnam takes place in America where civil rights have deteriorated into city riots, and an extraordinary number of the best and most talented students in America are exploring the frontiers of nihilism and drugs.

The Doves seemed to have arguments more powerful than the Hawks. So the majority of people in America, while formidably patriotic were also undecided and tended to shift in their opinion like the weather. Yet the Hawks seemed never too concerned. They held every power securely but one, a dependable consensus of public opinion. Still this weakness left them unperturbed—their most powerful argument remained inviolate. There, the Doves never approached. The most powerful argument remained: what if we leave Vietnam, and all Asia eventually goes Communist? all of Southeast Asia, Indonesia, the Philippines, Australia, Japan, and India?

Well, one could laugh at the thought of Australia going Communist. The Hawks were nothing if not humorless. If Communist China had not been able to build a navy to cross the Straits of Formosa and capture Taiwan, one did not see them invading Australia in the next century. No, any decent Asian Communist would probably shudder at the thought of engaging the Anzacs, descendants of the men who fought at Gallipoli. Yes, the Hawks were humorless, and Lyndon Johnson was shameless. He even invoked the defense of Australia.

But could the Dove give bona fides that our withdrawal from Vietnam would produce no wave of Communism through Asia? Well, the Dove was resourceful in answers, and gave many. The Dove talked of the specific character of each nation, and the liberal alternatives of supporting the most advanced liberal elements in these nations, the Dove returned again and again to the profound weaknesses of China, the extraordinary timidity of Chinese foreign policy since the Korean war, spoke of the possibility of enclaves, and the resources of adroit, well-managed economic war in Asia.

Yet the Doves, finally, had no answer to the Hawks. For the Doves were divided. Some of them, a firm minority, secretly desired Asia to go Communist, their sympathies were indeed with Asian peasants, not American corporations, they wanted what was good for the peasant, and in private they believed Communism was probably better suited than Capitalism to introduce the technological society to the peasant. But they did not consider it expedient to grant this point, so they talked around it. The others, the majority of the Doves, simply refused to face the possibility. They were liberals. To explore the dimensions of the question, might have exploded the foundation of their liberalism, for they would have had to admit they were willing to advocate policies which could conceivably end in major advances of Asian Communism, and this admission might oblige them to move over to the Hawks.

Mailer was bored with such arguments. The Hawks were smug and self-righteous, the Doves were evasive of the real question.

Mailer was a Left Conservative. So he had his own point of view. To himself he would suggest that he tried to think in the style of Marx in order to attain certain values suggested by Edmund Burke. Since he was a conservative, he would begin at the root. He did not see all wars as bad. He could conceive of wars which might be noble. But the war in Vietnam was bad for America because it was a bad war, as all wars are bad if they consist of rich boys fighting poor boys when the rich boys have an advantage in the weapons. He recollected a statistic: it was droll if it was not obscene. Next to every pound of supplies the North Vietnamese brought into South Vietnam for their soldiers, the Americans brought in one thousand pounds. Yes, he would begin at the root. All wars were bad which undertook daily operations which burned and bombed large numbers of women and children; all wars were bad which relocated populations (for the root of a rich peasant lore was then destroyed) all wars were bad which had no line of battle or discernible climax (an advanced notion which supposes that wars may be in part good because they are sometimes the only way to define critical conditions rather than blur them) certainly all wars were bad which took some of the bravest young men of a nation and sent them into combat with outrageous superiority and outrageous arguments: such conditions of combat had to excite a secret passion for hunting other humans. Certainly any war was a bad war which required an inability to reason as the price of retaining one's patriotism; finally any war which offered no prospect of improving itself as a war—so complex and compromised were its roots—was a bad war. A good war, like anything else which is good, offers the possibility that further effort will produce a determinable effect upon chaos, evil, or waste. By every conservative measure (reserving to Conservatism the right to approve of wars) the war in Vietnam was an extraordinarily bad war.

Since he was also a *Left* Conservative, he believed that radical measures were sometimes necessary to save the root. The root in this case was the welfare of the nation, not the welfare of the war. So he had an answer to the Hawks. It was: pull out of Vietnam completely. Leave Asia to the Asians. What then would happen?

He did not know. Asia might go to the Communists, or it might not. He was certain no one alive knew the answer to so huge a question as that. It was only in the twentieth century, in the upper chambers of technology land (both Capitalist *and* Communist) that men began to believe there must be concrete answers to every large question. No! So far as he had an opinion (before the vastness of this question) his opinion existed on the same order of magnitude of undiscovered ignorance as the Opinion of any Far Eastern expert. While he thought it was probable most of Asia would turn to Communism in the decade after any American withdrawal from that continent, he did not know that it really mattered. In those extraordinary World War II years when the Wasp admirals, generals, statesmen, legislators, editors, and corporation presidents had whispered to each other that the next war was going to be Christianity versus Communism, the one striking omission in their Herculean crusade was the injunction to read Marx. They had studied his ideas, of course; in single-spaced extracts on a typewritten page! but because they had not read his words, but merely mouthed the extracts, they had not had the experience of encountering a mind which taught one to reason, even to reason away from his own mind; so the old Wasps and the young Wasps in the power elite could not comprehend that Communists who read their Marx might come to reason away from the particular monoliths of Marxism which had struck the first spark of their faith. It seemed never to occur to the most powerful Wasps that one could count quite neatly on good Communists and bad Communists just as one would naturally expect good Christians and bad. In fact, just as Christianity seemed to create the most unexpected saints, artists, geniuses, and great warriors out of its profound contradictions, so Communism seemed to create great heretics and innovators and converts (Sartre and Picasso for two) out of the irreducible majesty of Marx's mind (perhaps the greatest single tool for cerebration Western man had ever produced). Or at least—and here was the kernel of Mailer's sleeping thesis —Communism would continue to produce heretics and great innovators just so long as it expanded. Whenever it ceased to expand, it would become monolithic again, mediocre, and malign. An ogre.

An explanation? A submersion of Asia in Communism was going to explode a shock into Marxism which might take a half century to digest. Between Poland and India, Prague and Bangkok, was a diversity of primitive lore which would jam every fine gear of the Marxist. There were no quick meals in Asia. Only indigestion. The real difficulty might be then to decide who would do more harm to Asia, Capitalism or Communism. In either case, the conquest would be technological, and so primitive Asian societies would be uprooted. Probably, the uprooting would be savage, the psychic carnage unspeakable. He did not like to contemplate the compensating damage to America if it chose to dominate a dozen Asian nations with its technologies and its armies while having to face their guerrilla wars.

No, Asia was best left to the Asians. If the Communists absorbed those countries, and succeeded in building splendid nations who made the transition to technological culture without undue agony, one would be forced to applaud; it seemed evident on the face of the evidence in Vietnam, that America could not bring technology land to Asia without bankrupting itself in operations ill-conceived, poorly comprehended, and executed in waste. But the greater likelihood was that if the Communists prevailed in Asia they would suffer in much the same fashion. Divisions, schisms, and sects would appear. An endless number of collisions between primitive custom and Marxist dogma, a thousand daily pullulations of intrigue, a heritage of cruelty, atrocity, and betrayal would fall upon the Communists. It was not difficult to envision a time when one Communist nation in Asia might look for American aid against another Communist nation. Certainly Russia and China would be engaged in a cold war with each other for decades. Therefore, to leave Asia would be precisely to gain the balance of power. The answer then was to get out, to get out any way one could. Get out. There was nothing to fear—perhaps there never had been. For the more Communism expanded, the more monumental would become its problems, the more flaccid its preoccupations with world conquest. In the expansion of Communism, was its own containment. The only force which could ever defeat Communism, was Communism itself.

Yet there was no likelihood America would ever withdraw from Asia. Rather there was the covert and unhappy intimation that we were in Vietnam because we had to be. Such was the imbalance of the nation that war was its balance. The burning of villages by napalm might be the index of our collective instability.

Mailer had been going on for years about the diseases of America, its oncoming totalitarianism, its oppressiveness, its smog—he had written so much about the disease he had grown bored with his own voice, weary of his own petulance; the war in Vietnam offered therefore the grim pleasure of confirming his ideas. The disease he had written about existed now in open air: so he pushed further in his thoughts—the paradox of this obscene unjust war is that it provided him new energy—even as it provided new energy to the American soldiers who were fighting it.

He came at last to the saddest conclusion of them all for it went beyond the war in Vietnam. He had come to decide that the center of America might be insane. The country had been living with a controlled, even fiercely controlled, schizophrenia which had been deepening with the years. Perhaps the point had now been passed. Any man or woman who was devoutly Christian and worked for the American Corporation, had been caught in an unseen vise whose pressure could split their mind from their soul. For the center of Christianity was a mystery, a son of God, and the center of the corporation was a detestation of mystery, a worship of technology. Nothing was more intrinsically opposed to technology than the bleeding heart of Christ. The average American, striving to do his duty, drove further every day into working for Christ, and drove equally further each day in the opposite direction—into working for the absolute computer of the corporation. Yes and no, 1 and 0. Every day the average American drove himself further into schizophrenia; the average American believed in two opposites more profoundly apart than any previous schism in the Christian soul. Christians had been able to keep some kind of sanity for centuries while countenancing love against honor, desire versus duty, even charity opposed in the same heart to the lust for power—that was difficult to balance but not impossible. The love of the Mystery of Christ, however, and the love of no Mystery whatsoever, had brought the country to a state of suppressed schizophrenia so deep that the foul brutalities of the war in Vietnam were the only temporary cure possible for the condition —since the expression of brutality offers a definite if temporary relief to the schizophrenic. So the average good Christian American secretly loved the war in Vietnam. It opened his emotions. He felt compassion for the hardships and the sufferings of the American boys in Vietnam, even the Vietnamese orphans. And his view of the war could shift a little daily as he read his paper, the war connected him to his newspaper again: connection to the outside world, and the small shift of opinions from day to day are the two nostrums of that apothecary where schizophrenia is treated. America needed the war. It would need a war so long as technology expanded on every road of communication, and the cities and corporations spread like cancer; the good Christian Americans needed the war or they would lose their Christ.

In his sleep did Mailer think of his favorite scheme, of a war which took place as a war game? of a tract of land in the Amazon, and three divisions of Marines against three divisions of the best Chinese Communists, and real bullets, and real airplanes, real television, real deaths? It was madness. He could not present the scheme in public without exercising the audience—they were certain he

212

had discovered the mechanism of a new and gargantuan put-on, no one could take it seriously, not even as a substitute for Vietnam. No, the most insane of wars was more sane than the most insane of games. A pity. Before he had gone to sleep, he had talked for a while with one of the guards, a mournful middle-aged Southerner with a high forehead, big jaw, long inquiring nose, and the ubiquitous silver-rimmed spectacles. The guard had been upset by the sight of so many college boys romping in the dormitory, pleasant looking boys, obviously pleased with themselves. So the guard had asked tentative questions about the war in Vietnam and how they all felt, and why they felt as they did, and Mailer tried to answer him, and thought it was hopeless. You could use every argument, but it was useless, because the guard didn't want to care. If he did, he would be at war against the cold majesty of the Corporation. The Corporation was what brought him his television and his security, the Corporation was what brought him the unspoken promise that on Judgment Day he would not be judged, for Judgment Day—so went the unspoken promise—was no worse than the empty spaces of the Tonight Show when you could not sleep.

Mailer slept. Given this portrait of his thoughts who would make book he did not snore?

8: WANITY

His suit was in poor shape by morning. There had not been a hanger nor a clothes rack, just a dark green locker next to every cot of the sort to be seen in a broken down gym—the locks were removed, the hooks were smashed, and the shelf had a layer of dust. He had been obliged to fold his suit about his shirt, and stuff the bundle onto the shelf—in the morning he made half successful efforts to

213

beat the marks of the dust out of his pants. His regimental tie, stripes of wide dark blue, and wide maroon, had been tied too often in a Windsor knot, and now needed pressing—he left it off, left off his vest, walked with open dirty white collar and wrinkled jacket to breakfast. Nor was he able to shave—there was, of course, no equipment. In a prison, the razor blades are counted.

He had thought of sleeping through. The call to eat came somewhere around seven, and he had not gone to bed until three, but in a place like this, one never missed an opportunity to see a new locale: each item in the schedule was an event. He had a hint of the psychology of the prison day—a man could keep his humor by refining his sense of confirmed expectation—raisin bread instead of white bread might be the largest surprise of the hour.

They walked down the cloistered arcade of new brick along the quadrangle, the last of the dew offering lights in the grass, the prison architecture appearing even more agreeable than the average of spanking new junior colleges on this fine October Sunday morning in Virginia, then marched into the cafeteria, where some Negroes—bona fide prisoners!—served them from the chow line with sidelong looks, fascinated by white men who would volunteer for this incarceration.

Breakfast was a small Dixie cup of canned or frozen orange and grapefruit juice, so concentrated with additive that it burned his throat. Then came three slices of raisin bread, margarine, corn flakes, milk, a slice of lemon cake with much soft icing, and a mug of coffee. He took it all. He was a ritualist about breakfast—he would eat the same breakfast all but ten days a year, and it was not much like this breakfast—his scrambled eggs were made ideally in subscription to a tried method—but it was obvious that for a day in prison, nothing was going to be particularly connected to anything else; if the night had felt like a journey in a smoking car, the morning might as well begin with lemon icing on the cake. But then just as the battered dark green lockers had given him a vista of precisely the sort of cheap gyms the regular prisoners in Occoquan would have known for years, so this sweet

214

starchy breakfast spoke of the ego-bulking hash-house foods of the poor—all that concentrate of sugar to cheer you up.

Back in the dormitory, the day was beginning. He lingered by the coffee urn, going over the paperbacks. Last night, true to a maxim he had formed in Bellevue that one should try in prison to read only the more difficult books, he had selected a paperback called *A Primer on Money, Banking, and Gold,* but the lemon cake had been bullion enough, and now he went again through the books on the automatic hope something interesting had been returned, but there was only the same litter of mystery stories by authors whose names changed with every book (years of contractual hanky panky in paperback houses must be concealed in this litter) and one book he might have looked at in another hour of boredom—a life of *Saint John Bosco—Friend of Youth.* Friend of who? Saint John Bosco must be the first saint of Camp.

The rumors were livelier this morning at the coffee urn. Something had gone on at the Pentagon. Prisoners had been brought in the middle of the night, and were installed now in another dormitory. Prisoners here claimed to have talked to them. Some of the new ones had been badly beaten by the Marshals. Everybody wanted to know how many had been arrested—calculations of the total varied from two hundred to four hundred, and groans replied to the low totals, cheers to the high—they were reacting to the score at a ball game. It was a natural reaction for any American, Mailer decided, but he could anticipate the horror of European revolutionaries, "These Americans," they would hiss, "cannot comprehend an historic occurrence unless it takes place by the numbers!"

Teague was lecturing again. It was not eight o'clock in the morning, and the sun came through the high windows in the high walls of the dormitory at an evocative angle —evocative of early morning studies in a college library. Yet, the Occoquan Free School for Transient Nascent Revolutionaries was in full swing, and First Preceptor Teague, a battery of siege guns in one vocal box, was battering the walls of assumption by which the National Mobilization Committee to End the War in Vietnam had incarcerated the revolutionary potential of the demonstration.

"The precise objective was never even defined," he heard Teague say to his fifteen or twenty auditors. "In order to hold his middle-class elements, and imbue the movement with a patina of respectability, Dellinger frittered away the opportunity to mobilize the real militants, who could have organized a concerted and *successful* attack on the Pentagon. As a result of such compromise, undefined at best, unscrupulous conceivably"—he held up a finger—"at worst, what has happened? The militants have been unsuccessful, and the moderate middle-class peace elements will be miserable tomorrow when the newspapers get done with their condemnations of the activities of those groups which wanted—and to a degree got—overt action."

There was much in what Teague said. It would probably not be far from his own summary. Why then did he resent him, feel the pinch of the hanging judge in his critical nerve? It must be Teague's certainty. Doubtless there had been something wrong in the style of the move on the Pentagon, but it would take him weeks to comprehend this March, and the events now taking place: it was only by forcing his mind to the subject that he could recognize something was still going on at the Pentagon—prisoner of his own egotism, some large vital part of the March had ended for him with his own arrest. He was poor material for a general indeed if he had no sense of the major combat twenty miles away.

He passed through a few conversations. A tall very thin man with an eroded face, and a pale consistent flame in his eye came up to him. (How many eyes had he seen in these last few days on fire with their own soul the better to purify it? or in the dread of not consuming it?) The tall man now introduced himself. He was Jim Peck, a name well-known in radical circles, for Peck had been the first of the Freedom Riders back in the late forties, one of the first Whites to be beaten by Southern policemen, to have his teeth smashed, his ribs kicked. He had respect for Peck, how could one not? yet he also had the instinctive withdrawal of a meat-eater before an ascetic.

The morning worked along. About ten, lawyers arrived and gave them orientation lectures in groups of six. The answers to their questions were scrupulous and empty of content, for no one knew exactly what the government was planning to do today. They were all given, however, one piece of advice most concrete—plead Nolo Contendere. Mailer objected. He wished to plead Guilty. He was after all guilty for a purpose which he wished to advertise, and Nolo Contendere had something soft about it to the ear, like copping a plea on a billy rubbed with olive oil. But the lawyer merely looked unhappy when he raised his objection, and answered blankly, "The Legal Defense Committee seems to think it's best to plead Nolo Contendere."

Where the devil was de Grazia? What kind of friend was he? But shortly after, prisoners began to be called, and they were told to take their belongings. They did not come back. Now the lawyers had word. The sentences appeared to be more or less standard. Regardless of the charge, Blocking a Roadway, Resisting Arrest, Entering a Forbidden Area, et cetera, et cetera, the fines were running at $25 and the sentences were for five days but suspended. Plus the written promise not to return to the Pentagon for six months. This did not seem unreasonable.

Then he saw Tuli Kupferberg sitting on a bunk. He had the impression Kupferberg had been called out some time ago; now he was back. It developed that Kupferberg had refused to agree to stay away from the Pentagon for six months—so he would have to serve his five days. Kupferberg was not particularly happy; with his beard and long hair, he did not think it was going to be altogether routine when the majority of the Pentagon protesters were gone, and he was then dropped in with the regular prison population. But he did not see any way out of it. To agree not to return to the Pentagon for six months was to collaborate with the government—what then had they been protesting?

Mailer listened to him with a dull ear. He hated to become enmeshed in these unmanageable connections between politics and personal morality. To a part of him, Kupferberg seemed absolutely right. "The essence of spirit was to choose that alternative which did not better your position, but made it worse." Mailer was quoting himself again, but not with pleasure, for he was getting ready to go against his own maxims. He knew that he wanted to get out of this jail, and as quickly as possible. Early this morning, he had put his name on the list for the telephone, and so had been able to make a call to his wife just a while ago. It had been a merry call. They were anxious to see each other, and she had brightened at the news he would almost certainly be out this day. They had laughed gently at Lowell's concern. Back in New York, he had called several times to express his worry. And Macdonald had called and left a message. "Tell Norman he's one up on me." The sunlight he could now see through the high dormitory window was about in balance with his memory (three days old) of her blond hair—which was one advantage of being a blonde—sunlight advertised you. Of course her hair was tinted delicately, but then which blonde was not? "A blonde is a girl who chooses to be blonde. She's an optimist. She thinks that life will turn out well for her." It had been perhaps his favorite scene in the play of *The Deer Park*. He was breaking all his own maxims—he was missing his wife much too much; he was full of hope that he would be out of this dormitory in another hour, and he was even quoting himself over and over.

But Kupferberg had left him with a moral dilemma. He had his answer of course. Nothing was accomplished by staying in jail—the point had been to get arrested, not to go to war against the sentence. Nothing would happen at the Pentagon for six months; so the promise would cost nothing. He found himself discussing the problem in just this light with several of the younger prisoners. Kupferberg's decision had presented everyone with a Sunday dilemma.

"But what," asked a bearded young sociology instructor (from a small college in Connecticut), "if something is planned at the Pentagon in the next six months?"

"Why, then," said Mailer, "we go to the Pentagon. This promise is probably unconstitutional anyway."

"I'm sure it is," said the instructor.

"Then why serve five days? They must know they're being unconstitutional. So you're collaborating with their trick."

Yes, his arguments were cogent, but his cool had most undeniably been cracked. There was the definite taint of an unholy desire to get out, as if to remain too long was dangerous. Seen from one moral position—not too far from his own—prison could be nothing but an endless ladder of moral challenges. Each time you climbed a step, as Kupferberg just had, another higher, more dangerous, more disadvantageous step would present itself. Sooner or later, you would have to descend. It did not matter how high you had climbed. The first step down in a failure of nerve always presented the same kind of moral nausea. Probably, he was feeling now like people who had gone to the Pentagon, but had chosen not to get arrested, just as such people, at their moment of decision, must have felt as sickened as all people who should have marched from Lincoln Memorial to the Pentagon, but didn't. The same set of emotions could be anticipated for all people who had been afraid to leave New York. One ejected oneself from guilt by climbing the ladder—the first step back, no matter where, offered nothing but immersion into nausea. No wonder people hated to disturb their balance of guilt. To become less guilty, then weaken long enough to return to guilt was somehow worse than to remain cemented in your guilt. There was something exorbitant in the divine breadth of this moral equation.

"But what," asked the sociology instructor, "if all of us were to serve the five days?"

"They would not rescind their demand that we stay away from the Pentagon." Did he really know? "Look," said Mailer, "we each have to do what we think we must do. I have to be back in New York. I think there are things I must do there which are more important." Kupferberg had put the day into depression; he was no longer in any degree fond of himself. So his fellow prisoners began to cloy the air of his mood. They were for the most part a fair group of young men, their faces were generally good, their minds seemed no more ridden with jargon than any gang of college students he might meet at a lec-

219

ture or a reading, but the sameness of this condition in the dormitory had gone on too long. About eleven, lunch had been served—a carton on the table of the same ham sandwiches they had had last night, a basket of apples, containers of milk with the taste of wax and milk. It was all mixed somehow with the company. He felt as if he had been on an all night party in a college dormitory with no girls, no booze, just lots of cigarette smoke and endless conversation. His own saliva tasted to him now of the air of a subway. A subtle hell offered its perspective—if you were an intellectual and a bad one, no matter how, you might end in some eternity like this, with nothing but the sounds of conversations already held to entertain the ear, nothing but books like *Saint John Bosco—Friend of Youth* to exercise the brain.

In the early afternoon a prisioner made his escape. At one end of the dormitory was a single door which led to the shower room and to a room beyond where there were several guards, a number of benches, and a desk. In this doorway, between the outer room and the long dormitory, a guard was posted, the only guard for these hundred beds. It had not been then too difficult. One of the kids at the other end had climbed up on top of a locker, and while the guard was being diverted by a prisoner, had slipped through the open window high on the wall above the locker and dropped to the ground outside. He had escaped. Everyone in the room was aware of it, everyone but the guard; the stale heat of the early afternoon, dull-odored and somnolent (with its hint of why factory mills would not necessarily thrive in the South) now took on a whiff of new breeze from the collective adrenaline of the prisoners. To the glee of some, was mixed the worry of others that their release would be delayed.

But in five minutes a squad of guards abruptly appeared, raced down the floor, inspected the window, moved the locker, and left—but with an additional guard posted at the far end of the dormitory where the prisoner had escaped. As the squad now moved back to the door, the leader of these guards, a short wiry man with a firm dry face, spoke to the prisoners at large. With a tight grin, and a jerk of his thumb in the direction of the field beyond the window where the boy had escaped, he said, "You know, we do have a man or two out there."

"But Officer," Mailer called out in his best country squire voice, "I thought you were a minimum security prison."

"Well, sir," said the guard, "we *was!*"

It raised his mood a hint, and when he went out to the front room to confer for a minute with a lawyer named Hirschkop who brought regards from de Grazia, he had an opportunity to see the escaped prisoner. They had just brought him in, a red-bearded young goat with a red look in his eye and a lithe stubborn spring to his moves. This spring was clear to see, for he was not cooperating, they were having to carry him in. Since he merely pretended to be limp, but in fact kept twisting his limbs and springing them free, the guards were having a poor time. A big middle-aged Negro in uniform at the desk went up to one of the guards so struggling, and said, "Let me take over for you. This damn kid's gonna hurt your hernia."

The guard, a tall skinny white man, shook his head. "Naw, I can manage him," he said. But he looked worried.

"Listen," said the Negro, "you let me have him now. You just take care of your hernia." So the prisoner was brought back with his legs held by the black man. Great cheers greeted them as they came into the dormitory.

But Mailer kept thinking of the guards. He had had a conversation the night before with a handsome young monitor who had been in the adjoining cell at the Post Office. He was one of the best prisoners, bright, strong, personable, a member of SDS—he had spent his summer at a teach-in in Oregon on the war, and yet his pleasure the night before was that they had managed to paste a great many stickers on their cell wall, and this monitor was laughing as he thought of how the hack would react when he had to read the slogans while cleaning the cell. Mailer was thinking of what his in-laws would feel for the hack, that poor hack with his store teeth, his misery that he had to work on the weekend. These middle-class kids, no matter the depth of their commitment, were also hav-

221

ing a game with the campus cop. But the guards were here to work out the long slow stages of a grim tableau —the recapitulation of that poverty-ridden rural childhood which had left them with the usual constipated mixture of stinginess and greed, blocked compassion and frustrated desires for power.

They were men, but the one secret route back, there down in the cellar of the hierarchies of schizophrenic ranch-house life in America, was by finding a life which recaptured the cold stringy gruel of their own parents in their own poor large family, step by step, degree by degree, dealing with prisoners everyday, doling out a kindness here one degree more kind than they had once received, dropping a stinginess there to get the barb of an old stinginess out, yes their relation to the poor Negroes and the poor whites in this workhouse was a parallel to their own childhood, of course, a slow solemn process of exchanging psychic equivalents in order to remake their nervous system. This horde of middle-class kids now descended on them had left such careful slow over-cautious work of reconstruction in a shambles, for the kids treated them like nannies, the kids were revolutionaries; to them the flesh was no better than the symbol of the uniform: how then could the doctor cure the disease if he was also buried in it? Stale thoughts. His detestation of prison came from the mark it left on the mind. He had been in the coop not twenty-four hours and his mind was already feeling stale.

Now he forced himself to listen to the lawyer Hirschkop, who was chatting with Teague and himself. It was with Teague that Mailer had been called out—just in time to see the Negro guard protect the white guard's hernia—Teague and he were apparently the most important prisoners left, for this new lawyer had introduced himself as Chief Counsel for the Demonstrators and he, for one, had answers, was definitive, showed confidence, a man about Mailer's height, but built like a young bull. A perfect fullback. His physique spoke of the ability to mount a good second effort, which was the term in football this season for being able to drive hard with the ball, and when stopped by tacklers, able to drive forward again before the whistle blew.

No need for a second effort now—he was merely giving them a quiet orientation, but Mailer was not unhappy he was there. If he had once thought he would be out in an hour after his arrest, the slow mounting weight of his detention all these inexplicable hours—what had happened to his priority?—had given him, not a panic, but a dull set of expectations.

Actually, Hirschkop's presence was enough to reassure him. He hardly listened. Instead, he was thinking of Teague who seemed to show no resentment to Mailer now. That morning he had helped to spoil a plan of Teague's. The free school had revealed a purpose. After hours of lecturing the night before and hours of lecturing in the morning, Teague had convinced a number of prisoners of a number of points. A letter was drafted to be released to the press, and Teague had read it aloud to the dormitory. It had contained something like eighteen items, and each item was critical of the National Mobilization. The letter ended by condemning the leadership.

Debate on Teague's proposal had sounded for ten minutes with much loud argument back and forth. In the beginning, Teague's new-forged allies showed promise of stimulating everyone to sign. Then came counter-arguments. Jim Peck had cried out, "Why this letter is divisive!" Mailer had made a curt speech. "Maybe there are ten million people in American today who think we're heroes. Can't we let them be happy for a few months before they find out we're not!" This speech seemed to make a small difference. Sentiment turned toward carrying such criticism to a meeting, rather than into a newspaper. Finally Teague decided to redraft the letter, and present the criticism intramurally. Mailer had thought Teague might resent his speech since he had obviously been working with this letter as his end. Mailer had done as much as anyone to thwart him. But Teague gave no sign of rancor. Teague was a professional.

As they were walking back to the dormitory, Mailer asked, "What would you have done if you had managed to get into the Pentagon and hold a corridor for a while?"

"Oh, I don't know," said Teague. "We could have painted the walls, created disruption generally."

Yes, it was a battle conceived unlike any other, for in a symbolic war, victory had no tangible fruit. Once again, Mailer wished he could be out of this prison in order to think. In prison his thoughts could only meander. There was an explanation to the attack on the Pentagon. It was somewhere in the shape of this event. If only he could brood on it.

In the afternoon sun, the air grew heavier, boredom took on dimension. There was the mounting pressure on the ear of a horsefly buzzing in a dirty room. New prisoners had arrived in the dorm, shock troops of a new wave of arrests, and their presence disturbed the atmosphere. The original cadre of prisoners had become respectable in these hours—they were virtually trustees of the dorm—so the new prisoners seemed raucous, of a different code, not pacifists and academics at all. Many of them had been in fights with Marshals; there were bandages and bloody heads, torn clothing, more: someting drunk and violent, full of pot, like spring rioters in a small college town ready to get into a rumble with the police. Mailer took a stroll the length of the dormitory and back—it was enough to verify his first impression.

"Hey, you Norman Mailer?" asked one rangy prisoner, grabbing his arm. There was a rollercoster in the boy's eye, a big Yahoo tone. He had obviously been in some action. He still was cocked on whatever he had taken.

"Yeah."

"We got to talk." The grip deepened, the eye was red.

He threw off the arm. "When the time comes, buddy." Through stale sweat, and all rancid prison air, he could feel adrenaline coming again. Half the kids who had just arrived would be his admirers. For want of a live Hemingway, he would be expected to serve as the poor man's Papa.

If half of these new kids proved to be admiring, they would certainly be the sort who couldn't bear an admiration until they had had a fight with it. If the admiration won, they could admire it even more—if it lost, they would be sad. Yes, Mailer decided, on the basis of past experience there was one good chance in three or four, he would be in a real fight before dark. That would certainly help him to get out, yes it would. He would get out of the dormitory and into isolation.

But now he was worrying—the one thing he had sworn he would not do in prison. He lay on his bunk, and made a determined effort to stay cool—all the while, his nerve for adventure, hitherto dormant this day, now urged him to circulate among the new prisoners, go looking for the trouble, sweat it right through. From experience, he knew that was the best and simplest way.

But prison had other rules. If he got into a bad fight, he would then be doubly in the hands of the authorities —what was worst about prison is that you must imprison your own best instincts, avoid anything which looked like action. Yes, the wise book of prison said, "Wait. By evening these new prisoners will look like the old ones. The air of the dormitory will grind them down. Saint John Bosco will grind them down."

Visions of his wife and family kept him on his bunk. Now one of the guards (or may it have been one of the lawyers?) brought in the Sunday papers. One of the prisoners began to read aloud, and as he did other prisoners with a pent and happy fury—happy because there was finally something to express—began to roar their responses in unison.

The restrained and carefully instructed troops at the Pentagon met provocation with a minimum of force.

"Bullshit!" shouted the prisoners happily.

They were pelted with rocks from the crowd and according to reliable Pentagon sources were the target of three tear gas grenades thrown by demonstrators. There was no retaliation in kind ordered by the army . . .

"Bullshit! Bullshit! Bullshit!" chanted the prisoners.
The boy read on through long news stories. Then through columns. He read Jimmy Breslin aloud.

These were not the kind of kids who were funny.
225

These were the small core of dropouts and drifters and rabble . . .

"Bullshit! Bullshit! Bullshit!" chanted the prisoners. At the end of the day, the only concern anybody could have was for the soldiers who were taking the abuse.

"Bull*shit!* Bull*shit!*" sang the prisoners happily.

He dozed to the sound of their chant, had a fantasy which belonged in *The Magic Christian*—he would buy a television station, and a commentator would read the news each day, and a chorus of street kids would give comments. Yes, the use of obscenity was indeed to be condemned, for the free use of it would wash away the nation—was American the first great power to be built on bullshit?

He had a private taste of it two minutes later. An odd boy, sly, lumpish, almost moronic, now took over. A Richmond newspaper in his hand, he had blundered onto an account of Mailer's arrest.

He read with the difficulty of a third grader. "When asked why he was arrested, the novelist smiled wainly."

"What?" asked Mailer, getting up from his cot.

"The novelist smiled wainly," said the boy in a mocking tone.

"Wanly," said Mailer and said no more for he could feel the amusement of the others at his anger.

"When asked why he was arrested," the boy repeated in a stilted voice, lip-reading with exaggerations, enjoying the round of theater he had created, "the novelist smiled wainly, and said, 'I am guilty.' "

Mailer took a not altogether playful swipe at the boy.

He remembered the reporter who had been running in front and behind of Leiterman's camera. The reporter had hung on his words. It had been his own best moment in all these days—he had never felt so fair a moment of dignity in his life, and now they had him smiling wanly, saying, "I am guilty." Were they incapable of giving any enemy a fair chance? If the reporter had been before him, he might have tried to tear him apart with his hands.

To calm himself, he spent time with a prisoner he

liked, a quiet soft-spoken small trim Texan from Houston who was a member of SDS. This prisoner never said much, but everything he said was sensible. They spent time idly, pitching pennies to a line in the composition floor. After a while the boy who had read from the newspaper, as if contrite, now came over and joined them quietly. Finally four of them played.

Now came a call from the front room. Mailer was wanted in court.

He put on his regimental tie, trying to hide the deep creases by using more of the wide tongue for the substance of his knot. The front of his tie came out nine inches long, the tail which he stuffed in his pants must have been twenty-six. Then he put on his vest most carefully to cover the asymmetry of these roots, and put on his cufflinks, mother-of-pearl cufflinks, no less! the fanciest cufflinks—might one lay the bet? ever to go into the filthiest cuffs, put on his jacket again, tried in the absence of a comb to flatten his hair with his hands, and feeling like the people's choice between Victor McLaglen and Harpo Marx, went through the dormitory shaking hands, gave a respectful goodbye to Tuli Kupferberg, and headed for the front room.

"Your lawyer is wearing sneakers," said the last of the prisoners.

9: MAILER, DE GRAZIA, HIRSCHKOP, AND SCAIFE

It was de Grazia. He was dressed in a corduroy jacket of moss green, pants of compatible lemon, a red shirt with a white collar. De Grazia's eye for color had even worked an art for he was wearing spotless white sneakers. In some triumph of the sartorial, they were suitable. Mailer did not know how de Grazia had succeeded—he had only to think of himself in a green corduroy jacket

227

with yellow slacks and white sneakers—well, he was not giving compliments yet. He was annoyed at de Grazia for having been invisible till now.

"Where's your tennis racket?" he asked.

But they were in fact friends. They were glad to see each other again. In the wash of events, they had each forgiven the other for Thursday night at the Ambassador.

"Have they talked to you about the plea?" de Grazia asked in his subtle hesitant voice.

"Well, all the lawyers said we should plead Nolo Contendere, but I'd like to plead Guilty."

De Grazia looked uneasy. "We don't want anything about your case to be special."

"Is something up?"

"Nooo." Lawyers, like doctors and literary agents, were obliged to be professionally assuring, but de Grazia was as obviously trying to warn him.

"Come on."

"No, I don't know any reason why it would make any difference. It's just . . ." de Grazia's instinct was to plead Nolo Contendere.

"I don't understand why it should make a difference," he repeated.

Without saying a definite word, with half-phrases and subtle clearings of the throat, hesitations which produced the announcement of nuances next presented by a nod of the head, or a light in the eye, de Grazia succeeded in passing the following unspoken exposition over to Mailer. It seemed that as in all massive legal operations, tacit arrangements to expedite passage of the sheer weight of cases . . . mmm . . . had resulted in certain unofficial agreements: the prisoners would waive their right to a jury trial, would accept the verdict of the U. S. Commissioner who was sitting in judgment, would plead Nolo Contendere, and would receive five-day suspended sentences. All prisoners convening to this tacit arrangement would be treated equally. "There's always the possibility . . . mmm . . . that's to say . . . specially you." It was clear. If he made himself a special case by pleading guilty, the Commissioner might not feel he was entitled to the tacit arrangement.

"Well, can't we see in court?"

De Grazia nodded. "We can try and . . . mmm . . . see what the feeling is."

"What kind of Commissioner have we got?" One of the other lawyers had indicated in one of the orientations that of the four Commissioners, two were good, one was fair, and one was—the lawyer had used the term—an animal.

"I think we have one of the good ones." De Grazia explained that he could not practice in Virginia, so he would be present as a Friend of the Court. If they ran into trouble, they would call on Hirschkop who was swinging from case to case in all four courtrooms, trying to take care of . . . um . . . the tender spots.

They walked out the front door to the arcade, Mailer making a point of saying goodbye to the guards, if only to surprise them. Then they walked to the end of the prison along the arcade, walked up a flight of stairs into a hallway, passed into a very small meeting room or office with seats for fifteen or twenty people in the rear and two desks in the front which served as the bench. There was another case being tried, so he and de Grazia sat down. He noticed Fontaine in the row behind and smiled.

A man with a narrow nondescript red face whispered in his ear. He heard a muttered name and the sound of *The Washington Post*. The stranger was a reporter. "Would you care to make a statement?"

"Not now. Later," he whispered back. It was exactly what would be expected of him that he would make a courtroom speech. Well, he wouldn't. He did not have to spend his life continuing to play their game.

He studied the Commissioner who happened to be wearing a red and blue regimental tie almost indistinguishable from his own. The Commissioner was a pleasant looking, well proportioned, well-built man not yet in his forties, with a low deep voice and a long sloping nose. Back of his high forehead, the crown of his scalp was without hair—he had the half-bald head which seems to come often to athletes. Hearing his accent, Mailer decided he was a Virginian who well might have gone to Princeton. With the half-bald head, he would have proved suitable for any number of commercials requiring gentry on television. But his brown eyes (as Mailer saw them

229

from up close, when he was called and stood in front of the desk) were thoughtful, even bottomless—one could not begin to tell if compassion, concern, or a profound philosophical condemnation looked out of them.

De Grazia spoke for Mailer as they stood side by side. "Commissioner Scaife, Mr. Mailer is interested in entering a plea of . . . um . . . Guilty, but would like if possible to inquire if this would alter the treatment . . . ummm . . . consideration of his case."

The Commissioner looked back at them. Since he was seated on the level, and they were standing, he had to look up at them. But it did not seem to bother him. His eyes were extraordinarily calm, yet very attentive. "I do not think," he said, "that I can answer your question, since that would offer a premature suggestion of the sentence which is obviously improper before hearing the plea."

That was enough for Mailer, it was enough for de Grazia. They looked at each other. There had been something grave and indeed all too bottomless in Commissioner Scaife's voice. "Your honor, in that case, I would like to plead Nolo Contendere." His voice had been all right, but he had not known until the moment he spoke whether it would betray him. He had felt surprisingly short of breath all the while he had stood before this Commissioner. Standing before the Bench always affected him so; whether this was due to some unconscious and conceivably well-placed notion of Judgment, or whether he was finally and fundamentally criminal, a devil indeed, he did not know. Still his voice had been all right. That was just as well. Scaife's eyes blinked back once, then stared dispassionately into his eyes. He found to his surprise that he liked this Commissioner, he liked him as much as any man he had met in the last few days. Indeed they were staring into each other's eyes as equals.

New maxim: if the judge stares thoughtfully into the eyes of the arraigned, he is probably a hanging judge.

"Mr. Mailer," said the Commissioner, "I view your case with somewhat more seriousness than the average case before me today. You are a mature man, responsible for your ideas, well-known, and you exert influence upon many young people. I think a man in your position should not act as a bad example, so I view your offense with greater concern. It is quite possible to exercise your Constitutional rights of protest and dissent without breaking the law. Therefore, I am going to fine you fifty dollars, and give you a sentence of thirty days in jail." He paused, continued to look at Mailer, who continued to look back, and added, "Of these thirty days, twenty-five will be suspended."

Five days. It sat like the sound of the word cancer on the small available area of his soul. Not to get out in the next ten minutes, when he had been so ready to get out, so foolish as to drop his guard. And a sense of woe at what a martyr this would make him, and for so little. To have his name cheered during a season at every deadly dull leftist meeting to raise money—he would trade such fame for a good hour's romp with the—yes, doomed *pater familias*—with the wife and kids.

De Grazia was now pleading his own incompetence to argue for Mailer in a court in Virginia, since he was a District of Columbia lawyer. He requested the assistance of Mr. Hirschkop. The Commissioner answered that the plea had been entered and judged, but on the motion that the defendant was not properly represented, he would listen to further argument by Mr. Hirschkop.

So began a legal contest. It was not important, for nothing was at issue but a few days in jail, yet Hirschkop fought the case for the next twenty minutes as if the hill before him might determine the outcome of the war. And Mailer, now invited to sit down in the rear of this small room by the Commissioner, followed with attention as if there was indeed much more than five days at stake, and he could hardly say why. He detested entertaining any thought which would encourage paranoia in himself, he had indeed gone through these hours in jail with a determined and much diminished sense of himself. Next to his vanity, was a disproportionate modesty—he had actually believed he would be arrested and released with no particular attention paid to him. If he had been moved when one of the prisoners told him demonstrators had heard the news of his arrest while they were still marching on the bridge, he had not attached the fact of his name on radio to anything of such concrete administrative impor-

231

tance as his sentence. He was invariably surprised when authorities took him seriously. Now, he had no idea if the Commissioner had given him this special sentence, different from the others because Scaife was a serious man who had, conceivably, read his books, and decided he was a sophisticated menace to the general welfare of the nation, or whether—and he did not entertain the feel of this—there had been a suggestion from somewhere else to hold him for five days. He did not like the idea of encouraging any paranoia, but he also did not like five days in jail at all. Not now. Did they wish him to be under surveillance next to a good agent, or were they capable of concocting a nasty accident in a corridor, a piece of petty Oswalderie? This seemed vastly far-fetched, but then he had been hearing the ugliest rumors about Vietnam, of men shot in the back on patrol, and worse. Certainly, since the assassination of Kennedy, no political prisoner could necessarily trust an American jail again, not even a political amateur for a routine five days. So he listened with care to the argument. If the government wanted him in for five days, then—government being the agent of war in Vietnam, and so his enemy—he certainly wanted to be out.

Hirschkop's dark hair and powerful short body put double weight back of every remark. He spoke quickly, clearly, with a mixture of brightness, boyishness, and did not believe many of the more pious sentiments he was obliged to express—what he did believe, what stood out about him, was his love of law as an intricate deceptive smashing driving tricky game somewhere between wrestling, football, and philosophy—what also stood out was his love of winning, his tenacity, his detestation of defeat.

He began, much to Mailer's profound embarrassment, by pleading that the sentence be reduced since Mailer had offered no violence in his arrest, had been a model prisoner since, had cooperated with the guards, had helped to maintain decorum among his fellow demonstrators, and had talked some of them into cooperating with the court!

Where had he gotten all this—these half-truths, these indigestible distortions, these pious legalisms about the

232

good prisoner? If not for the impossible social situation of denying his lawyer in court, he would have stood up.

But this motion was quickly denied.

Hirschkop then argued that the sentence was untypical and more punitive than any other for similar cases, and so should be vacated.

The Commissioner turned to the U. S. Attorney, a tall pale Negro named Mason, and asked his opinion. The U.S. Attorney replied that the specific ground for the greater sentence had been stated by the Commissioner. The Commissioner said he would deny the motion.

Hirschkop then moved that the initial plea of Nolo Contendere be withdrawn on the grounds of inadequate counsel. This involved the 6th Amendment and the right to effective counsel. Commissioner Scaife denied the motion.

It was not at all easy to follow but it was interesting. Hirschkop kept attacking with his high-pitched, eager, peppy voice. He would come up with a new argument, he would work it under the eyes of the Commissioner, his voice reacting to every hint of interest or annoyance he could extract from Scaife's impassive face, he was like a wildly successful salesman with an impossibly difficult buyer, there was by now a contest between them, the full equivalent of a show of strength, man to man, full leverage of one man against the full arm of the other. Under the legal dialogue seemed to proceed another. "I'm going to get this guy out today," went the unspoken dialogue of Hirschkop. "You don't know me, Scaife, I'm a persistent guy."

"I'm pretty stubborn myself, friend. You may get this man out, but you'll have to work. Cause he's not getting out on this Commissioner's pity."

"Don't need it. I'm going to show you that the bag of the law is a bottomless bag."

There was of course another battle, the natural face-off between a tough Jew and a well-made son of Virginia gentry—that was in it as well.

"I'll bewitch you, Commissioner, with my legal speed."

"Haven't lost an eye on you yet, Phil."

Well, said Hirschkop, since he was not allowed to get

rid of the sentence or withdraw the plea, he now asked for permission to withdraw the waiver of rights on the ground that the waiver of rights had been given on the implied assurance that the sentence would be moderate, and this tacit assurance had not been kept.

The Commissioner conferred with the U. S. District Attorney and announced that this motion was also denied.

Each time Hirschkop would finish an argument, Scaife would consider it, confer formally with the U. S. Attorney, turn back to Hirschkop, and in a voice resolutely empty of content, neutral as a spirit level, would declare somewhat sepulchrally that this motion was also denied. Each time Hirschkop would recoil back, then bore forward again with a new motion.

After this last one, however, he shifted tactics. Now, he announced he would appeal the case. He asked for bail.

The unspoken dialogue resumed:

"I was wondering how long it would take you get to that."

"If you weren't out to burn my poor novelist, I'd have sprung him already. What did they do—pass the word down?"

"You, my friend, will never know."

"I'm getting him out on bail."

"Wait—you haven't got him out yet."

A second U. S. District Attorney now entered the argument. The Defendant, he remonstrated, had no right to bail unless he had already appealed, or could prove the right to bail on substantial Constitutional grounds.

Hirschkop then argued that the Defendant was prepared to make appeal, but had obviously no opportunity to file appeal.

In that case, said the U. S. District Attorney, bail could not be granted.

"They're going out of their way to keep you in," murmured de Grazia in Mailer's ear. He had been alternately getting up to confer with Hirschkop and coming back to sit beside Mailer.

"Your honor," said Hirschkop, "in precisely these circumstances I was able to obtain bail for H. Rap Brown in the United States District Court in Richmond on September 18, 1967. I was allowed by the court to file notice of appeal which was then accepted as proper basis for appeal bail because it is a Constitutional right."

At this point, the argument grew more complex. Hirschkop kept shuttling between points which involved the procedural rights of a prisoner filing appeal in a Commissioner's Court, and basic substantive rights to bail on Constitutional grounds. The items came so fast, and with such dexterity in their passes and leaps that Mailer while he could not begin to keep up with each detail, was able to study the growing sense of uncertainty on the part of the U. S. Attorney, as if to maintain his resistance here might open the danger of entrapping the government in an untenable legal position which could occasion some future ruling by a higher court to weaken the authority of such a court as this. In that uneasy area, through that precise anxiety, was the breach made. For the first time, the U. S. Attorney took a backward step. He went to a second line of defense. "Commissioner Scaife," he stated, "to file notice of appeal, an appropriate form must be used. We do not have such forms here on Sunday. Defendant will have to be kept over until tomorrow."

They would have him then for another night in jail. But it was also a way of signifying to the Commissioner that bail could not be withheld on primary grounds, but now only on a technicality.

Hirschkop smiled at the Commissioner, and ducked his head, and came forward again. Mailer could hear him citing some particular clause in some book pertinent to courts of this nature which allowed one to file, when proper forms were not available, the same kind of papers in handwritten form.

The Commissioner read the clause. He pressed his lips together carefully, as if to signify the conclusion of an event. Then he opened them. He looked relaxed, so relaxed that Mailer wondered if he were not relieved that a way had been found to keep him out of jail this night. "All right," Scaife nodded, "you may file notice of appeal."

Hirschkop stated that he would have to borrow the

G.S.A. book which offered a model of the proper form —the U. S. Attorney gave him this; and he would need a pencil—which the Commissioner supplied; and a piece of paper—the Court Stenographer tore a sheet off her pad and passed it to him. These transactions completed, Hirschkop, de Grazia, Mailer, Fontaine, and two reporters went into the next room and Hirschkop opened the borrowed book with obvious good humor and began to write out the formal notice of appeal.

"They were really trying to sock it to you," said the reporter sympathetically. But his voice was false, provocative.

"I don't know," said Mailer.

"What's it to them to have you in jail for a few days?"

He didn't answer. He would give this reporter nothing until he decided what he wished to say.

Back in the courtroom, the bail asked by the U. S. Attorney was $500. Hirschkop had the opportunity to do an encore: conditions were clear for a virtuoso—he entered a plea that the prisoner be let out on his own recognizance. Under the provisions of the Federal Bail Reform Act, *responsible* persons were given this privilege. The Commissioner asked on what ground could Counsel establish Defendant's right to said provision of the Federal Bail Reform Act? Hirschkop then pointed out that the Commissioner had given the thirty-day sentence to the Defendant on the ground that he was a mature and responsible individual.

Now Commissioner Scaife's lips pressed very tight together. When he opened them, he began to smile, indeed he could not keep from smiling, his silent laughter grew larger and larger, as if when all was said there was no lawyer like a good Jewish lawyer, and it might be a pleasure to lose a game so well played. "All right," he said quietly, "pending appeal we will then release the Defendant on his own recognizance."

Standing at the bench, signing the last papers, Mailer, prompted by some shade in the late afternoon air of lost Civil War protocols in Virginia, spoke to the Commissioner. "Mr. Scaife," he said.

"Yes," said Scaife looking up.

236

"Some day in quieter times I hope we have the opportunity to meet and discuss some of these matters."

"Yes, Mr. Mailer," said Scaife, "so do I."

10: THE COMMUNICATION OF CHRIST

Five minutes later was a scene of congratulation on the grass outside the open arcades of Occoquan. He had signed papers, gone through a few small formalities, and now stood in front of Leiterman's camera, speaking into the microphone held by the sound man, Heiss, while the reporters from *The Washington Post* stood by with pads in their hands, taking every word he said, and he spoke slowly at the rate of dictation he might have used with a new stenographer.

John Boyle, the Presbyterian Chaplain at Yale, was also there. Released yesterday, he had come out to Occoquan today, and he and Mailer greeted each other with warmth, next to old buddies now on the impetus of their bust. But he had also greeted Leiterman with warmth, Leiterman with his faithful camera—how many hours had Fontaine and Leiterman and Heiss been waiting for his release, and in the open celebrative sentiment of being free of jail, and out on that last unexpected high hurdle— funds of great affection now for de Grazia also listening to his speech before the camera, and for Hirschkop now back in some other courtroom, working no doubt with the same dedicated ferocity to gain a verdict for the next prisoner, Hirschkop, the most unexpected bonus of the day, yes he could even forgive Hirschkop for those tons of unreconstructed schmaltz about Mailer the model prisoner, yes, in this resumption of the open air after twenty-four hours, no more, there was a sweet clean edge to the core of the substance of things—a monumentally abstract remark which may be saved by the concrete observation that the air was good in his lungs—not often could Mailer count on such sweet air. He felt a liberation from the unending disciplines of that moral ladder whose rungs he had counted in the dormitory while listening to Kupferberg, no, all effort was not the same, and to eject oneself from guilt might yet be worth it, for the nausea on return to guilt could conceivably prove less: standing on the grass, he felt one suspicion of a whole man closer to that freedom from dread which occupied the inner drama of his years, yes, one image closer than when he had come to Washington four days ago. The sum of what he had done that he considered good outweighed the dull sum of his omissions these same four days. So he was happy, and it occurred to him that this clean sense of himself, with a skin of compassion at such rare moment for all—yes, even for noble Commissioner Scaife and the dour U. S. Attorneys, no, not quite them, not quite, but go on—this sense of nice expectation and shining conception of his wife, and regrets for the guards, and pride in the prisoners, too much, much too much, it must come crashing soon, but still—this nice anticipation of the very next moves of life itself (and all for just an incredibly inexpensive twenty-four hours in jail) must mean, indeed could mean nothing else to Christians, but what they must signify when they spoke of Christ within them, it was not unlike the rare sweet of a clean loving tear not dropped, still held, oh he must be salient now, and deliver the best of himself to these microphones and reporters, and in respect to Boyle, pick up some of the Chaplain's language, why not? Some message from the Marchers at the Pentagon had to reach America and Americans.

So he made the following speech:

"Today is Sunday, and while I am not a Christian, I happen to be married to one. And there are times when I think the loveliest thing about my dear wife is her unspoken love for Jesus Christ." Unspoken it was, most certainly. She would wonder if he was mad when she read this, for outside of her profound observance of Christmas Eve and her dedication to decorating a Christmas tree, they never talked about such matters. As a child, she had rarely gone to church, but he knew what he meant—some old pagan spirit of her part Swedish blood must have carried Christ through all the Southern exposures of her mixed part Indian blood, crazy American lass, one-time mouther of commercials on television, mother of his two —would they be mighty?—boys, angel or witch, she had a presence like silver, she was on all nights of the full moon near to mad, and he loved her for that quality he could never explain—her unexpected quixotic depths of compassion, yes the loveliest thing about his dear wife was her unspoken love for Jesus Christ.

"Some of us," said Mailer to the reporters and the photographer and the microphone, "were at the Pentagon yesterday, and we were arrested in order to make our symbolic protest of the war in Vietnam, and most of us served these very short sentences, but they are a harbinger of what will come next, for if the war doesn't end next year," then said he, feeling as modest as he had felt on the steps of the Department of Justice, "why then a few of us will probably have to take longer sentences. Because we must. You see, dear fellow Americans, it is Sunday, and we are burning the body and blood of Christ in Vietnam. Yes, we are burning him there, and as we do, we destroy the foundation of this Republic, which is its love and trust in Christ." He was silent. Wow.

And Boyle gave him a sidelong look, as if to say, "Watch it, old buddy, they put junior reverends in the cuckoo house for carrying on." But Boyle looked pleased. And the reporters looked pleased. And Fontaine and Leiterman, Leiterman particularly, looked ecstatic, for the end of their movie might be there.

They drove back to Washington in de Grazia's car, and Mailer changed at the hotel, called his wife, caught a shuttle, had a merry ride back with Fontaine for there were hordes of young girls on the flight and the air between New York and Washington was orgiastic with the breath of release, some promise of peace and new war seemed riding the phosphorescent wake of this second and last day's siege of the Pentagon, as if the country were opening into more and more on the resonance of these two days, more that was good, more that was bad, and Mailer met his wife at P. J. Clarke's for dinner, but their luck was poor: an old girl friend of the novelist passed by, tapped him possessively on the hair, and so he spent the evening in a muted quarrel with his wife, the actress, Beverly Bentley.

And a few days later saw his immortal speech on Christ as it was printed in *The Washington Post*. There was no mention of the scene outdoors on the grass. The story went like this:

> Novelist Norman Mailer using a makeshift courtroom to deliver a Sunday sermon on the evils of the Vietnam war, received the only prison sentence yesterday as justice was meted out in wholesale lots for hundreds of anti-war demonstrators.
>
> In his courtroom speech, Mailer said, "They are burning the body and blood of Christ in Vietnam."
>
> "Today is Sunday," he said, "and while I am not a Christian, I happen to be married to one. And there are times when I think the loveliest thing about my dear wife is her unspoken love for Jesus Christ . . ."
>
> Mailer said he believed that the war in Vietnam "will destroy the foundation of this republic, which is its love and trust in Christ." Mailer is a Jew.

It was obvious the good novelist Norman Mailer had much to learn about newspapers, reporters, and salience.

11: SKINS AND HIDES

Still he was not injured unduly. His hide was hard. He laughed when he read the red bordered story in *Time* about his scatological solo at the Ambassador Theater—

he laughed because he knew it had stimulated his cause. And as the days went by, he contracted to write an account of the March on the Pentagon, and wrestled with the difficulties of how to do it, and appeared on a television show and amazed himself. For if he had been half as conservative as Russell Kirk in prison, he was half as militant on television as H. Rap Brown.

Then he began his history of the Pentagon. It insisted on becoming a history of himself over four days, and therefore was history in the costume of a novel. He labored in the aesthetic of the problem for weeks, discovering that his dimensions as a character were simple: blessed had been the novelist, for his protagonist was a simple of a hero and a marvel of a fool, with more than average gifts of objectivity—might his critics have as much!—this verdict disclosed by the unprotective haste with which he was obliged to write, for he wrote of necessity at a rate faster than he had ever written before, as if the accelerating history of the country forbade deliberation. Yet in writing his personal history of these four days, he was delivered a discovery of what the March on the Pentagon had finally meant, and what had been won, and what had been lost, and so found himself ready at last to write a most concise Short History, a veritable précis of a collective novel, which here now, in the remaining pages, will seek as History, no, rather as some Novel of History, to elucidate the mysterious character of that quintessentially American event.

Book Two

THE NOVEL AS HISTORY: THE BATTLE OF THE PENTAGON

1: A NOVEL METAPHOR

The Novelist in passing his baton to the Historian has a happy smile. He has been faster than you think. As a working craftsman, a journeyman artist, he is not without his guile; he has come to decide that if you would see the horizon from a forest, you must build a tower. If the horizon will reveal most of what is significant, an hour of examination can yet do the job—it is the tower which takes months to build. So the Novelist working in secret collaboration with the Historian has perhaps tried to build with his novel a tower fully equipped with telescopes to study —at the greatest advantage—our own horizon. Of course, the tower is crooked, and the telescopes warped, but the instruments of all sciences—history so much as physics —are always constructed in small or large error; what supports the use of them now is that our intimacy with the master builder of the tower, and the lens grinder of the telescopes (yes, even the machinist of the barrels) has given some advantage for correcting the error of the instruments and the imbalance of his tower. May that be claimed of many histories? In fact, how many novels can be put so quickly to use? (For the novel—we will permit ourselves this parenthesis—is, when it is good, the personification of a vision which will enable one to comprehend other visions better; a microscope—if one is exploring the pond; a telescope upon a tower if you are scrutinizing the forest.)

The method is then exposed. The mass media which surrounded the March on the Pentagon created a forest of inaccuracy which would blind the efforts of an historian; our novel has provided us with the possibility, no, even the instrument to view our facts and conceivably study them in that field of light a labor of lens-grinding has produced. Let us prepare then (metaphors soon to be mixed—for the Novelist is slowing to a jog, and the Historian is all grip on the rein) let us prepare then to see what the history may disclose.

2: SYMBOLIC SEARCH

The cadres of that citizens' army later to march on the Pentagon were composed of a coalition which could never have come together ten years before, and were in fact held in a kind of suspension on this occasion only through what is considered—by reasonable consensus—the extraordinary abilities of the Chairman of the National Mobilization to End the War in Vietnam, David Dellinger, editor (it may be recollected) of the anarchist-pacifist magazine *Liberation*. Yet his previous experience for such mobilizations was surprisingly not very great. Assistant to A. J. Muste for years, it may also be recalled that he inherited some of the Reverend's prestige when Muste died in February 1967 while working on preparations for the peace parade in New York that spring. Consequently, Dellinger organized the April parade, rally, and assembly in the plaza of the UN of a host of peace groups whose number was probably so high as a quarter of million people. By *The New York Times* estimate, this support proved twice as large as a massive counter rally in May of patriotic groups who chose to support the war in Vietnam. While *The New York Times* was not altogether confirmed in this estimate, since the *Daily News* and some radio networks chose to reverse the size of both rallies, finding the patriotic rally to be double the protest rally in numbers, the count of *The New York Times* was more generally believed, and the April March was therefore seen as a great victory. But when its size and success proved to have an absolutely discernible lack of effect on foreign policy, and the war in Vietnam escalated again, an open conference was held in Washington at the Hawthorne School on May 20 and 21 of the National Mobilization Committee. With the exception of Dellinger who was then in Hanoi, some of the figures attending were the Reverend James Bevel, one of the leading organizers of the April March and aide to Martin Luther King; Professor Sidney Peck, a co-chairman of the Mobilization and chairman of the Cleveland Area Peace Action Council; Professor Robert Greenblatt, national coordinator of the Mobilization and an early founder of the campus antiwar teach-ins; and representatives from numerous moderate peace groups, SNCC, SDS, Socialist splinter parties, even a couple of Communists. On the rising enthusiasm which followed the New York March it was contemplated by many at this meeting to have what would probably be the greatest rally in American history. In Washington in the fall, they would attempt to gather a million people. That was the magnetic number originally discussed, and the key slogan drafted at this May meeting was "Support Our Boys in Vietnam—Bring Them Home Now." The date was even picked: October 21; it seemed the best conjunction of a number of factors—the weather would still be good, there would be ample time after Labor Day to get out word of the action, and yet not so late that exam schedules would keep college students away. Already there was vague talk of civil disobedience. Still, the date, October 21, was about the only detail which was to remain constant.

Now, at this early point, a few comments already intrude. It seems obvious that the idea for such a massive rally probably derived from the success and the organizational mechanics of the April March rather than in response to the lack of political effect that March had had on the Johnson Administration—indeed there was hardly time to measure the effect. It is possible that if the April March had produced a noticeable de-escalation of the war, future peace rallies might have been more conciliatory—as likely, they would have turned militant. In fact, it probably made no real difference. Just as a study of foreign policy usually succeeds in depressing any lover of democratic process because foreign policy is encapsulated and therefore self-governing, so political life on the American Left tends to have an inner development which bears little relation to subtle changes in the external political context. Severed from the trade-union movement by Right Wing labor leaders' raids in the early years of the Cold War, the American Left—until the rise of the Negro civil rights movements—was in this interregnum a profoundly middle class phenomenon filled with bitter family rifts, great propriety, academic foundations, intellectual rigidity which reacted to cataclysmic political changes outside the way a patient reacts to an operation (misery, nausea, and convalescence) and much skill in internecine organizational war (not unlike the scheming which goes into the rewriting of a will). There was—as in many middle class families—a middle class excess of compulsive orality, an extraordinary love of debate in meetings; just as the family lends itself to a vigorous if sterile set of speeches by its members in which—if the family is sufficiently unhappy—each can have the floor for ten minutes to describe his own views, resentments, private sufferings, and sacrifices, so too for Left Wing life during the interregnum. The fifties were a profoundly unhappy period for the Left Wing; in the sixties with Cuba, civil rights, Kennedy, Berkeley, the Great Society, and the war in Vietnam, the new blood of Negro movements and youth movements brought life back to the Left, but only for a period. By 1965 the Negroes were disaffected, even profoundly bored with Left Wing rhetoric which seemed to match little in their own imperatives, the youth were obviously contemptuous of the Old Left. By the time of the April March, the rifts were profound between the races and the generations. But the huge and unexpected success of the April March, its unanticipated size—no one had secretly believed they would attract a quarter of a million people—had given new hope to the Old Left, which, being thus profoundly middle class (and hence committed to the logic-of-the-next-step) had entered, infiltrated, invigorated, and doubtless inspired many middle class

248

peace movements. There are political alliances which are attractive, just as there are others which are dutiful. By the rudest existential measure, attractive alliances are not un-sexy, dutiful alliances are deadening. Any coalition of the New Left and the Old, or the New Left and the Black Militants was dutiful, and sometimes near to unendurable. On the other hand, coalition between the New Left and the hippies, or the Old Left and the middle class liberals in the peace movements was attractive for ideas developed from such meetings, hopes, enthusiasms, even agreeable surprises—which last is next to manna in the life of an Old Leftist since the orthodoxy of his mind leaves not much room for surprise. Perhaps the deepest and most natural of these new alignments was between the peace liberal and the peace, or Old Leftist; each excited the other—the liberal, bringing along his mass movement, was the equivalent of a wealthy heiress to the poor Old Leftist; the Old Leftist was a virile but most conventional (and manageable) principle of adventure in the somewhat deodorized orchards of comfortable middle class liberal life. So even a year or more before the October March of 1967 in Washington was discussed, the future schisms were shaping: the Black Militants were moving off by themselves, the Old Left was investing itself deep in the liberal purlieus of mass peace, and the New Left and the hippies were coming upon the opening intimations of a new style of revolution—revolution by theater and without a script.

Under these uneasy conditions, one may wonder at the practical judgment of men who meet in Washington in May to call for a rally in October which will assemble a million people. It is not really as unsound psychologically as it seems, any more than it is mentally unsound for the head of a middle class family to announce on his best day of the year, "Honey, I'm going to make a million yet!" Without one such fierce element of the fantastic, middle class life is insupportable. The same may be said of the old Left Wing life. Without the ability to believe for a magical minute at a meeting that a million people will rally, without such inner intimations of glory (from the speech—not the fulfillment of the event) life on the Left

Wing would be a drab parade of mimeograph machines, meetings, economic sacrifices, organizational tension, and that auditory deadening of the senses produced by Left Wing rhetoric. The Old Left lived for their imagination; their imagination was founded on the apocalyptic moment —not for nothing had Lenin pointed out that there were ten years which passed like an uneventful day, but there was also the revolutionary day which was like ten years.

So plans for a rally to bring a million men and women to Washington were discussed, and the near to absolute impossibility of the project was cushioned by a growing sense of apocalypse in American life. If everything was altering at an unpredictable rate, so might a mass outcry against the war build over the months of the summer.

But the summer of 1967 was not favorable for the building of such a vast response. The Arab-Israeli war in June divided the Old Left one more time. Many of the Old Left and many members of the liberal peace groups were Jewish, and enraptured with Israel; more of the Old Left, also Jewish, remained true to the rigorous coils of certain more or less Trotskyist and Communist positions, which left them therefore beached as apologists for Nasser (a miserable position since he had bragged of the future burning of Israelis). Worse, the Black Militants were almost entirely for the Arabs. The New Left in its turn was therefore seriously divided. Unity had obviously not been encouraged.

Then came Negro riots near a scale of war in the ghettos of at least a dozen major American cities. If the Old Left was thrilled at the militancy, it was also disturbed at the brutality. Plekhanov, teacher of Lenin, first editor of *Iskra,* architect of revolution on the Russian model, was appalled by the actual presence of the Soviet soldier at his doorstep—so was the Old Left by the criminally suggestive cool of Black Power, by the snipers, the Molotov cocktails thrown from the roof tops. On the other hand, the New Left was impressed. Young, college-bred, middle class, they felt the militancy of the blacks as a reproof to their own secure relatively unthreatened mass demonstrations. The center of pressure to mount an exciting weekend in Washington began then to pass from the

Old Left and the peace groups to the New Left and the youth groups. Where the Arab-Israeli war had divided liberals from Old Leftists, and the Negro riots had quenched some of the militancy of the peace group liberals, the New Left was in a state of stimulation, and the hippies, dedicated to every turn of the unexpected, were obviously—as always—ready for anything.

For many of these reasons therefore, the projected March on Washington was in the doldrums. Money to support it was hardly dribbling in, Dellinger had been on visits to Hanoi and thus otherwise occupied; enthusiasm among peace groups was not high. At this point Dellinger called in Jerry Rubin from Berkeley to be Project Director for the March. Rubin had enormous stature among youth groups and Under-Thirties, second perhaps only to Mario Savio. Rubin had organized Vietnam Day at Berkeley (the first mass protest of the war) had led marches in Berkeley designed to block troop trains, then massive marches in Oakland, had served a thirty-day jail sentence, and had appeared at a House Un-American Activities Committee hearing in an American Revolutionary War uniform. He had also run for Mayor of Berkeley on a platform opposing war and supporting black power and the legalization of pot, collecting in the process 7,385 ballots or 22 percent of the vote.

It was a way of announcing to the various groups in the National Mobilization that the October event in Washington was now striking out into that no-man's-land between organized acceptable dissent and incalculable acts of revolution. As will be seen shortly, some most radical possibilities were already in Dellinger's mind, but to call on Rubin was in effect to call upon the most militant, unpredictable, creative—therefore dangerous—hippie-oriented leader available on the New Left. It is to Dellinger's credit that he most probably did not do this to save the March, since there was no doubt that, doldrums or no, a peaceful demonstration of large proportions could always have been gotten together; the invitation to Rubin was rather an expression of Dellinger's faith in the possibility—a most difficult possibility which only his own untested gifts as a conciliator could have enabled him to

251

envisage—of a combined conventional mass protest and civil disobedience which might help to unify the scattered elements of the peace movement. When Rubin arrived in New York, Dellinger's project was at the time conceived as follows: there would be an assembly, then a march past the White House down Pennsylvania Avenue to the Capitol where demonstrators who wished would enter Congress and there commit acts of civil disobedience. There was even talk of investing Congress and taking it over, establishing, if only for an hour, a People's Congress. But Rubin did not like the revolutionary aesthetics of this plan—he argued with Dellinger that the proposal, while on the surface most attractive, was nonetheless a move at once too radical and too soft. It was too radical because the Capitol could not successfully be occupied, and the alternate plan—for demonstrators to petition their Congressmen—was pathetically soft.

In Rubin's opinion, Congress was not a source but a servant of the real power in America. So Congress did not inspire the thought of real confrontations between real enemies, it did not stir the imagination to awe and dread and admiration. In fact, for good or ill, Congress was an agreeable symbol to the vast majority of Americans. Rubin had therefore brought another idea. On the West Coast they were talking of a March on the Pentagon which would encircle it, invest it, disrupt it, and conceivably paralyze its actions for a few days. Such a move would have symbolic meaning in America and around the world, for the Pentagon was the symbol of the American military, and so was hated wherever U.S. forces were resented or despised at home or abroad.

Discussions ensued. It was later to be a subject of much amusement, and an interesting sidelight into the revolutionary differences between the visionary West and the practical East that the idea of invading the Pentagon began in California, yet the knowledge was obliged to come from New York that the Pentagon was not even in Washington, D.C., but Virginia, and the bridge or bridges across the Potomac would be therefore the place where police could stop the demonstrators with no difficulty at all.

A visionary may however always defeat a practical suggestion, for he absorbs any necessary kernel of the detailed from the aura of the other debater: splendid, said Rubin, if the police should halt the March to the Pentagon on the bridge, the demonstrators could turn back and create massive disruption in the Capitol!

A few days later, about the middle of August, Rubin, Robert Greenblatt, coordinator of the Mobilization, and Fred Halstead of the Socialist Workers party (whose view would be not unrepresentative of the moderate peace groups) went out to the Pentagon to study its geography and suitability for a march, a rally, and the projected civil disobedience. Their report to a meeting of the Administrative Committee of the National Mobilization was not unfavorable and the committee approved the shift from the Capitol to the Pentagon.

A number of such trips were yet to be made, a number of committee members were to walk through the Pentagon in the following weeks. They were to have the opportunity then to study a most bewildering opponent, for the strength of the Pentagon is subtle. It is not even a building one needs a pass to enter, and on an average working day no guards are visible. Nor is there any easily identifiable objective within the building. Long exceptionally monotonous corridors with doors to evenly spaced small offices off them lead into other equally undistinguished halls. Of course the Administration Entrance faces north onto a triangular piece of lawn called the Mall (which will figure prominently in this history) and back of it are the offices of some of the most important men in America, the Secretary of Defense, the Chiefs of Staff. If the halls on four of the five floors of the Administration wall are lined with paintings related in the main to military and naval matters (of the sort which could have been all-but-accepted for a *Saturday Evening Post* cover during World War II) and if the offices are larger here, and have reception rooms and carpet, if in these Administration corridors the walls are painted a modestly bright yellow, and there are even short stretches of wall with walnut paneling, still by no measure can anyone claim that the taxpayer's money is being wasted for extravagant interior decoration in the Pentagon.

At the other end of the building is a gloomy, ill-lit chamber half the size of the Port Authority Bus Terminal in New York and it serves as a sort of roofed-over plaza. It is the shopping center for the Pentagon. A vast cafeteria is off this immense gallery, and shops of every variety, stairways to buses and taxis, airplane reservation desks, men's and women's clothing shops, a Brentano's bookstore, gift shops—doubtless there is a souvenir shop. This is the only center of interest. Each of the five walls of the Pentagon is probably as long as the Louvre, so it is doubtful if there was ever another building in the world so huge in ground plan and so without variation. It would therefore be one thing to attack the Pentagon—it would be another to immobilize it. What could one do inside? —there were no redoubts to take unless the shopping center and cafeteria could qualify as targets, or perhaps the office of the Secretary of Defense at the other end of the building. In fact, it hardly mattered. Regardless of how many military conversations might be bandied about the possibility of occupying the Pentagon for a few hours or a few days, it must have been secretly evident to the committee members (each to himself) that a mass march to the Pentagon announced in advance was not going to be able to enter the building in any conclusive fashion. The approaches by road were too few, the doors in each wall were also too few and too small, and the five concentric rings of the building with their lateral corridors, and corridors on axes (like a spider web) and the sum of five floors on top of one another made up a total of somewhere between one hundred fifty and two hundred corridors varying in length from two hundred to perhaps a thousand feet long, or somewhere near to twenty miles of passageway. If twenty thousand people worked in the offices, cubbyholes, and warrens off those indistinguishable corridors, twice that number of demonstrators might be needed to paralyze the entire building. For the Pentagon, architecturally, was as undifferentiated as a jellyfish or a cluster of barnacles. One could chip away at any part of the interior without locating a nervous center.

It was nonetheless an historic moment when these re-connoitering vanguards of the Mobilization Committee went into the Pentagon to study its vulnerability to attack, historic not for the magnitude of the events which were to derive from this visit, but historic as a paradigm of the disproportions and contradictions of the twentieth century itself. Nineteenth-century generals would not have been permitted to explore the fortress they would attack, but they would have known its storehouse when they took it. Now recapitulate the problem at the Pentagon: an enor-mous office building in the shape of a fortress housed the military center of the most powerful nation on earth, yet there was no need for guards—the proliferation of the building itself was its own defense: assassination of any high official in the edifice could serve only to augment the power of the Pentagon; vulnerable to sabotage, that also could work only for the fortification of its interest. High church of the corporation, the Pentagon spoke exclusively of mass man and his civilization; every aspect of the building was anonymous, monotonous, massive, inter-changeable.

For this committee of revolutionary explorers, the strangeness of their situation must have been comparable to a reconnaissance of the moon. They could enter the Pentagon without difficulty, walk wherever they pleased —although not without attracting attention quite soon, for if most of them looked like responsible executives and experts, Rubin's hair was brushed out like a Black Mili-tant's in five inches every direction from his head; they could nonetheless explore their target, debate their ap-proach (even debate aloud if need be in these corridors filled as much with moving people as a busy subway sta-tion) they could even if they had wished probably have paid a call on the Secretary of Defense to inform him of their project, yet it was impossible to locate the symbolic loins of the building—paradigm of the modern world in-deed, they could explore every inch of their foe and know nothing about him; the twentieth century was in the proc-ess of removing the last of man's power from his senses in order to store power in piled banks of coded knowl-edge. The essence of coded knowledge was that it could

255

be made available to all because only a few had the code to comprehend it.

Nonetheless, they had many discussions as to which wall of the Pentagon to approach on the day. The west wall adjacent to Washington Boulevard and the helicopter pad, had too small an entrance, the southeast wall was similarly undistinguished, and overprotected by a formidable spaghetti of superhighways and cloverleafs, the river entrance on the east was militarily impossible since a narrow ramp here crossed over Jefferson Davis Highway into the building—as well try to lead ten thousand men into a castle by a drawbridge. Of the five walls, two then were left: the southwest wall by the South Parking Area, and the Administrative Entrance on the north wall.

Early sentiment was for entering by way of the South Parking Area which was close to the Pentagon, indeed confronted it from not fifty yards away. Here the entrances were numerous, the approaches broad, and the building most difficult to defend, for not two hundred feet behind the doors was the shopping center and the cafeteria, where a host of passageways debouched. The shopping center, although at one end of the Pentagon, was the nearest equivalent to a major crossroads. If they succeeded in reaching its great open floor, they could strike out in any number of directions, indeed in all directions —there would be no single narrow corridor to stop them.

On the other hand, the South Parking had serious disadvantages. The demonstrators would have to march half around the Pentagon to reach it, and such a long move might be easy to harass or delay; also, the southwest face of the Pentagon was the least inspiring—it looked like what it was, a loading platform (it was here from the barred-windowed bus that Mailer had studied the Marshals) an open maw for the tons of food and supplies which came in every day, the mountains of garbage which went out. To attack here was to lose some of one's symbolic momentum—a consideration which might be comic or unpleasant in a shooting war, but in a symbolic war was not necessarily comic at all. There was something absurd in throwing oneself upon the Pentagon in order to capture the cafeteria and the shopping center. Besides, if it would be easy to strike out in all directions from the floor of this enormous gallery, so would ambush upon them be equally available—troops could come from half a hundred entrances; the projected battle might therefore be too rapid, and pinch off any possibility of a massive sit-in for forty-eight hours.

So the north wall with its Administrative Entrance was eventually chosen. It was the main approach to the Pentagon, and the most attractive. Access roads curved up from Jefferson Davis Highway and Washington Boulevard to the large square of asphalt in front of the entrance steps and the Egyptian columns. Below was another flight of steps which led to two ramps descending to the Mall. An army could meet on that grassy area for a rally, then move forward for acts of civil disobedience and/or disruption with a full view of the edifice.

Be it said that the government, for altogether different reasons, was soon to offer the same area to the Mobilization.

3: CAUTIONARY CRAFTS

Back in New York, there were now weekly Steering Committee meetings; every two weeks, then every week, the Administrative Committee would get together to make basic decisions. They would meet in apartments, or members' houses, or in rented halls, or at the Free School in New York. Representatives from Women Strike for Peace, the New York Parade Committee, the Chicago Peace Council, the Student Mobilization Committee, the Ohio Area Peace Action Council, and pacifists, veterans' groups, Communists, Trotskyists, returned volunteers from the Peace Corps in Vietnam were present. The difficulties of coalition, always present, were now agitated.

The more liberal, which is to say the less radical peace groups were intimidated by the specter of a large unruly civil disobedience, yet if pushed by such fears in the direction of not collaborating with the March on the Pentagon, they faced the other side of the dilemma—their refusal would split the peace movement. So enormous pressure was never put entirely upon Dellinger to settle for a massive peace rally which would forego civil disobedience, and he was able to draft a plan: the demonstration would be two-pronged—a mass march and rally would be followed by acts of civil disobedience for those who wished to engage in them. It was obvious that much time and much energy must have been spent by Dellinger in assuring the gentler and more prosperous peace groups that the civil disobedience would almost certainly be "mild," and they would be protected from unwilling involvement in the civil disobedience. Therefore, in designing this two-pronged action, certain contradictions were in-built. Yet Dellinger had no desire to take such a large action without including the peace groups. From beginning to end, Dellinger envisaged the struggle against the war as a mass movement—how else to impress the power elite in Washington if not with a dedicated mass? The power elite knew better than anyone how difficult it was to rouse Americans to acts of dedication by now—hence, envisaged as a mass movement, Dellinger was obliged from his own point of view to have the peace groups. Besides, one could not avoid the inevitable recognition that the major source of funds would be precisely these same moderate peace groups. The demonstration was eventually to cost $65,000, the money to go in rent for offices in New York and Washington, for ads, for rented sound equipment, costs of telephone (huge), mailings, travel, buttons, even the modest expense of staff salaries—perhaps ten people working for $50 a week. In addition the National Mobilization was in debt as much as $15,000 from the costs of the April March. So Dellinger could never afford to dispense—even if he had wished—with the potential financial support of the more middle class peace groups.

Viewing these matters from without, it could of course

be asked why an organizer would be interested in the more militant aspect of the demonstration when it was obvious the forces who wanted the more active varieties of civil disobedience, like outright disruption, although a minority in numbers, would create most of his problems, assure him a hostile press, exhaust huge funds of time and energy in placating his right wing, probably compromise him hopelessly in middle positions, and finally remain even hostile and uncoordinated to the National Mobilization Committee. Avoiding any certainty as to his private reasons, speculations are possible on the natural desire of a middle-aged revolutionary to remain in contact with the youth groups, as well as Dellinger's own natural militancy. Not by nature, or by his own history, a conciliator or compromiser, he had been involved for years in small not uncourageous actions of civil disobedience. It is possible he would have been even more militant if not for his trips to Hanoi which had left him with the conviction that ending the war had first priority in America, and unity was thus the obligatory strategy. This last conviction could lead one to nothing but mass movements, if not for the fact that there were hard objective practical reasons for quitting passive protest and entering active civil disobedience, for taking on the slogan, "From Dissent to Resistance." The fragmented condition of the Left after the summer of 1967 was certain to hold down the number of participants. Yet, another mass protest against the war would be meaningless unless many times the size of previous efforts; the peace movement, if not growing, would become a predictable figure in the tapestry, to be discounted by the power elite rather than respected. A protest movement which does not grow loses power every day, since protest movements depend upon the interest they arouse in the mass media. But the mass media are interested only in processes which are expanding dramatically or collapsing. Active civil disobedience was therefore essential to give glamour and publicity to the demonstration—a page-one story for Washington must instead become a page-one story for the world. Then, the ante would be up, and the results unpredictable

—the peace movement would seem far from subsiding into the tapestry.

Besides, Negro civil rights had prospered (until the beginning of the war in Vietnam) by the existence of their most militant groups. The value of the Black Muslims to Martin Luther King must have been considerable—he did not even have to say to the ADA, "If not me, it may be them." In contrast, white radical movements had invariably made their alliances with white liberal movements, so they lacked the threatening discomposing cutting edge of an ultra-Left movement which was potentially violent. It had become commonplace to remark that young people would not travel to just another march and rally. Civil disobedience was therefore vital to the advertisement of the March, as vital to the needs of the Mobilization Committee as money, and masses of demonstrators.

On August 28 at the Overseas Press Club in New York, a press conference was held to announce the March and its intention to close down the Pentagon on Saturday, October 21, by blocking entrances and doorways. The effort would be continued through Sunday, and if possible through Monday. At the press conference table sat Monsignor Rice of Pittsburgh; Father Hayes of the Episcopal Peace Fellowship; Gary Rader, former member of the Green Berets, now a pacifist; Abbie Hoffman of the Diggers' Free Store in New York; David Dellinger, Jerry Rubin, and Robert Greenblatt of the Mobilization; Amy Swerdlow of Women Strike for Peace; William Pepper, executive director of the National Conference for New Politics (about to have their convention in Chicago); Carl Davidson of SDS; Lincoln Lynch of CORE; Fred Rosen of The Resistance; Lee Webb, co-director of Vietnam Summer; Dick Gregory, and—to everyone's surprise—H. Rap Brown of SNCC.

Reverend Hayes spoke to the press for the Moblization and announced that the giant coalition group which grew out of the Spring Mobilization "is beginning to organize a confrontation in Washington on October 21–22 which will shut down the Pentagon. We will fill the hallways and block the entrances. Thousands of people will disrupt the

260

center of the American war machine. In the name of humanity we will call the warmakers to task.

"This will be a weekend of unified activities. Individuals will act on their consciences and in their own personal styles. Not all people will take part in the massive sit-in at the Pentagon, and we are not asking people to come to Washington solely on this basis. Those who do not block the Pentagon will surround it in a massive peace-in of picketing, vigiling, music, drama, and rallies. We will bring a community of protest, expressing joy and affirmation of man, to a place whose only business is wholesale murder. This confrontation will be massive, continuing, flexible, and surprising."

This was putting the best, most liberal, and most constructive face on the projected activity, but the newspapers could also quote Dellinger—"There will be no government building left unattacked" (although the attacks "will be nonviolent"); Rubin—"We're now in the business of wholesale disruption and widespread resistance and dislocation of the American society"; Hoffman—"We're going to raise the Pentagon three hundred feet in the air"; and H. Rap Brown—"I would be unwise to say I'm going there with a gun because you all took my gun last time. I may bring a bomb, sucker."

This press conference naturally attracted huge attention in the press, most of it critical or mocking. The snide reaction was that the demonstrators would attempt to close down the Pentagon on a day (October 21 was part of a weekend) when it was already closed down, which was not quite true, for several thousand of the Pentagon's employees were present on any normal Saturday. That reaction was less significant than the dismay of the moderate peace groups through the country who on reading of this press conference were left shocked, fearful, and antagonistic. But these negative reactions were whipped to a fury by the September 1 issue of the *Mobilizer*, newsletter of the Mobilization, which began with an editorial written in fire—

The American people today live in a country which has developed the world's most murderous military

261

machine. We live in a society which trains its sons to be killers and which channels its immense wealth into the business of suppressing courageous men from Vietnam to Detroit who struggle for the simple human right to control their own lives and destinies. *We Americans have no right to call ourselves human beings unless, personally and collectively, we stand up and say NO to the death and destruction perpetrated in our name.*

—and was backed with articles on Black Power, Rebellion, Resistance, plus an article by Keith Lampe "On Making a Perfect Mess" which included some of the following items

A thousand children will stage Loot-Ins at department stores to strike at the property fetish that underlies genocidal war.

As the network cameras wheel in for classic counter-demonstrator footage, the BOMB PEKING picket signs will be flipped to say "Does LBJ suck?"

During a block party in front of the White House a lad of nine will climb the fence and piss, piss. . . .

The first thousand copies of this issue were rushed to Chicago to be distributed at the convention of the National Conference for New Politics where the language induced a profound shudder in every middle class element of the white Left, old and new. A storm of protest, indignation, and horror came back on the Mobilization. At a tense meeting of the Steering Committee, people like Al Evanoff, a co-chairman of the Mobilization and a trade-unionist in department-store organizing, could point to the item on looting in department stores as an example of why he could not even distribute the issue to the members of his union. The general consensus of the older people on the Steering Committee was that this newsletter would not mobilize support but would destroy it. It was voted to suppress the issue, and a new issue containing a mild statement of aims written by Sidney Peck in the form of questions and answers, and directed obviously at women's groups and moderate peace groups, was hurriedly put out. From this point on, the Berkeley group which had been the inspiration for the first issue was conceivably in decline.

Dellinger had left for Czechoslovakia after the press conference on August 28. He came back in September to a period of near chaos and conflicting demands. The moderate peace groups, put in a panic by the nihilistic possibilities of the March on the Pentagon, now began to push their demands. They wanted a clear and adequate separation between the March and rally activity, and the civil disobedience and/or disruption which would follow (in order that people who wished to protest the war but did not want to be arrested or endangered could also join). They insisted that Mobilization's press releases project a tone more peaceful, less militant. It was also understood that they would not give large support to the venture unless Dr. Spock could be induced to join it.

Of course these moderate peace groups were often radical themselves in some part, and were not opposed to "outright lawbreaking" if it was symbolic, peaceful, controlled—but the presence of these demands implicated Dellinger in a series of promises, details, and works of personal energy whose objective result was to inhibit any real mass approach to massive disobedience. Dellinger was now obliged to act in part as an agent for the interests of the peace groups even though their intent was critically less militant than his own. It could not have been the happiest position.

The scene now shifts to Washington, and negotiations with the government. A curious period begins.

4: AN ARBITRATED AESTHETIC

In the beginning, any question of jurisdiction must have been moot. It is safe to assume that no particular arm of the authorities would welcome the responsibility of negotiating with the demonstrators. A call to the Chief of the Park Police in Washington, D.C., inspector Beye, was made by the Mobilization Committee, and when it was explained what they wanted, Beye called a small meeting at which appeared a representative of the Metropolitan (D.C.) Police, Beye for the Park Police (who were responsible for order at such monuments as Lincoln Memorial), a Department of the Interior representative, another from the General Services Administration (responsible for the protection and maintenance of all government buildings), and a man from the Pentagon to represent the Defense Department. It was a quiet business meeting. While all must have been more or less aware of the muted end which would take place finally in the isolation cells of the D.C. jail, the conversation was limited on this first meeting to a discussion of the proposed route of march, and the incidental problems attached for the authorities—such as precisely where jurisdiction would pass from one police force to another. Before the meeting was over, however, a man representing the Department of Justice exclaimed, "Do you expect us to allow this to take place?" The meeting broke up shortly afterward. No word came back from any representative of the government.

Mobilization waited ten days, then called Inspector Beye. He suggested they communicate with Harry Van Cleve, the general counsel for GSA—the General Services Administration. Van Cleve had been selected to have jurisdiction for the government. He met with the committee shortly after, and a pattern of meetings was begun. Before they were finished perhaps eight meetings took place in late September and October, and indeed some details were to be argued until the very last night over such matters as the road to be permitted for the March from the Virginia side of the bridge to the Pentagon.

In these meetings, Van Cleve would come with an assistant who never spoke. The committee, being a coalition, would arrive at meetings with as many as ten people. Dellinger, after his return, and Rubin and Greenblatt were at next to all the meetings, and others appeared if they happened to be in Washington on the day, or were interested in a specific point. De Grazia, as head of the Washington Lawyers' Committee, was sometimes there, and Brad Lytle of the Committee for Non-Violent Action, Dagmar Wilson of Women Strike for Peace, attorney Morton Stavis, Sue Orrin of the Mobilization's Washington office, and occasionally Fred Halstead of the Socialist Workers' Party and Sidney Peck.

The first meeting with Van Cleve was perfunctory, and consisted of little more than an exchange of basic information, but in the next meeting, on October 6, Van Cleve, for the GSA (now representing the Park Police, Metropolitan Police, Defense Department, etc.) gave the following offer: the government would allow a rally at Lincoln Memorial, a march to the North Parking Area of the Pentagon, and a rally in the parking lot. But if the Mobilization did not relinquish all plans to break the law, the government would not even allow a rally.

At this point there was nothing to negotiate. The two parties were obviously not at all close to one another. Members of the Mobilization therefore left, and went back to their office, a three-story house at 2719 Ontario Road N.W., where a number of them got on the telephone to speak to different groups around the country. The response which came back was militant, for the reaction was that the Johnson government was now entering a period of suppression. Sentiment was for having the rally anywhere in Washington or Virginia—wherever the police intervened, massive disruption would occur. The

265

demonstrators could move out in every direction and put Washington in disorder. The response was militant even from the Southern Christian Leadership Conference. Martin Luther King was ill these days, in need of rest, and in need of time to rebuild the SCLC, but his assistant, Andrew Young, assured the Mobilization that King would be there in such a case. One didn't pick the day of the revolution. Feeling among the more moderate peace groups was then surprisingly strong. Men like Julian Bond, Dr. Spock, William Sloane Coffin, Jr., and Don Duncan indicated their determination to speak at the rally. It looked as if Rubin might yet have his epic of disruption.

Hundreds of phone calls had been made all over the country, however, and it is not easily believable that no one of the lines suffered from wire tap. Even if there were no informers or government agents among the visitors to Mobilization House (also unlikely, since the high incidence of spies in Left Wing movements was by now accepted as a chronic joke) it must be close to certain that the government was aware of the shift in sentiment, for at the next meeting of the GSA and the Mobilization, Van Cleve came in with a different set of suggestions. In contrast to the first meeting, Van Cleve was proper, even cordial at the second. The new offer proposed that the demonstrators assemble at Lincoln Memorial, go over Arlington Memorial Bridge, proceed on a road to be determined, to a rally in the North Parking Area, and then at a certain hour, those who wished could cross over the four-lane dual Jefferson Davis Highway, enter the Mall in front of the Administration Entrance, and climb the first rows of steps. This offer, made at the second meeting, was actually close to the final agreement drafted on the night before the March. All the essential elements, even the ground plan of the combat which ensued on October 21, was here indicated.

Now the conversations between Van Cleve and the Mobilization Committee were limited to technical matters and specific points, no longer acrimonious affairs. The mood in the room—but for such occasional and unexpectedly unusual elements as Rubin's mane of hair and the costume of a hippie whom he brought in one day—was not too dissimilar, although probably less intense, than an arbitration proceeding between a corporation and a union. No one can of course repress the wit who would point out that any time two bodies of men whose names end in Mobilization and Administration get together, even a revolution can be negotiated, and for fact Dellinger and Van Cleve had similarities in their personal style, since both men were civil, well-spoken, able to appreciate the nuances of the opposite view, and could with no difficulty have acted as contending parties at an Ivy League faculty meeting.

In fact, the meetings could have served as another paradigm of American civilization in this decade of the twentieth century, for two groups with absolutely incompatible ends and an irretrievable lack of final resolution between them, were nonetheless adjudicators in effect with one another over the few small items of common ground which were negotiable, and this through its sheer instrumentalism—since it is somewhat more difficult to take militant action after negotiating quietly with one's enemy for weeks—was to work to pacify and finally curtail the more unmanageable aspects of the Antiwar March.

Debate now proceeded over the finest points—the hour of the rally at the North Parking, the specified time when demonstrators could move on to the Mall, the special regulations—those for example who left the Mall after 7 P.M. on Saturday could not come back till noon the next day. So went a host of small points. The Mobilization asked for a rally at Lincoln Memorial and were granted it, adjustments of the area on the steps above the Mall permitted to the demonstrators were made, the duration of the permit was in question, and the access road.

It was to a degree incredible, as every paradigm of the twentieth century is incredible. Originally the demonstrators were saying in effect: our country is engaged in a war so hideous that we, in the greatest numbers possible, are going to break the laws of assembly in order to protest this impossible war. The government was saying: this is a war necessary to maintain the very security of this nation, but because of our tradition of free speech and

267

dissent, we will permit your protest, but only if it is orderly. Since these incompatible positions had produced an impasse, the compromise said in effect: we, the government, wage the war in Vietnam for our security, but will permit your protest provided it is only a little disorderly. The demonstrators: we still consider the war outrageous and will therefore break the law, but not by very much.

Each side was compromised, each side was, on the face of their professed attitude, absurd. Yet each party had the most pressing practical concerns to force them into collaboration. Dellinger had his moderate peace groups; Van Cleve, the interest of the government. An open white riot in the streets of the Capital after the summer riots in the Negro ghettos would telegraph a portrait of America to Global Village as an explosively unstable nation, therefore a dangerous nation on whom to count for long-term alliances since the explosiveness gave every sign of increase. Moreover, the possibility of a number of white Americans seriously wounded or killed by police, troops, or U. S. Marshals after the government's refusal to permit civil disobedience was even worse to contemplate. A concrete disaster of international publicity could result, especially if the police were too brutal. (And the police might be ultimately less manageable than the wildest of the demonstrators.) It would be undeniably safer to permit civil disobedience. The problem was to limit its intensity.

Van Cleve's position became simple. He had to look for every nuance of negotiation which would reduce the potential for violence of the demonstrators. So the choice of road and time of day and rally areas became critical. If the impact of this oncoming attack, part symbolic, part concrete, depended upon the quality of the revolutionary aesthetic—the revolutionary image, if you will, presented to the marchers as they came within range of the Pentagon—then the government, through Van Cleve, would do their best to dim that image. (They would also do their best to restrict the number of hours, even minutes, that the majority of demonstrators could be active at the Pentagon.) So subtle engagements were fought by Van Cleve to restrict any entrance to the Mall until four P.M. Perhaps he knew the buses would be going back to New

York at five, perhaps—this is sheer speculation—perhaps charter bus operators in New York were given the idea an early departure from Washington was desirable.

Since Dellinger in his turn was committed to two groups at once, and was therefore obliged to work in the opposed directions of what might be ultimately more violence or less violence, and since he was a man personally opposed to violence (as a Quaker) and had therefore no particular habits for comprehending its subtleties, the inference is large that Van Cleve from this point probably scored more for the government than Dellinger for the Moblization.

Each small point the government requested was small indeed, too small to break off negotiation. The nightmare confronting Dellinger would be the press treatment of the Mobilization if a break occurred on what would seem an absurdly minor point—the choice of a road. Who could explain that to the mass media? Mobilization wanted Washington Boulevard or Jefferson Davis Highway for their March from the bridge, since each large road had a bold unimpeded view of the Pentagon almost all the way —the government insisted on Boundary Channel, a narrow side road now under repair and with—it may be remembered—but a restricted view on one occasion of the building. The Mobilization, ideally, if it had been free to create the maximum of civil disobedience, would have been obliged to insist on the Pentagon Mall rather than the North Parking Area for their rally, since there was every difference in the sense given of the objective. A powerful orator speaking on the Mall would have been able to point to the Pentagon a hundred yards away across the grass—how different from the blurred view across wire fence and four-lane highway of a rally held in an oil-stained parking lot more than a thousand feet away.

The Mobilization was to request the Mall for their second rally a number of times, but in that economy of barter which characterizes negotiation, they did not make an issue of it—rather it was a point they were ready to relinquish in return for other points: the assumption is that a part of the coalition did not really desire the Mall. Like Van Cleve, they assumed the disruption would be less in the North Parking.

It had been decided that a first rally would be held at Lincoln Memorial rather than just an assembly. This was necessary to raise money (and in fact $30,000 was to be collected during the speeches). The length of this speakers' program grew under the pressure of every group which wished to be represented on the podium—there was as well, no doubt, the unspoken assumption by the moderates that hours of speeches would reduce the possibility of violence. (Never had a more middle class group, more fundamentally opposed to violence, assembled in great numbers on an occasion whose precise novelty was that it promised precisely to be violent!)

Now there was pressure from the moderates to have another rally at the North Parking with more speeches. As far back as the second week of September, Dr. Spock and representatives from Women Strike for Peace were arguing that the rally had to be held at Lincoln Memorial in order for women and children to be able to attend in freedom from disorder. (Also, the moderates thought it was essential to separate one rally completely from any civil disobedience, so that those who did not wish to go to the Pentagon would not be forced to.) On the other hand, the second speakers' rally at the North Parking had been planned from the beginning; it was now kept (despite the glaring possibility of many superfluous speeches) on the theory that those who did not wish to participate in civil disobedience would still need an *activity* (the influence of the progressive school is everywhere) on their arrival at the Pentagon, otherwise they might not march over the bridge. But obviously the parking-lot rally following in the wake of a two-hour speech-fest at Lincoln Memorial was another deterrent to large civil disobedience.

Rubin and Dellinger were by now at considerable odds. At every point where the government had dulled the aesthetic, Rubin wished to brighten it—so he had wanted the rally in the Mall, had wanted to resist the choice of roads, had accepted with some unhappiness the limitation to one bridge—for the sight of two friendly armies coming together at the approaches to the Pentagon would prove inspiring, besides there would be more troops present at once—had wanted one rally, not two, and a plan to divert people back to Washington if opportunities at the Pentagon were small, he had been particularly unhappy with the late hour—4:00 P.M.—accepted from the government for the commencement of the "protest." So he had pleaded and/or argued with Dellinger that the government was all but compelled to negotiate an agreement and was therefore bluffing. Breaking negotiations would only make the government concede their points. It is likely Rubin felt the frame of reference had gotten away from him, and that the demonstration would end as another mass rally with interesting but essentially minor gestures of civil disobedience. So the difference between these leaders was by now fundamental. From Rubin's point of view, the concept had come a long way down from his first proud promise of "wholesale and widespread resistance and dislocation of the American society."

And Dellinger? We must speculate again. He had fulfilled his promise to the moderates, and so had been unable to go very far in the direction of a mass, symbolic, and prestigious pageant of nonviolent civil disobedience, but he had brought off the preparations for an unprecedented rally and action—it had been finally his responsibility, his nightmare if disaster struck and tens or hundreds of people were killed. Besides it is possible he had been true to both factions. The moderates had not been betrayed by him, the limitations upon civil disobedience were subtle and many. But they were not hermetic. Far from it. If an extraordinary potential for civil disobedience and disruption existed among the younger groups—and no one really knew—it would find any number of ways of flowing over the restraints. He had succeeded in fashioning therefore an action which was at once penned and open-ended—for the character of the civil disobedience still remained undefined, and that was an achieve-

271

ment. The government had been obliged to collaborate on details of an oncoming battle against its own jurisdiction, property, and troops. Medieval concepts of war seemed to be returning, or was it primitive contracts for war?

5: A PERSPECTIVE OF BATTLE

We can pass over the mood of Washington in the few days before the March, the sympathetic and somewhat coordinated actions of protest in other parts of the country for the week preceding October 21, we may skip over the last meetings of the government and the Mobilization Committee, the denunciations in Congress, the bill which was passed on Friday October 20 to protect the Capitol building from men carrying arms! And the scoldings and adjurations of newspaper editorials which remonstrated with the peace movement to remain peaceful. No, one we must give, it is from *The New York Times* on the day of the March.

> It will be totally unnecessary for paratroopers or police or demonstrators to provoke each other, in the exercise either of duty or of self-expression today—and it will be tragic if they do.
> The demonstrators will be betraying their own ideals if they follow those extremists who would deliberately turn this rally into a field of violence.

On Friday and Saturday morning, there were front-page stories in the Washington papers on the arrival of troops, and a comic story on LACE, the hippies counterindicant for MACE. A man named Augustus Owsley Stanley, III, had made it. His statement was that LACE "makes you want to take off your clothes, kiss people and make love."

Much enjoyable copy on hippie plans to attack with marbles, noise-makers, water pistols. They would jam gun barrels with flowers. They would try to kidnap LBJ and wrestle him to the ground and take his pants off.

Let us move then to the Pentagon. The speeches at Lincoln Memorial were done, and a mass of people, calculated by *The New York Times* as fifty thousand, walked over Arlington Memorial Bridge in the next two hours. Waiting for them at the Pentagon or engaged in police work on the route were the following forces; 1,500 Metropolitan Police, 2,500 Washington, D.C., National Guardsmen, about 200 U. S. Marshals, and unspecified numbers of Government Security Guards, and Park, White House, and Capitol police. There were also 6,000 troops from the 82nd Airborne Division flown in from Fort Bragg, North Carolina, the same 82nd Airborne which had once parachuted into Normandy on D-Day and was now fresh from Santo Domingo and the Detroit riots. MP units had been flown in from California and Texas, the U. S. Marshals had been brought from just about everywhere—Florida, New York, Arizona, Texas, to name a few states—it was to be virtually a convention for them. In addition, 20,000 troops stationed nearby were on alert.

For the army of the demonstrators, no precise figures are available; government estimates were low and Left Wing estimates were high. The April March in New York had suggested a rule of thumb: the police estimate multiplied by four might be as close to the real number as the Left Wing estimate divided by two and a half. Thus a real crowd of 200,000 people would be described as 50,000 by police and a half million by the sponsors. In Washington these discrepancies had less thunder in the gap. A quote from *The New York Times*

The joint estimate by the police and the military was that a maximum of about 55,000 persons had attended the Lincoln Memorial rally that preceded the March. A *New York Times* employee assigned to make a head count estimated the marchers who crossed Memorial Bridge at more than 54,000.

273

Assuming this last figure is close to a real count (on the basis that a literal count was actually made, and that the *Times* is presumably an intermediary point of view in this dispute) we can then assume that somewhere between 75,000 and 90,000 people were at Lincoln Memorial, for if 54,000 crossed the bridge, at least 10,000 must have stayed behind, and this is not to include the people who came to Lincoln Memorial in order to be there, listened to a few speeches, and departed, no historic oratory intercepting them. That number could have been as many as twenty or thirty thousand although it was doubtless not so great.

Now another quotation from the *Times*.

The Defense Department said that it had made aerial photographs of the crowd at the Pentagon and had arrived at a maximum estimate there of 35,000 persons through military photo-interpretation techniques.

In other words, 19,000 of the 54,000 demonstrators who crossed the bridge suddenly decided not to continue on to the Pentagon! No, it is obvious the Defense Department is speaking (assuming their estimate has any value at all) of the maximum crowd at any one time, for since it took several hours to cross the bridge (how interesting in this light becomes Rubin's lost desire for two bridges) some of the crowd was leaving while others were arriving.

At any rate, we have an army of at least 35,000 amateur soldiers consisting of doctors, dentists, faculty, veterans groups, housewives, accountants, trade unionists, Communists, Socialists, pacifists, Trotskyists, anarchists, artists, and entertainers, no, even historians may have a joke—there was no more than a smattering and a sprinkling of such professionals at the Pentagon. Present in the majority were college students from all over the East, and high school students and hippies and Diggers and bikers. And—we come to the beginning of the battle—a striking force of shock troops. There was a group which had arrived with a real idea of combat in mind. It was in fact that same advance of hundreds of men carrying placards

274

and flags and standards whose approach on a half-run across the North Parking Area had so impressed Mailer with its resemblance to a photograph by Mathew Brady.

This group consisted in fact of two groups, the Students for a Democratic Society, and a considerably smaller group of unattached elements who had once called themselves the Revolutionary Contingent, but had been unable to function together because of many arguments on the proper style of their militancy, i.e. whether to use Vietcong flags or some of the specialized techniques of Japanese students such as snake dances for breaking through police lines. Once, the Revolutionary Contingent had consisted of the Committee to Aid the National Liberation Front, the Black Mask, and other high-fragmentation sects, but now no alliance was left, other than their agreement to work together at the Pentagon. In preference to a new name, let us however still call them the Revolutionary Contingent. (It was to this group, incidentally, that Walter Teague was attached.) That the Revolutionary Contingent happened to be in the vanguard was not surprising, but the body of the striking force remained the SDS, and that was significant, for the SDS, sharing apparently the detestation of some on the Left for the mass rally and the Great Left Pall, had a practice never to take part in large demonstrations. The Students for a Democratic Society did their work in the field—they organized in the colleges and went to live in the ghettos. They were an American form of the nineteenth-century back-to-the-people movements among Russian intellectuals.

But when on October 6 Van Cleve first stated that the government would not allow civil disobedience in any form, SDS decided to work for the March. (Thus, this first announcement of government repression had helped to bring in not only Dr. Spock on the right but SDS on the left of the Mobilization.) In the two weeks which followed, however, SDS's enthusiasm cooled over some of the compromises. Yet in the week before the March, it still appeared as if the government and the Mobilization might be able to come to no agreement on details, and so the government would not grant the Mobilization Com-

275

mittee a rally and parade permit. If our history has deliberately made little of such last-minute dramas, it is because all emphasis here has been in the other direction; it was assumed that once the government permitted some kind of assembly on the Pentagon steps with a recognition of the likelihood of civil disobedience, the rest was negotiation and detail. That is an advantage of history—it can assume that certain supposedly dramatic issues were never in doubt, even though last-minute agreement on the specific road to the Pentagon was never made, and there were threats on both sides through the last week to break off negotiation. It is obviously safe to assume then that the atmosphere around the headquarters of the Mobilization Committee was dramatic. Without a permit, some violent confrontation between demonstrators and the authority would be inevitable. So SDS kept up word to its members that Washington was very much an active front, worthy of their activity. They got ready for the March.

SDS was, however, nothing if not wary of the Mobilization Committee and its tail of cautionary bureaucratic moderate peace groups. SDS did not wish to compromise its own militancy and its own view of civil disobedience, confrontation, and resistance by falling into the toils and instrumentalisms of the others. So it formed a temporary alliance to go into action with the Revolutionary Contingent. They would get themselves in the vanguard of the March—it was their militancy the line of notables may have been feeling most directly behind them—and, once on the Virginia side of the bridge, would separate from the other marchers and proceed by their own private route, running most of the way for a mile, through the woods to the North Parking Area where they would assemble and make their charge. Elements of SDS were lost on the rush, but determined not to wait and in fact obviously determined to start the combat before the second rally at the North Parking Area had well begun (in order to break what they considered the ridiculous petty legalities of the agreement: talk from 3 P.M. to 4; fight from 4 to 5!) the Revolutionary Contingent and SDS had charged across the parking area and made an assault on the military police barrier at a point considerably to the left (all directions will be given from the point of view of the demonstrators facing the Administration wall of the Pentagon) indeed far to the left of the Pentagon itself, so far to the left that if they had broken through, they would probably have been forced to try to cross the ramp which went over Jefferson Davis Highway into the River Entrance, and from there might have tried to circle back to the asphalt plaza in front of the Administration Entrance, or might simply have continued on into the Pentagon itself by the River Entrance. In any case, they were stopped. There were barriers, there were troops, they were winded by their run all the way from Arlington Bridge, "the crowd was not yet mad enough to back them up," as Teague was to put it later (although if it was an angry crowd they desired for a base, they could hardly have expected much support from the empty reaches of the North Parking at that early stage) and they were charged by MPs with rifles and sheathed bayonets. It is possible that bayonets were in panic unsheathed —reports of such bayonets appear here and again in accounts, none remotely verifiable, even the hour in doubt; but for whatever reason, the vanguard of this militant striking force certainly faltered, and abruptly fled backward in panic. (Precisely the retreat which was to discover Mailer's own panic of MACE.) Teague, carrying the N.L.F. flag in the forefront, was at this point lost. Someone grabbed his flag. Teague struggled to get it back, and was thereupon arrested, but the flag was left in his possession. Shortly afterward, Mailer, picking a point still further to the left of the charge of the SDS and the Revolutionary Contingent, stepped over the line and was, as described, arrested, brought over the ramp to the River Entrance, and deposited in a Volkswagen where he was soon to meet Teague and the Nazi.

Let us go back to the alliance between the Students for a Democratic Society and the Revolutionary Contingent (which alliance for the sake of brevity we may as well begin to call SDS-Contingent). They had obviously been charged for combat for days, and such tension in men who are determined, usually succeeds in concealing from themselves the extent of their fear. In combat which comes after long spiritual preparation, there is an instant of relaxation in the very first moment altogether dangerous to dedicated troops—all the fear they have denied can now flood them. They can panic and flee—the inner preparation has been too great. (One must, after all, contemplate the extent of that fear, made up in part of sustained political brooding about the nature of American brutality at home and abroad—they were now going to confront this brutality; the very imagination which stimulated them to think radically now had added its exaggerations to the possibilities of reprisal.) Where the dedication is serious, however, the recovery is quick. Furious with themselves at this first rout, they now reassembled, conferred among themselves, moved past the Fugs, climbed the embankment which bordered the four-lane Jefferson Davis Highway, broke down the newly erected wire fence which restrained them to the Parking Area, gathered numbers from arriving unattached demonstrators, and crossed the highway, entered the Mall, went up the long diagonal steps in the face of the stone wall which separates the asphalt plaza of the Administration Entrance from the Mall, then climbed the approach steps, pushed back the MP line, and broke through it at the head of the stairs to fan out and occupy the left side of the plaza, only—so far as can be determined from the conflict of reports—to be immediately cut off from the main body on the stairs and the center of the plaza by a bracing of MPs and U.S. Marshals who virtually separated the two groups, thereby making passage from the left side of the plaza back to the stairs impossible. Still, this group which overflowed the plaza on the left was to retain these positions until morning by which time arrests and the attrition of departures had emptied their salient. More centrally located, the group in the center of the plaza and stairs was to hold their position for thirty-two hours, a perfectly legal position by the terms of the GSA contract, although no one on the line, troops or demonstrators, were too aware of this, and illegalities on both sides in relation to this line abounded. The estimates of Left Wing and underground newspapers put the number of demonstrators on the left of the plaza at 2,500, and

278

the number on the central plaza, entrance stairs, and diagonal steps leading to the stairs as double. Since underground papers seem to pride themselves on being even more inaccurate than their enemies, the rule of thumb previously suggested would put no more than one thousand demonstrators in the "illegal area" of the plaza and a maximum of two thousand on the "legal" stairs, steps, and center of the plaza.

Let us not however go another step into developments until we have fortified our picture of the situation. Far away, a quarter of a mile away, across the Mall, the four-lane highway, a wire fence, and a small intervening hill, the rally is taking place in the North Parking and somewhere between ten and twenty thousand people, nervous, bored, uncertain whether they are relieved or disappointed that so little seems to be taking place, are out there receiving the long tasteless unleavened bread of fiery political speeches, the apogee of this irony achieved by the most militant speech of them all, made by Carl Davidson, the interorganizational secretary of SDS (even SDS had its table of organization) who said, "Repression must be met, confronted, stopped, by whatever means possible." The next major demonstrations would arm to disrupt draft induction centers. "We must tear them down," he said. "Burn them down, if necessary." That was strong stuff. Over the hill, across the highway, along the Mall, up the steps, the first heads were being cracked by the clubs of the Marshals, while some true hearts of the orally-oriented Left were listening to their fourth hour of oratory—how much of one's own saliva must have been tasted by now.

Younger spirits were now breaking down a new section of fence between the Parking Area and the highway in order to get to the Mall. The monitors made impotent efforts to hold them off. "You're not supposed to go over there until later," they shouted through their bullhorns while people crossed. All the while, marchers in that long line of 54,000 people taking two hours to cross the bridge (it is possible Chaplain Boyle was being released from Alexandria Post Office as the last marcher reached the Pentagon) were trickling into the Parking Area, listening in confusion to the speeches (for many of the marchers must like Mailer have foreseen a dramatic confrontation with a line of soldiers for himself) and then looked about them for the next move. Meanwhile, rumors were arriving and passing through the crowd of the action at the Pentagon itself. As speakers continued, the crowd began to diminish—now thousands were going through the gap in the fence, crossing the highway, and invading the Mall. The legal time of entry on the Mall arranged by Van Cleve had been 4 P.M., the first attack had come earlier, but the majority of demonstrators, being present at the Parking Rally, did not cross over to the Mall until 4:30, being thus left with not much more than an hour of daylight.

Meanwhile, in the vanguard, on the asphalt plaza and on the Pentagon steps, not a great deal was happening, yet everything was happening. The military situation had not altered appreciably, although a few significant events took place, notably three: first, a member of SDS, Tom Bell, succeeded in climbing an isolated wall of the plaza bordering the steps accompanied by his bullhorn. He was thus in position to talk to the groups isolated on the left side of the plaza from the steps. When a Marshal or an MP (accounts conflict) attempted to pull him down, he pushed him off—to the cheers of the demonstrators watching—and proceeded to serve as communications center. He also proceeded—well grounded doubtless in Trotsky's *History of the Russian Revolution*—to talk to the troops. This was to be the first of many speeches to be made to them, and the content of these speeches must eventually be given, for the most conventional and original aspects of Left polemic were to be presented by different speakers, some professional, some—girls, for instance, opening buttons on their blouses—improvisational. More of that, later.

The second significant event in this relatively constant military situation was that some of the demonstrators, having overrun the restraining lines of rope in their push through to the plaza, now began to use them. Tying knots in the ropes, they lowered them over the wall to the Mall where young demonstrators, anxious to join them, now began to climb up. Since the wall was built of massive bevelled blocks of stone, it was not altogether difficult to hold on to the rope, and climb up, using the serrations for toe-holds. Still, it had risk, a fifteen-foot drop on one's back at worst, and so the men who climbed were full of good morale on reaching the top and probably inspired the next and third significant action which is that a group probably composed in the main of SDS-Contingent on the plaza saw a side entrance door to the left of the main Administration Entrance guarded only by six MPs. Since only a relatively thin line of MPs were on the line to restrain them here, a small group, perhaps twenty-five, made a quick push, broke the line, broke through the MPs, and actually entered the Holy of Holies—they were in the Pentagon racing down a corridor.

Not for long! Troops had been brought into the Pentagon the night before, they had slept on cots in the corridors of the building (which is not unlike laying out one's mattress in Lincoln Tunnel). Confined inside, suffering the tension of endless hours waiting for unseen anarchists, bomb-throwers, Communists, poison gassers, poison in the water, nymphomaniacs, drug addicts, insane Negroes, and common city folk to inundate them under their human wave in these drear corridors, one can only guess—unless there are films—at the unmitigated fury with which the few demonstrators were clubbed and kicked, arrested, and carried off.

One can of course ask why so few felt obliged to attempt the sortie, and no one behind to follow them; the answers cannot be definitive. But two factors apply. One is the extraordinary demand for initiative on the side of the demonstrators if they were to do anything at all. Anyone who has passed through the educational system of America is in unconscious degree somewhere near half a patriot. (We may reduce the fraction when considering progressive schools.) The brain is washed deep, there are reflexes: white shirts, Star-Spangled Banner, saluting the flag. At home is corporation land's whip—the television set. Who would argue there are no idea-sets of brave soldiers, courageous cops, great strength and brutal patriotic skill in the land of authority? Obvious remarks, but it is precisely this huge and much convinced unconscious part of oneself which a demonstrator has to move against when he charges with his small part of an army into a line of MPs close-packed, arms locked; anxiety washes the will with its dissolving flood. Demonstrators may break off at the last moment. Moreover, one moves forward unarmed into men who hold clubs or rifles. One does not even know the guns are unloaded—these are amateur soldiers so innocent of war they do not know enough to deduce that if there are no magazines loaded into the rifles, there can be at most but one round in the chamber. It was not so easy, therefore, when the moment came to charge into the Pentagon.

In any case, the group on the plaza was already divided. SDS-Contingent was now separating (in the centrifuge of revolutionary activity) back into SDS and the Revolutionary Contingent. They now had a different ideas of how to proceed. SDS was for consolidating the ground gained by sitting down. Bell at the bullhorn was telling demonstrators to sit on the theory that the troops were being baited, and people could be trampled on the steps if there was a charge and a panic. SDS, profoundly influenced by the ideas of Che Guevara, was now opposed to any further violent confrontation at this point for they thought it would be suicidal—it was not Guevara's maxim to confront a superior military force from fixed positions.

The Revolutionary Contingent on their side (the two factions mixed and arguing with one another on the stairs and the plaza) were for pushing actively against the line of MPs and attempting to breach them—either some deep principle of martyrdom was involved (some revolutionary mystique of an initial blooding) or they were working on dubious military principles, since a breach in the MPs' line would serve to advantage only if thousands could follow through behind them, and those thousands were not available. Since they were cut off from all reinforcements on the Mall, the first push, in the military sense, should have been through the troops holding the access road off Jefferson Davis Highway. A breach there would have opened the left side of the plaza to the tens of thousands on the Mall whose only way of reaching them now was by climbing the ropes on the fifteen-foot wall. But then the Revolutionary Contingent produced at once the bravest and most ineptly directed troops of the demonstrators' army.

Let us recapitulate their errors. They assembled too soon, and they attacked too soon. Knowing they were the only dedicated troops (but for SDS) they might have done better to have reconnoitered the ground, waited for thousands of marchers to arrive, next established lines and zones of communication between the Mall and the Parking Area, and then with latent armies ready, even looking for action, they could have charged suddenly, hoped to make a major breach, and might have counted on tens of hundreds to follow them. It could of course be argued that their early attack succeeded precisely because it was early, but then they only gained a small illegal area of the left side of the plaza beyond the steps. To enter the Pentagon in numbers, which was the real objective of the Revolutionary Contingent, would have been possible only if they were the point of attack for some determined available mass of hundreds, preferably thousands of demonstrators ready to follow in their wake.

At any rate, if this is the military situation with which we are left, let us now take a look at the front line, at the six inches of no-man's-land across which troops and demonstrators—in the closest use yet of this word—confront each other.

6: A PALETTE OF TACTICS

It is on this particular confrontation that the conceit one is writing a history must be relinquished. Doubtless it has been hardly possible to ignore that this work resides in two enclaves, the first entitled History As a Novel, the second here before us called The Novel As History. No one familiar with husking the ambiguities of English will be much mystified by the titles. It is obvious the first book is a history in the guise or dress or manifest of a novel, and the second is a real or true novel—no less!—presented in the style of a history. (Of course, everyone including the author will continue to speak of the first book as a novel and the second as a history—practical usage finds flavor in such comfortable opposites.) However, the first book can be, in the formal sense, nothing but a personal history which while written as a novel was to the best of the author's memory scrupulous to facts, and therefore a document; whereas the second, while dutiful to all newspaper accounts, eyewitness reports, and historic inductions available, while even obedient to a general style of historical writing, at least up to this point, while even pretending to be a history (on the basis of its introduction) is finally now to be disclosed as some sort of condensation of a collective novel—which is to admit that an explanation of the mystery of the events at the Pentagon cannot be developed by the methods of history —only by the instincts of the novelist. The reasons are several, but reduce to one. Forget that the journalistic information available from both sides is so incoherent, inaccurate, contradictory, malicious, even based on error that no accurate history is conceivable. More than one historian has found a way through chains of false fact. No, the difficulty is that the history is interior—no documents can give sufficient intimation: the novel must replace history at precisely that point where experience is sufficiently emotional, spiritual, psychical, moral, existential, or supernatural to expose the fact that the historian in pursuing the experience would be obliged to quit the clearly demarcated limits of historic inquiry. So these limits are now relinquished. The collective novel which follows, while still written in the cloak of an historic style, and, therefore, continuously attempting to be scrupulous to the welter of a hundred confusing and opposed facts, will now unashamedly enter that world of strange lights and intuitive speculation which is the novel. Let us, then, fortified by this clarification, this advertisement of intentions, move up to the front, to the six inches of no-man's-land between the U. S. Army and the demonstrators.

It is safe to say that the beginning of this confrontation has not been without terror on each side. The demonstrators, all too conscious of what they consider the profound turpitude of the American military might in Asia, are prepared (or altogether unprepared) for any conceivable brutality here. On their side, the troops have listened for years to small-town legends about the venality, criminality, filth, corruption, perversion, addiction, and unbridled appetites of that mysterious group of city Americans referred to first as hipsters, then beatniks, then hippies; now hearing they are linked with the insidious infiltrators of America's psychic life, the Reds! the troops do not know whether to expect a hairy kiss on their lips or a bomb between their knees. Each side is coming face to face with its own conception of the devil!

Let us give the literal picture. At this early stage, before the demonstrators were to sit down, a close-packed line of MPs with clubs, backed by another line of soldiers, was supported further by separate U. S. Marshals a few feet behind them, arrayed like linebackers—it could not have been unself-conscious. In other places of tension and at other times, soldiers were to advance with rifles, with sheathed bayonets, with tear gas, but this had not happened yet on this front where the line of standing demonstrators was composed of a mix of SDS-Contingent with a greater number of unattached young demonstrators caught in the suction of the action. Posed against the lines of soldiers, already some historic flowers were being placed insouciantly, insolently, and tenderly in gun barrels by boys and girls.

Of course the rhetoric of the Left had been consistent in referring to these troops as innocent victims of the military machine, and there is the real possibility that some fraction of the soldiers may have been secretly sympathetic to the demonstrators. The following is from an allegedly unedited tape of an interview with a soldier who had been at the Pentagon. "Around 40 percent of all the military is in favor of your demonstration. This is a big point that I

285

have found. They go out there, and around 30 percent are just out to hurt anybody, beat anybody up they can, just because they have a rifle and all this other stuff. However, 30 percent of them are sort of serene about the whole thing, and they couldn't care less. They have a job to do and that's all."

Since this interview was printed in the *East Village Other,* one cannot be certain it exists; psychedelic underground papers consider themselves removed from any fetish with factology. Still the dialogue has its ring—"sort of serene" is not an easy remark to make up. In any case, if the soldiers at this hour were not generally, by all accounts, interested in brutality, they were certainly fascinated by their foe, and when the minutes of confrontation went by and then the first hour, there began some lessening of woe and some lessening of the soldiers' extraordinary attention; the true literal fear of losing their lives began to go away from them. They had been sent out after all with God knows what orientation. "Well, men," says the major, "our mission is to guard the Pentagon from rioters and out-of-march scale prearranged-upon levels of defacement, meaning clear? well, the point to keep in mind, troopers, is those are going to be American citizens out there expressing their constitutional right to protest—that don't mean we're going to let them fart in our face—but the Constitution is a complex document with circular that is circulating sets of conditions—put it this way, I got my buddies being chewed by V.C. right this minute maybe I don't care to express personal sentiments now, negative, keep two things in mind—those demos out there could be carrying bombs or bangalore torpedoes for all we know, and you're going out with no rounds in your carbines so thank God for the .45. And first remember one thing more—they start trouble with us, they'll wish they hadn't left New York unless you get killed in the stampede of us to get to them. Yessir, you keep a tight asshole and the fellow behind you can keep his nose clean."

If the troops were relieved that a pullulating unwashed orgiastic Communist-inspired wave of flesh did not roll right over them, and that in fact the majority of demonstrators right there before them were not unlike in appearance the few quiet long-haired cool odd kids they had never quite gotten to know in high school, the demonstrators in their turn were relieved in profounder fashion that their rank of eyes had met the soldiers, and it was the soldiers who had looked away. They looked across the gulf of the classes, the middle classes and the working classes. It would take the rebirth of Marx for Marxism to explain definitively this middle class condemnation of an imperialist war in the last Capitalist nation, this working class affirmation. But it is the urban middle class in America who always feel most uprooted, most alienated from America itself, and so instinctively most critical of America, for neither do they work with their hands nor wield real power, so it is never their lathe nor their sixty acres, and certainly never is it their command which is accepted because they are simply American and there, no, the urban middle class was the last class to arrive at respectable status and it has been the most overprotected (for its dollars are the great nourishing mother of all consumer goods) yet the most spiritually undefended since even the concept of a crisis in identity seems most exclusively their own. The sons and daughters of that urban middle class, forever alienated in childhood from all the good simple funky nitty-gritty American joys of the working class like winning a truly dangerous fist fight at the age of eight or getting sex before fourteen, dead drunk by sixteen, whipped half to death by your father, making it in rumbles with a proud street gang, living at war with the educational system, knowing how to snicker at the employer from one side of the mouth, riding a bike with no hands, entering the Golden Gloves, doing a hitch in the Navy, or a stretch in the stockade, and with it all, their sense of élan, of morale, for buddies are the manna of the working class: there is a God-given cynical indifference to school, morality, and job. The working class is loyal to friends, not ideas. No wonder the Army bothered them not a bit. But the working class bothered the sons of the middle class with their easy confident virility and that physical courage with which they seemed to be born—there was a fear and a profound respect in every middle class son for

287

his idea of that most virile ruthless indifferent working class which would eventually exterminate them as easily as they exterminated gooks. And this is not even to mention the sense of muted awe which lived in every son of the urban middle class before the true American son of the small town and the farm, that blank-eyed snub-nosed innocent, bewildered, stubborn crew-cut protagonist of all conventional American life; the combination of his symbolic force with the working class was now in focus here.

Standing against them, the demonstrators were not only sons of the middle class of course, but sons who had departed the middle class, they were rebels and radicals and young revolutionaries; yet they were unbloodied, they felt secretly weak, they did not know if they were the simple equal, man for man, of these soldiers, and so when this vanguard confronted soldiers now, and were able to stare them in the eye, they were, in effect, saying silently, "I will steal your élan, and your brawn, and the very animal of your charm because I am morally right and you are wrong and the balance of existence is such that the meat of your life is now attached to my spirit, I am stealing your balls." A great exaltation arose among the demonstrators in that first hour. Surrounded on the plaza and on the stairs, they could have no idea of what would happen next, they could be beaten, arrested, buried in a stampede, most of them were on the mouth of their first cannon, yet for each minute they survived, sixty seconds of existential gold was theirs. Minutes passed, an hour went by—these troops were more afraid of them than they were afraid of the troops! Great glory. They began to cheer. Those who were not in the first row yelled insults, taunted the soldiers, derided them—the demonstrators in the front looked into the soldiers' eyes, smiled, tried to make conversation. "Hey, soldier, you think I'm a freak. Why am I against the war in Vietnam? Cause it's wrong. You're not defending America against Communism, you're just giving your officers a job." Some of the dialogue was better, some was worse, some was face to face, some by bullhorn to the troops—technology land at the front. The dialogue was to change character yet, become more intimate, more awful, more excruciating for the soldiers, and the demonstrators; it was to go on for thirty-two hours of close-up dialogues across the line of confrontation, first standing, then—in response to the fear of stampede—sitting, faces inches apart, the demonstrators speaking softly, the soldiers under orders silent, some soldiers trembling—there were reports of officers coming up to say, "Steady, soldier!" and of soldiers here and there specifically relieved, even unconfirmed stories of three soldiers who took off their helmets and joined the demonstrators.

Of course this was only the first hour of thirty-two, and involved but the first line; three or four rows back the condition was different, one was safer, more anonymous —one's abuse could have more bite for considerably less cost. And down in the Mall a different condition existed, one of excitement, bewilderment, interest, anticipation. Cut off from the demonstration on the stairs or the plaza by the press of the crowd at the base one had only to ignore the possibility of climbing the ropes and there was no way one could not in good conscience declare one had done his best. Of course, there were confrontations here as well. Where soldiers cut off the access roads, demonstrators from the Mall were pressing against them. Here the attitude was more ugly. Here soldiers were not cutting people off from the Pentagon, but from their own demonstrators, so the imperative to get through was more direct, the fear of being stampeded was less—there was all the Mall to run out into. Therefore the inability to mount a charge to break the soldiers' line was less excusable, closer perhaps to cowardice—hence the ugliness of the crowd. And indeed far out in the Mall, isolated altogether from other soldiers, were very small detachments on now unknown details, three soldiers here, five there. Newspaper stories referred to them, Breslin reported they were reviled and tormented unmercifully; when it got dark a few soldiers were beaten up—so goes the story. It may be well to quote Breslin here.

Taste and decency had left the scene a long time before. All that remained were these lines of troops and packs of nondescript kids who taunted the soldiers. The kids went to the bathroom on the side of the Pentagon building. They threw a couple of rocks through the first-floor windows. The soldiers faced them silently. From the steps, a captain in the Airborne kept calling out through a bullhorn.

"A Company, hold your ground, A Company," his voice said. "Nobody comes and nobody goes. Just hold your ground, A Company."

The mob on the grass in front of the soldiers began chanting. "Hold that line, hold that line."

There was no humor to it. These were not the kind of kids who were funny. These were the small core of dropouts and drifters and rabble who came to the front of what had started out as a beautiful day, one that would have had meaning to it. They turned a demonstration for peace, these drifters in raggedy clothes, into a sickening, club-swinging mess. At the end of the day, the only concern anybody could have was for the soldiers who were taking the abuse.

On the steps leading from the grass to the blacktop the kids taunted the troops and kicked at them.

"Hit them—they won't hit back," somebody yelled.

A scraggly bearded guy in a blue denim jacket shrieked. He ran up with a flag holder and swatted a soldier in the back.

Whatever it was that this peace march had started out to be, it now became an exercise in clawing at soldiers. And it lasted into the darkness.

In contrast let us now dare to give an extract from Gerald Long's account in the *National Guardian*. It is not a paper famous for its lack of bias and the account here is obviously partisan, but its virtues are to be brief and vivid.

Some demonstrators near the entrance and a good number behind the front lines urged the crowd forward, into a clash with the troops who were standing with rifles at the ready. A debate ensued. SDS leaders, also among the first near the doors, grabbed portable loudspeakers and urged the crowd to sit down. ("It would have been a bloodbath," SDS leader Greg Calvert commented later. "A thousand people could have been killed if they attempted to storm those lines unarmed. We regarded those urging the crowd forward as left adventurers and tried to stop them. We succeeded.")

A company of MPs materialized from the right, running awkwardly like puppets. They stopped in front of the ramp, regrouped, leveled their rifles and marched forward. Unbelieving demonstrators just gaped at them, stunned, confronted for the first time by the guns of "our boys." Then something remarkable happened. People began laughing. Someone threw yellow flowers at the MPs, who by now had stopped, frozen, guns pointed at young men and women their own age.

Every time the troops moved forward to push demonstrators away from the ramp, scores, hundreds of youths would sneak behind them—up the ramp. The MPs were enveloped. People were standing with faces just inches from the barrels of M-14 semi-automatics and an occasional single barrel shotgun.

The MPs executed an about-face, seeking to clear out the demonstrators who ran behind them. A youth refused to be moved. A rifle butt landed in his stomach. He grabbed the rifle. Several youths grabbed rifles. Four helmets were stolen. A demonstrator was slugged. An MP was slugged.

White-helmeted federal marshals, impressed for service from the calm of courtrooms, moved forward, clubs swinging. It seemed to this observer— both in this incident and for the next 30 or so hours —that the marshals aimed particularly at women.

Each time the action stopped in a particular spot, demonstrators sought to speak with the soldiers, who were under orders not to respond. "Why are you doing this?" a demonstrator asked. "Join us" the soldiers were asked. It was obvious that some of the troops were weakening. A few soldiers seemed ready to faint. "Hold your lines, hold your lines," a captain repeated harshly, over and over, to the soldiers.

A girl confronted a soldier, "Why, why, why?" she asked. "We're just like you. You're like us. It's them," she said pointing to the Pentagon. She brought her two fingers to her mouth, kissed them and touched the soldier's lips. Four soldiers grabbed her and dragged her away, under arrest. The soldier she had spoken to tried to tell them that she hadn't hurt him.

It may be obvious by now that a history of the March on the Pentagon which is not unfair will never be written, any more than a history which could prove dependable in details!

As it grew dark there was the air of carnival as well. The last few thousand Marchers to arrive from Lincoln Memorial did not even bother to go to the North Parking Area, but turned directly to the Mall and were cheered by the isolated detachments who saw them from a ledge of the wall at the plaza. Somewhere, somebody lit his draft card, and as it began to burn he held it high. The light of the burning card traveled through the crowd until it found another draft card someone else was ready to burn and this was lit, and then another in the distance. In the gathering dark it looked like a dusting of fireflies over the great shrub of the Mall.

By now, however, the way was open again to the North Parking. The chartered buses were getting ready to leave. That portion of this revolution which was Revolution on Excursion Ticket was now obliged to leave. Where once there had been thirty thousand people in the Mall, there were now suddenly twenty thousand people, ten thousand people, less. As the busses ground through the interlockings of their gears and pulled out into a mournful wheezing acceleration along the road, so did other thousands on the Mall look at one another and decide it was probably time to catch a cab or take the long walk back to Washington—they were in fact hungry for a meal. So the Mall began to empty, and the demonstrators on the steps must have drawn a little closer. The mass assault was over.

A few thousand, however, were left, and they were the best. The civil disobedience might be far from done. On the Mall, since the oncoming night was cold, bonfires were lit. On the stairs, a peace pipe was passed. It was filled with hashish. Soon the demonstrators were breaking out marijuana, handing it back and forth, offering it even to the soldiers here and there. The Army after all had been smoking marijuana since Korea, and in Vietnam— by all reports—were gorging on it. The smell of the drug, sweet as the sweetest leaves of burning tea, floated down to the Mall where its sharp bite of sugar and smoldering grass pinched the nose, relaxed the neck. Soon most of the young on the Mall were smoking as well. Can this be one of the moments when the Secretary of Defense looks out from his window in the Pentagon at the crowd on the Mall and studies their fires below? They cannot be unreminiscent of other campfires in Washington and Virginia little more than a century ago. The Secretary of Defense is by all report a complex man, a reader of poetry —does he have a secret admiration for the works of Robert Lowell as he stands by the window?

But what has happened to Lowell, to Macdonald and Lowell, to Dellinger, to Dr. Spock, and Father Rice, and Lens, and all? We must move on.

7: AN END TO ORIENTATION

When Macdonald and Lowell were turned back by the MPs, they went down the length of the North Parking to the speakers' rally and stayed there for the duration of the speeches. When this second rally was done, the leaders decided to join the others, and commit their acts of symbolic civil disobedience at which, presumably, the notables would be arrested. So Dave Dellinger, Dagmar Wilson, Dr. and Mrs. Spock, Noam Chomsky, Sidney Lens, Barbara Deming, Macdonald, and Lowell left the North Parking. Drifting through the Mall, entering dialogues with young demonstrators, or holding impromptu press conferences which would be forced to emphasize their unhappy distance from the action (and the press of the demonstrators on the steps might have been difficult to pass through) were alternatives which offered no grip —Dellinger wisely led the contingent past the Mall to a small grassy area, now untenanted but for soldiers, between Washington Boulevard and the west wall of the Pentagon. Here he planned to open another arena of action by engaging the troops in a teach-in. On their arrival, Dellinger suggested that those who had not spoken at the rally should talk to the soldiers. Father Rice spoke. Then Noam Chomsky. While he was speaking a line of soldiers left the west wall of the Pentagon and advanced gently on the notables, moving forward slowly, expressionlessly, and with a lack of violence which was bewildering, for they passed silently through the figures about Dellinger without striking any of them, indeed making every effort not to touch them. A larger crowd of students who had accompanied Dellinger's and Spock's contingent fled however before the soldiers, despite Dellinger's shouts through the bullhorn for them to hold ground, since the soldiers were not intending violence. But this group of demonstrators fled. Perhaps it was the movies they had seen of armies of zombies, perhaps it was the vitiated state of their liver after four hours of speeches—it was evident, no matter how, that rhetoric hand in hand with reason put no spirit of war into revolutionary boys. The notables, however, were made of firmer stuff—they turned around and began to address the soldiers who had passed by them. When this became apparently absurd—where does the teach-in begin on a man's back?—they turned about again, and walked once more toward the wall of the Pentagon. Now more soldiers suddenly double-timed out of an entrance, rifles at high port. Caught between two lines of soldiers, the ends pinched off, the notables were surrounded. The soldiers were silent.

Dr. Spock began to speak to the troops. He told a story which was obviously one of his favorites. He had received a letter not so long ago from a soldier who wrote to him from Vietnam in tones which condemned the war. Dr. Spock wrote back only to have his letter returned with the legend, "Verified deceased."

Now a Negro sergeant who had commanded the advance of the first line of troops came back, and said to the second line, "All right, push 'em out now."

The soldiers advanced, the notables sat down. Dr. Spock kept talking, and a flurry in which no account is clear took place. In the course of it, Dellinger, Dagmar Wilson, and Chomsky were arrested. Spock was not, although he made efforts to be arrested—it is conceivable the Marshals were under orders to leave him alone. Macdonald and Lowell were passed by. When it was all over, and some had been copped, and some hit by clubs (or rapped with the ends—for the Marshals were not conspicuously brutal here) Lowell, Macdonald, and a few others found themselves alone. The storm had passed. They left, unhurt, and eventually went home, Lowell to begin a long poem a few days later. (When next Mailer saw him a month later, 800 lines had already been written!) At this moment, however, in this history, it can only be said that the leader of the March on the Pentagon and the great majority of notables, all being obviously expendable, were now out of all action and/or away from the fray.

This excursion to the flank and arrest were not uncharacteristic of Dellinger's leadership in the weeks preceding the March. If Dellinger had been doing his best to be true to his principles and at the same time elucidate the maximum of practical advantage possible in the constructed situation which conciliation must obligatorily produce, he had on this occasion fulfilled just such a limited maximum. Not feeling determined to be with the demonstrators on the line, since the arrest of the notables would be in his mind a superior aim, he had made his own attack in an illegal area, and had attempted to teach the opposing soldiers. When this produced the order to push them out, Dellinger managed to get himself arrested, not easy in the face of the military's obvious policy of *random* arrest, and was out of jail in the same evening, also not so automatic (if Mailer's experience is to be the scale of measure). He was able therefore to be present at a press conference where he could claim a "tremendous victory." The protest, he was reported to say, marked the beginning of a "more militant mood, a more persistent mood, a more insistent mood." If the second half of the proposition was almost certainly correct, the first half did not necessarily precede it, for at the opposite end of the spectrum of Left opinion, bitter old veterans might have been remarking that out of such "tremendous victories" concentration camps were born. In fact it would not have mattered too much what did happen—Dellinger, like any leader of such a Mobilization, would have been bound to claim an enormous victory. It is this he could have told Rubin on the night before the March—if we are to make the unwarranted assumption that such cynicism was actually in his conscious head—he could (or if not Dellinger, another leader) could have thought that what happened at the Pentagon would not matter short of the most incredible victory—such as McNamara joining the demonstrators—or the most abysmal defeat, a paralysis of all activity before the sight of the troops. Anything less than these alternatives would produce the same predictable results—each side would claim a great victory for its own principles, the press would be naturally on the side of the authority (although much which was favorable to the other side would be *leaked*) and the Left Wing and underground press and word of mouth would be sure to distort, enrich, ennoble, purify, and finally transpose the real history of the events to their own need; the real victory or defeat could be measured later by the militancy, money, and mass available for the next big operation. In the meantime he had appealed to the conscience of America, to the middle-class conscience at any rate, he had appealed through the attraction of the mass of numbers of the people who had attended, the numbers arrested, and the names of the notables. So he could have told Rubin

—if he had been thus cynical and by all evidence he was not—that the important thing, the only thing, was to have an action at the Pentagon, because that, given the processing methods of American newspapers, would be the only thing to come out of the event. Since the American Revolution must climb uphill blindfolded in the long Capitalist night, any *thing* which was publicity became a walking stick.

Rubin in such a dialogue could possibly have answered that although he agreed in part with Dellinger—there was still no real victory unless the troops at the front could leave with the conviction that something magical had been won. Rubin was a mystic, a revolutionary mystic—his roots were in Bakunin: so he believed that the chaos which followed disruption would force a crisis, force the government to overextend itself, and so would polarize the country and develop the strength of the Left who could build new values, new community, new power. So he must also have believed that nothing could be gained in the future which did not proceed from the truth of a victory whose light could be seen in the eye, that a war of publicity unillumined by inner victory was a war in a wallow with gobbets of dung, but that a true victory, if it came to only a few of the best of the very last hundred of the troops, would put a radiance in the seed of their oncoming night. An extraordinary multiplication of the romantic, but it was not Rubin's apocalyptic vision alone—it had been seen before by men so vastly different (but for the consonants of their name) as Castro, Cortes, and Christ—it was the collective vision now of the drug-illumined and revolutionary young of the American middle class.

8: AN AESTHETIC TESTED

One might say, the rest is detail; but it is not, not quite, certainly it is not. The real climax on the steps of the Pentagon was yet to occur.

The night went on. As the remaining demonstrators realized they were alone, and no longer linked to the eighty- or hundred-thousand-headed force of men and women around the reflecting pool, or the fifty thousand at the Pentagon, but were instead down to a few thousand of the true, the adventurous, and the dedicated, their massive bourgeois complement now gone (not unlike the departure of an obese and wealthy mother-in-law) as they sensed that they were a smaller force, even by count of heads, to the troops around, about, and inside the Pentagon, so they knew that now the war could become more serious, now their true weapons could show.

The campfires were lit, the pot—as already described —was passed; what prehistoric forms the dark bulk of the Pentagon must have taken from its spark, how the figures studying them with field glasses from the roof must have looked—how much like gargoyles on the ridge of a cathedral. Action was on in the night. Hungry, thirsty, the demonstrators were being fed—impromptu self-elected Diggers had organized transportation service for food and water. Beer came in, sandwiches, it was Saturday night—Saturnalia came in: couples began to neck on the grass, some awed by their audacity, some stimulated by the proximity of the Pentagon. Others, using spray cans, crayons, paints and brush began to write slogans on the stone wall of the Mall, the pier, the sides of the ramp. "WAR SUCKS" went one of the signs, "PENTAGON SUCKS" went another, "FUCK WAR" went a third.

There was much to be made of this in the newspapers when all was done, and much to be made of the litter on the grass. That might have been a mistake—the litter. An army which leaves its litter behind could form the habit of leaving its dead behind, but the signs! they were easier to defend, for the legend "PENTAGON SUCKS" would reach the troops, it would reach every unit in the Army before a month, and they would be a new breed of American soldiers if they did not laugh.

In the meantime the Army was not inactive. On the left access road where the Diggers had established a base in the chain of food transportation, tear gas was used by the troops—there seems no doubt of this. Too many eyewitness reports appeared in too many newspapers—indeed some reporters entered a night briefing in the Pentagon hardly able to see from tears in their eyes caused by gas discharged from canisters by soldiers, just in time to hear the Army deny they had used tear gas. Of course, some of the demonstrators had used tear gas too; so would swear Jimmy Breslin; so admitted one of the March leaders. It would in fact have been unlikely if out of this citizens' army of angelic and vicious children and youth, not one of that pill-ridden, electronically oriented, chemically-grounded generation had not brought some gimmicks with gas. How else to play? That army of hippies and bikers would not be so unfrightening when their inventive pop-art genius turned to the craft of the nuisance weapon. Twenty years of comic strips were twenty years of surrealist seed.

The girls were now taunting the soldiers on the line. Something had happened with the line. Now soldiers were being rotated rapidly, sometimes by the half-hour—no relationship between troops and soldiers was to be permitted to grow. Perhaps for good cause. Earlier in the day, a couple of Negro demonstrators were reported to have taunted a Negro soldier until he had finally been obliged to hang his head, turn it away. One can conceive of the dialogue.

"Hey, nigger, how long you going to kiss Mr. Charlie's who-who-who? Going over to Vietnam, going to be nigger hero, huh? Going to have your photograph in a honkie paper, that right, is that right? Hey, Mr. Big, give us some skin, take your fat black hand off that honkie asshole rifle and give us some skin. You're the man! You're the man!"

Yes, they had skinned him with that Negro irony which could separate the most weathered hide from the most determined flesh—the wisdoms of torture were in their skill—how could any U. S. Army dare to put many Negroes on a line, if an army of black and white demonstrators would be there to face them, no, the troops might break and no one would know where—the loss was bitter on this night that the Black Militants pursuing their own revolution were dispersed in the black ghetto of Washington rather than here. The Blacks had their own army to form, the Black Left had more power over the White Left than over black people—besides, some instinct in the Blacks had them wary of the New Left's automatic acceptance of technology land (the New Left tended to think technology land was acceptable except for its management by corporation land; the Black Left now interested in discovering itself had unruly jungle intuitions that technology land and corporation land might be the same).

With Negroes or without, fraternization on the line continued. Draft cards continued to be burned—each one a flutter of anxiety in everyone's heart, a release of fire on wings. Contemplate the humiliation to a college student if he hates the war and keeps the card in his wallet—how it says to him each time he looks for an address: you are yellow, buddy, for you keep me. So the cards burned one by one through the night, each man sitting in his position on the steps, the plaza, or the Mall, with his own card burning inside him, his stomach a glut of elation and woe as each new card went up from the dark in flame, suddenly it is his own, he—wild revolutionary youth, conservative middle-class boy, keeper of draft cards—his schizophrenia is burning and the security of the future with it. He looks for a girl to kiss in reward.

Sex, fear, the lift of first courage, the lightness of freedom, the oncoming suffocations of dread, the wild swinging ache or the somnolent drift of the pot, the biting cold of the night, the Civil War glow of the campfire light on all those union jackets, hippies on the trail of Sergeant Pepper—the U. S. Army looking out on a field of fires heard demonstrators talking to them, crying, "Join us, join us," demonstrators talking in low voices, "Why do you stay in uniform? Do you like the helmet on your head, is that it? Do you like obeying officers you hate? Join us. We have everything. Look. We are free. We have pot, we have food we share, we have girls. Come over to us, and share our girls"—a generosity of Eskimos and the New Middle Class which these soldiers of the working class and the small town would not be quick to comprehend—who gives his girl away, would be their question. And the answer—a fag! Yes, the hippies offered much, perhaps they offered too much.

The girls conducted their war. They had been walking in view of the soldiers, talking to the soldiers, standing in front of them, studying them, putting flowers in their barrels, smiling—some were gentle and sweet, true flower girls; others were bold and with the well-seasoned and high-spiced bitch air of fifty Harlem pickup lovers in a year, not saying how many whites—they unbuttoned their blouses, gave a real hint of cleavage, smiled in the soldier's eye, gave a devil laugh, then a bitch belly laugh at the impotence of the man's position in a uniform, helpless to reach out and take her. And the Marshals behind the soldiers, tense as police dogs, wheeling up and down the line, glaring at demonstrators, rapping their clubs against their hands, dying for their own precise kind of action.

Once in a while an arrest would be made. It seemed never to make much sense. A seated demonstrator might touch a soldier by accident, the Marshal would reach through the soldier's legs, grab the demonstrator, pull him through, another Marshal would join him, a quick beating, a move off to the waiting wagon or truck. All day, the arrests had made no sense. There had been in the beginning an obvious attempt to hold arrests down, then a wave of arrests when SDS-Contingent took the corner of the plaza, then this long period from dark to midnight with random scattered meaningless arrests.

There was meaning in it. The deepest sort of technological meaning: the technique of avoiding martyrs in riots. The essence of that technique is to arrest at random. The arrested hero having done nothing in particular feels like a victim or a fool. Upon his release, his friends treat him like a hero. But he is the sort of hero who must end by disappointing them. That is part of the technical wisdom of random arrest. It also disrupts, since no preparation for self-protection can be made, no sense of slow immersion into the possibility of arrest is possible, and the growth of rumor is exaggerated—for random arrests seem always more brutal than more logical arrests. In fact they are more brutal.

One element of these arrests was however not random at all. A startling disproportion of women were arrested, and were beaten in ugly fashion in the act. Dagmar Wilson, the leader of Women Strike for Peace, was treated more brutally by the Marshals than any of the male notables. She was hardly alone. Over and over, eyewitness account after eyewitness account gives brutal deadening news of the ferocity with which Marshals and soldiers went to work on women. But let us move into these accounts.

Some time after midnight, the press was called into the Pentagon for a final press conference before going home. The Secretary of Defense had left, the television was gone. There was an hiatus in the coverage of the event. It was a moment which somebody in command had obviously anticipated. New columns appeared from the building: the soldiers who had been on the line were replaced. The new soldiers were veterans of Vietnam. Such men had been on the plaza since dark, but this detachment seemed specially trained, a fierce cry away from the more frightened reserves who had been first on the line in the afternoon, and had lost that confrontation of the two lines of eyes in the first hour. The strength gained by the demonstrators then was now to be tested in quite another fire. What came to be known as the Battle of The Wedge was here begun. Let us get news of it by an extract from an eyewitness account by Margie Stamberg in the Washington *Free Press*.

When the paratroopers with their M-14 rifles, bayonets, clubs, and stone faces appeared, the bull horns set up a call for reinforcements from those resting at the campfires below.

Note that the bullhorns seem to set up an immediate call. How palpable must have been the shift in mood.

A tight resistance of row upon row of people sitting with locked arms was formed. Then the squeeze began. We saw at first individuals in the front lines being dragged out behind the troop lines and carried away. Suddenly, the troops which had been in single rows in front of the crowd formed into a wedge on the right side. Their tactic apparently was to split the group in two and force them to move back. No explanation was given for the sudden action. Paddy wagons rolled up, soldiers with tear gas guns appeared among the troops, and from the mall behind, other troops began to form.

Slowly the wedge began to move in on people. With bayonets and rifle butts, they moved first on the girls in the front line, kicking them, jabbing at them again and again with the guns, busting their heads and arms to break the chain of locked arms. The crowd appealed to the paratroopers to back off, to join them, to just act human. They sang the "Star Spangled Banner" and other songs: but the troops at this point were non-men, the appeals were futile.

The pleas of SDS people on the bull horns to convince the group to pull back in the face of a tactically deadened situation went unheeded. And so we sat. Some individuals left, but most remained. To leave was to leave one's brothers and sisters to get clubbed, yet to passively remain in the locked chain was also to participate in the senseless brutality. The victory of before was forgotten. In the dark the paratroopers began to move.

As they clubbed the marked person, usually a girl, in the first row, and dragged her away, the ranks in back closed in tighter. The person in the row behind became the front, was subjected to blows and kicks, dragged away, and the troops went on to the third row. Then the fourth, the fifth, the sixth rank, and so on until the people were finally separated into two groups. One hundred people were methodically beaten and carried away to the paddy wagons.

The wedge beat through to the last line, and the resistance was broken. Those left, who had been locking arms, stood up and waited quietly to be taken to the paddy wagons which continued to arrive. No one was leaving now; the thousands there prepared for arrest.

One cannot articulate the agony of those who sat and watched this go on slowly for hours amidst the songs, the pleas, the tears, and the impotent curses of "Motherfucker!" and "Bastards!" from those who could not leave yet could not resist.

When the resistance had been broken, the brutality stopped, the crowd prepared for arrest, word came that McNamara had arrived at the Pentagon. When this was announced on the bull horns, the troops stopped attacking immediately. Sidney Peck of the National Mobilization Committee took the bull horn from SDS and begged the troops to stop until the person responsible within the Pentagon for the massacre order could be found for an explanation. Peck insisted we had been given a permit to remain on the steps which the troops were violating. This speech, to many of us, was a funeral oration. All during the day the legality or illegality had been superfluous; the permit, a petit-bourgeois hang-up for those who had come to confront the warmakers. We didn't want the brutality to stop BECAUSE we had a permit; if it was to stop it must stop because we had beaten them, or they had carried the last one of us away.

The lines of resistance were composed of people of varying political stance. United in the community of the day but unlike those who had stormed and held the lines earlier, many of them felt that one could not leave the slaughter, but must passively remain to make a personal witness, a penance through

304

suffering, for the horrors committed to our Vietnamese brothers. In spite of the feeling of many that this sentiment was a selfish and indulgent personal catharsis irrelevant to the real war abroad, one could not leave those who wished to stay. So we stayed until the troops backed off upon McNamara's arrival. The resistance was broken. People, stunned at what they had seen and that they were still alive, began the long walk home.

Let us have another account from the same newspaper. It is by Thorne Dreyer.

The second phase of the demonstration was pretty much a bad scene. And I'm not sure why. For one thing, they kept changing the troops. Whenever we'd start really talking to the guys, they'd move them out. Maybe they finally brought in their "crack" troops. Lots of people left. It got dark and cold. But this is most important: There was a tactical vacuum. We were in a box.

Suddenly we were defensive and scared. We sang "We Are Not Afraid." Earlier, we did not have to sing it. There was no communication with the troops now. We chanted, "Join Us!" and "We Love You" and it was meaningless rhetoric. People kept bringing more and more food and we gorged ourselves and that food became really obscene. We started bickering and began to sing "We Shall Overcome" and were right back in that liberal bag. There were a few people who were totally committed to getting their scalps torn open, and a few who thought it would be tactically best to leave, and a hell of a lot who were scared shitless, but just didn't know what to do. There were lots of young kids who had really been moved by the spirit of the thing and weren't about to leave if leaving meant a defeat. And at that point I guess it would have.

The cops began to get really brutal, moving into the group in a wedge and smashing heads with billy clubs. These beautiful little hippie chicks had tears

305

streaming down their faces, but they weren't about to move. These kids were really brave. And I began to resent the "super-militants" who created so much pressure to stay. Because that was nothing but goddam bourgeois politics. At this point we had moved from confrontation right back to symbolic protest.

People have to come to terms with what violence means. It's not something to groove on and cleanse your soul with. Using violence in a situation where you do not have the instruments of violence, or at least an equal strategic position, is insane. It is poor guerrilla strategy and it is likely to get you killed.

Earlier in the afternoon we were in a good strategic situation. We took them by surprise, we had massive numbers, we were confident. It is quite possible that, after we had gained all we were going to, we should have had a massive victory march out of that place. Sure, this is second guessing. I didn't figure it that way then, and I'm not sure now that it would have been better. But I do feel very strongly that we took two steps forward and one step back.

The brutality by every eyewitness account was not insignificant, and was made doubly unattractive by its legalistic apparatus. The line of soldiers would stamp forward until they reached the seated demonstrators, then they would kick forward with their toes until the demonstrators were sitting on their feet (or *legally* speaking, now interfering with the soldiers). Then the Marshals would leap between their legs again and pull the demonstrator out of the line; he or she would then be beaten and taken away. It was a quiet rapt scene with muted curses, a spill in the dark of the most heated biles of the hottest patriotic hearts—to the Marshals and the soldiers, the enemy was finally there before them, all that Jew female legalistic stew of corruptions which would dirty the name of the nation and revile the grave of soldiers like themselves back in Vietnam, yes, the beatings went on, one by one generally of women, more women than men. Here is the most brutal description of a single beating by Harvey Mayes of the English Department at Hunter.

One soldier spilled the water from his canteen on the ground in order to add to the discomfort of the female demonstrator at his feet. She cursed him—understandably, I think—and shifted her body. She lost her balance and her shoulder hit the rifle at the soldier's side. He raised the rifle, and with its butt, came down hard on the girl's leg. The girl tried to move back but was not fast enough to avoid the billy-club of a soldier in the second row of troops. At least four times that soldier hit her with all his force, then as she lay covering her head with her arms, thrust his club swordlike between her hands into her face. Two more troops came up and began dragging the girl toward the Pentagon. . . . She twisted her body so we could see her face. But there was no face there: All we saw were some raw skin and blood. We couldn't see even if she was crying—her eyes had filled with the blood pouring down her head. She vomited, and that too was blood. Then they rushed her away.

One wonders at the logic. There is always a logic in repression, just as there is always a logic in the worst commercial. The logic is there for a reason—it will drive something into flesh.

The logic here speaks of the old misery of the professional soldier, centuries old. He is, at his most brutal, a man who managed to stay alive until the age of seven because there were men, at least his father, or his brothers, to keep him alive—his mother had drowned him in no oceans of love; his fear is therefore of the cruelty of women, he may never have another opportunity like this —to beat a woman without having to make love to her. So the Marshals went to work; so did those special soldiers saved for the hour when everyone but themselves and the Marshals was gone from the Pentagon. Now they could begin their beatings. (The hundred arrested in the Battle of The Wedge arrived at Occoquan and were deposited in other dormitories before Mailer was even asleep.)

Yes, and they beat the women for another reason. To

humiliate the demonstrators, to break them from their new resistance down to the old passive disobedience of the helpless sit-in waiting one's turn to be clubbed; they ground it into their faces that they sat there while their women were being taken off and no one of them or group of them dared to charge for all that hour. It is the worst hour at the Pentagon for the demonstrators—and the worst hour for the speakers on the bullhorn who quieted the militants who wanted to make some sort of charge. Yes, it was a difficult hour—the working class had plucked all stolen balls back. Great cheer. With rifles and clubs they had plucked them back. It is a large blemish on the demonstrators that they were supine in The Wedge, but it is comprehensible. There is a dead nerveless area on the Left, comprised of the old sense of paralysis before the horror of the gas chamber. There are very few on the Left who do not live with the partial belief their own life someday will end in such a way—perhaps that is why they are hung like a string of fish on the power of the public speech for all occasions. In a crowd listening to a speech, perhaps they are then farthest from the nightmare of fetching up one's last salts in the incredible ballooning suffocations of the last gas. Perhaps it is better to die each public evening by such an inch. One wonders why no musicians were playing as the clubs came down—just motherly legalistic injunctions from the bullhorn; motherly! the clubs of the Marshals, the butts of the rifles of the soldiers came down with more force. Kill the mothers! All the while, rumors passed. A demonstrator was already dead they heard—then next that they were all to be taken away and beaten one by one. Now the rumors changed. At X hour, a charge would come down on them. They would be clubbed to death.

It was still possible to leave. It was possible every inch of that slow advance of The Wedge for demonstrators to leave. But they sat there expecting to share the fate of the girls and the boys being beaten now. So it is not altogether shameful. If they did not defend their allies by action, they defended another ideal by their presence, by their refusal to flee. And the pot had deprived them of force. The Wedge had come on their slide down from elation into the long bad stoning of their collective head as mental connections begin to miss and reports of new small brain damage reach the home of the mind. Apathy. Depression. Then the battle of The Wedge. The American Army had known when to strike.

They were shriven in the hours till dawn. Rumors went through the cold night and the forty degrees of darkest early morning that the charge would be coming or a new Wedge. They were down to four hundred demonstrators, a hundredth of the force which had come to the Pentagon —they were out on the cold exaltation of having survived, of having remained—they were therefore tempted to stay and stay, to stay to the very end. They were now engaged in that spiritual test so painful to all—the rite of passage. Let us ruminate with them and contemplate the dawn.

9: THE AESTHETIC FORGED

The few hundred demonstrators still left in vigil on the stairs of the Pentagon in those dark hours after The Wedge and before the dawn were being exercised in all those nerves which lead to the moral root—a physical and spiritual transaction whose emotions are, at worst, so little agreeable as the passage of the dentist's drill toward the nerve canal of a tooth. It was bitterly cold, and they slept huddled together, beggared by discomfort, even occasional acts of petty viciousness. A sergeant went down the line at 5 A.M. pouring cold water from his canteen on the sleeping bodies.

Generally, however, there were few incidents. The Wedge had left no desire for more fight on either side. The Army had been guilty of illegal activity and knew it: the section of plaza they emptied during The Wedge had clearly belonged by the terms of the GSA contract to the area provided for demonstrators—so a few officers must now have been contemplating their actions nervously—the hippies and pacifists still remaining on the stairs could not have felt even an instant of security. In the early morning hours, rumor must have been a leaden dread, stories of what was certain to come next must have sunk into the heart—their journey into the dawn of Sunday was not routine. Cowardice lives in waves, in congealed layers, in caverns of the psyche, in treacheries of fear next to the boldest moves; it also lives encysted in all the firmest structures of the ego. How many of these demonstrators, certain at the beginning of the night by the firm conviction of their ego that they would not leave until morning, must have been obliged to pass through layers and dimensions and bursting cysts of cowardice they never knew to exist in themselves, as if each hour they remained extracted from them a new demand, a further extension of their moral resolve, another rung up that moral ladder which Mailer had glimpsed in Occoquan and had made haste to refuse. Yes, the passage through the night against every temptation to leave—the cold, the possibility of new, more brutal, and more overwhelming attacks, the boredom, the middle-class terror of excess (if one has done two or three good acts in a row, it is time to cash them in) the fear of moral vertigo (one courageous action resolutely following another without compromise and without cease must end in the whirlpool of death) yes, even the fear that if they remained through the night, they would be obliged to remain through the morning, the afternoon, and the evening of the next night, and even then! would there be ever an end? yes, the passage through the night brought every temptation to leave including the thundering schisms of muttered political argument in the dark—the proud advertisements of the new resistance had been ground back to the old masochistic tramping grounds of the sit-in—an argument which was undeniable, and could have prevailed, except if they left, and no one was at the Pentagon then but the soldiers through the night, well what unseen burning torch of which unknown but still palpably felt spirit might expire?

310

no, this passage through the night was a rite of passage, and these disenchanted heirs of the Old Left, this rabble of American Vietcong, and hippies, and pacifists, and whoever else was left were afloat on a voyage whose first note had been struck with the first sound of the trumpet Mailer had heard crossing Washington Monument in the morning. "Come here, come here, come here," the trumpet had said, and now eighteen hours later, in the false dawn, the echo of far greater rites of passage in American history, the light reflected from the radiance of greater more heroic hours may have come nonetheless to shine along the inner space and the caverns of the freaks, some hint of a glorious future may have hung in the air, some refrain from all the great American rites of passage when men and women manacled themselves to a lost and painful principle and survived a day, a night, a week, a month, a year, a celebration of Thanksgiving—the country had been founded on a rite of passage. Very few had not emigrated here without the echo of that rite, even if it were no more (and no less!) than eight days in the stink, bustle, fear, and propinquity of steerage on an ocean crossing (or the eighty days of dying on a slave ship) each generation of Americans had forged their own rite, in the forest of the Alleghenies and the Adirondacks, at Valley Forge, at New Orleans in 1812, with Rogers and Clark or at Sutter's Mill, at Gettysburg, the Alamo, the Klondike, the Argonne, Normandy, Pusan—the engagement at the Pentagon was a pale rite of passage next to these, and yet it was probably a true one, for it came to the spoiled children of a dead de-animalized middle class who had chosen most freely, out of the incomprehensible mysteries of moral choice, to make an attack and then hold a testament before the most authoritative embodiment of the principle that America was right, America was might, America was the true religious war of Christ against the Communist. So it became a rite of passage for these tender drug-vitiated jargon-mired children, they endured through a night, a black dark night which began in joy, near foundered in terror, and dragged on through empty apathetic hours while glints of light came to each alone. Yet the rite of passage was invoked, the moral lad-

311

der was climbed, they were forever different in the morning than they had been before the night, which is the meaning of a rite of passage, one has voyaged through a channel of shipwreck and temptation, and so some of the vices carried from another nether world into life itself (on the day of one's birth) may have departed, or fled, or quit; some part of the man has been born again, and is better, just as some hardly so remarkable area of the soul may have been in some miniscule sweet fashion reborn on the crossing of the marchers over Arlington Memorial Bridge, for the worst of them and the most timid were moving nonetheless to a confrontation they could only fear, they were going to the land of the warmakers. Not so easy for the timid when all is said.

But of course this rite of passage was hardly to end as yet. The morning came; very cold, very quiet, unexciting. Demonstrators left, all but a token force. Were there even a few hundred? The others rushed to places for a few hours' sleep, then returned. By ten in the morning, two thousand may have been back. The day was different. There was not much militancy now, but long speeches, different somehow from the speeches of the day before, because the listeners moved now on the currents of the night before and the bloodyings. Now and again draft cards were burned, and for a part of the day Gary Rader, once a member of the Green Berets, gave a speech which was thought by many to be the best hour of them all.

Night was on. The demonstrators were entering the last few hours of their march on the Pentagon. They were tired, exceptionally tired, they felt vulnerable—their aggression, their ability even to defend themselves now used up by endless calls over the hours for more adrenaline; yes the mood was pacifistic, almost saintly, but very weak. In the night, they were all close to each other. Quietly. They were waiting. The walls of the Pentagon bulked large.

Fifteen minutes before midnight, a voice boomed out of a loudspeaker in the wall. To the demonstrators it sounded like the voice of the Pentagon. Big Brother had come to be heard.

"The demonstration in which you are participating,"

312

said the voice, "ends at midnight. The two-day permit which was agreed to by leaders of the demonstration and GSA expires at that time. All demonstrators must depart from the Pentagon grounds at midnight." A silence. "All persons who wish to leave voluntarily can board buses on the Mall." A pause. "Those demonstrators who do not leave voluntarily by midnight will be arrested and taken to a federal detention center. . . . All demonstrators are urged to abide by the permit." So the government remained to the end what it had been from the beginning: a part legalistic, a part cooperative, and a part threatening —or is it rather—a part in the area of the non-negotiable?

There was a short silence, hardly time for the demonstators to do more than reckon with the fact that another rung in the rite of passage had been presented. But again the Voice spoke out of the Pentagon wall. "I say again to you. The demonstration in which you are participating. . . ." and the same speech was read to the same conclusion. Thirty-four demonstrators accepted the offer to leave.

Let us quote from the *Washington Star*. For once, a newspaper account seems to agree with eyewitness reports. One must, of course, as always, beware of adjectives and estimates of number. Adverbs are to be shunned.

During its last hour the demonstration seemed no menace to the helmeted legions still facing them across a single-strand rope barrier. The crowd was down to its last 200.

Repeatedly, almost pleadingly, the march's leaders at that hour had reminded the soldiers and the marshals—by loudspeaker—that arrests should be made non-violently to fulfill a supposed promise.

At 11:46 an amplified voice echoed across the helmeted troops and federal officers and out to the now-tense 200.

"The demonstration in which you are participating ends at midnight."

313

"I say again to you. The demonstration in which . . ." and on to a second full reading.

This done, there was a moment of silence. Then, "No," a muted chorus from the demonstrators. Then, more lustily, the chant: "Hell no, we won't go, hell no, we won't go."

Almost immediately, 57 helmeted U.S. Marshals filed out of the Pentagon, across the Mall, and behind the front line of MPs.

The crowd started singing, mournfully, "We Shall Overcome." Most sat down, immediately in front of the first MPs. A futile attempt at "God Bless America," then more "We Shall Overcome.'

And then again, from the loudspeakers: "Attention all demonstrators. The demonstration in which . . ." It was repeated twice then, with the added notice that "It is now 11:55 P.M."

"God Bless America" issued from the protesting remnant, their number diminished by the 34 who had accepted the ride to freedom.

SECOND BUS DRIVES OFF

The announcement came again, this time with the notice: "It is now 11:58 and a half P.M." And then: "It is now 12 P.M."

A minute passed, and the second "Freedom bus" drove off. There was some shuffling about at the east end of the Marshals' line, but still no fulfillment of the arrest notice.

The closed vans, Occoquan-bound, began moving into position at two minutes after 12. And then the troops tightened around in a triangle, and the Marshals moved in on the demonstrators, now singing "This Land Is My Land," and then "Glory, Glory Hallelujah," and finally—over and over—"We Shall Overcome.'

It was a curious last act. Almost conversational. Said a priest to a Marshal: "Don't club that boy; this is non-violent." And there was no clubbing. Said a bearded boy to a soldier: "I am going limp." He did, and the soldier obligingly lifted him.

The arresting went so smoothly then that the vans could not be moved up fast enough to accept the prisoners.

After six vans, two panel trucks and that one unused "freedom bus" were loaded and driven off, it was over.

"It was over." Jerry Rubin who had been on the steps and the Mall for twenty-eight of the thirty-two hours was among the last to be arrested.

Troops, marching off the Mall after the anti-war crowd had been taken away, got a round of applause from their comrades on the line, the U.S. Marshals.

Within 20 minutes after the jail-bound vans had gone, two sweeper trucks had collected the debris left by the two-day campers—tomato juice cans, an empty bottle of expensive gin, a few tattered hippies' togas, stacks of paper and discarded magazines, a paperback book entitled "Irrational Man," and assorted remnants of food.

That same newspaper story had quoted a Pentagon spokesman's reaction to charges of brutality by Pentagon marchers: "We feel," said the spokesman, "our action is consistent with objectives of security and control faced with varying levels of dissent." *Consistent with objectives of security and control! levels of dissent!* One is speaking of a government process—the removal of sediment—a natural by-product of the forces of freedom invoked by the processes of government. The spokesman was speaking in totalitarianese, which is to say, technologese, which is to say any language which succeeds in stripping itself of any moral content. For if the spokesman had said, "We were trying to keep order against varying degrees of violence and insurrection," the speaker could have been asked, "What kind of violence? Insurrection in the name of what? and against which order?"

There are negative rites of passage as well. Men learn

in a negative rite to give up the best things they were
born with, and forever. How much must a spokesman
suffer in a negative rite to be able to learn to speak in
such a way?

10: THE END OF THE RITE

When the count was made, there proved to be one
thousand arrests. It was not a small number; it was not
an enormous number—it was certainly a respectable
number to be arrested over thirty-two hours in protest of
a war. Six hundred had charges pressed. The others were
taken to the back of the Pentagon, photographed, and
driven away in buses to be released on the street. Of the
six hundred arrested, no felony charges for assault were
brought in, indeed only a dozen were charged with assault, only two went to trial, and both were acquitted.
   Yes, the end seemed to have come, and the immediate
beneficiary of the March could be nobody other than the
President of the United States. Lyndon Johnson made a
point to have his picture taken Saturday sitting at a table
on the White House lawn with Hubert Humphrey, Dean
Rusk, and Orville Freeman. The caption informed that he
had spent the day in work. Headlines on Monday: "LBJ
Hits Peaceniks." He had sent a memorandum to Defense
Secretary McNamara and Attorney General Clark. "I
know that all Americans share my pride in the man in
uniform and the civilian law enforcement personnel for
their outstanding performance in the nation's capital during the last two days. They performed with restraint, firmness and professional skill. Their actions stand in sharp
contrast to the irresponsible acts of violence and lawlessness by many of the demonstrators."
   The press was, in the aftermath, antagonistic to the

March. Some measure of the condemnation and the abuse can be indicated by quoting Reston of the *Times* who was not immoderate in his reaction. Nor untypical.

It is difficult to report publicly the ugly and vulgar provocation of many of the militants. They spat on some of the soldiers in the front line at the Pentagon and goaded them with the most vicious personal slander.

Many of the signs carried by a small number of the militants, and many of the lines in the theatrical performances put on by the hippies, are too obscene to print. In view of this underside of the protest, many officials here are surprised that there was not much more violence.

The rest of the stories went about that way.

Emphasis was put on every rock thrown, and a count was made of the windows broken. (There were, however, only a few.) But there was no specific mention of The Wedge. Indeed, stories quickly disappeared. No features nor follow-up a few days later. In six weeks, when an attempt was made in New York to close down the draft induction centers, it seemed that public sentiment had turned sharply against resistance. The Negro riots had made the nation afraid of lawlessness. Lyndon Johnson stood ten percentage points higher in the popularity polls —he had ridden the wave of revulsion in America against demonstrators who spit in the face of U.S. troops—when it came to sensing new waves of public opinion, LBJ was the legendary surfboarder of them all.

It probably did not matter. Ever since he had been in office, the popularity of LBJ had kept going up on the basis of his ability to ride every favorable wave, and had kept going down on the unwillingness of the war in Vietnam to fulfill the promises his Administration was making. So his popularity would go up and down again. There would be many to hope it did not go up in the last week before election. In the demonstrations in New York in December against the draft centers, Teague was arrested for carrying a knife—to anyone who had listened to his verbal militancy in jail it seemed altogether likely that a knife was not his weapon, and he had been framed. And a month later, Dr. Spock, and Coffin, and Marcus Raskin, and Michael Ferber, and Mitch Goodman were indicted by a grand jury for advocating resistance to the draft law. Such advocacy was a felony—their sentences, if guilty, could run to five years.

Mitch Goodman called a meeting at Town Hall. Five hundred and sixty people (including Allen Ginsberg, Noam Chomsky, and Mailer) signed statements implicating themselves legally to aid and abet draft resisters. Macdonald, Lowell, and Paul Goodman had already signed such statements. They could now all receive the same sentence. So the weekend in Washington which had begun with a phone call from Mitch Goodman gave promise of ending in Harrisburg or Leavenworth.

But probably it was in Occoquan and the jail in Washington, D.C., that the March ended. In the week following, prisoners who had chosen to remain, refused in many ways to cooperate, obstructed prison work, went on strikes. Some were put in solitary. A group from the Quaker Farm in Voluntown, Connecticut, practiced noncooperation in prison. Among them were veterans of a sleep-in of twenty pacifists at the Pentagon in the spring before. Now, led by Gary Rader, Erica Enzer, Irene Johnson, and Suzanne Moore, some of them refused to eat or drink and were fed intravenously. Several men at the D.C. jail would not wear prison clothing. Stripped of their own, naked, they were thrown in the Hole. There they lived in cells so small that not all could lie down at once to sleep. For a day they lay naked on the floor, for many days naked with blankets and mattress on the floor. For many days they did not eat nor drink water. Dehydration brought them near to madness.

Here was the last of the rite of passage, "the chinook salmon . . . nosing up the impossible stone," here was the thin source of the stream—these naked Quakers on the cold floor of a dark isolation cell in D.C. jail, wandering down the hours in the fever of dehydration, the cells of the brain contracting to the crystals of their thought, essence of one thought so close to the essence of another

318

—all separations of water gone—that madness is near, madness can now be no more than the acceleration of thought.

Did they pray, these Quakers, for forgiveness of the nation? Did they pray with tears in their eyes in those blind cells with visions of a long column of Vietnamese dead, Vietnamese walking a column of flame, eyes on fire, nose on fire, mouth speaking flame, did they pray, "O Lord, forgive our people for they do not know, O Lord, find a little forgiveness for America in the puny reaches of our small suffering, O Lord, let these hours count on the scale as some small penance for the sins of the nation, let this great nation crying in the flame of its own gangrene be absolved for one tithe of its great sins by the penance of these minutes, O Lord, bring more suffering upon me that the sins of our soldiers in Vietnam be not utterly unforgiven—they are too young to be damned forever."

The prayers are as Catholic as they are Quaker, and no one will know if they were ever made, for the men who might have made them were perhaps too far out on fever and shivering and thirst to recollect, and there are places no history can reach. But if the end of the March took place in the isolation in which these last pacifists suffered naked in freezing cells, and gave up prayers for penance, then who was to say they were not saints? And who to say that the sins of America were not by their witness a tithe remitted?

11: THE METAPHOR DELIVERED

Whole crisis of Christianity in America that the military heroes were on one side, and the unnamed saints on the other! Let the bugle blow. The death of America rides in on the smog. America—the land where a new kind of man was born from the idea that God was present in every man not only as compassion but as power, and so the country belonged to the people; for the will of the people—if the locks of their life could be given the art to turn—was then the will of God. Great and dangerous idea! If the locks did not turn, then the will of the people was the will of the Devil. Who by now could know where was what? Liars controlled the locks.

Brood on that country who expresses our will. She is America, once a beauty of magnificence unparalleled, now a beauty with a leprous skin. She is heavy with child —no one knows if legitimate—and languishes in a dungeon whose walls are never seen. Now the first contractions of her fearsome labor begin—it will go on: no doctor exists to tell the hour. It is only known that false labor is not likely on her now, no, she will probably give birth, and to what?—the most fearsome totalitarianism the world has ever known? or can she, poor giant, tormented lovely girl, deliver a babe of a new world brave and tender, artful and wild? Rush to the locks. God writhes in his bonds. Rush to the locks. Deliver us from our curse. For we must end on the road to that mystery where courage, death, and the dream of love give promise of sleep.